Performing the Reformation

O | R | S Oxford Ritual Studies

Series Editors

Ronald Grimes, Radboud University Nijmegen
Ute Hüsken, University of Oslo
Eric Venbrux, Radboud University Nijmegen

Ritual Efficacy
Edited by William S. Sax, Johannes Quack, and Jan Weinhold

Performing the Reformation
Barry Stephenson

Performing the Reformation

Public Ritual in the City of Luther

BARRY STEPHENSON

UNIVERSITY PRESS

2010

OXFORD
UNIVERSITY PRESS

Oxford University Press, Inc., publishes works that further
Oxford University's objective of excellence
in research, scholarship, and education.

Oxford   New York
Auckland   Cape Town   Dar es Salaam   Hong Kong   Karachi
Kuala Lumpur   Madrid   Melbourne   Mexico City   Nairobi
New Delhi   Shanghai   Taipei   Toronto

With offices in
Argentina   Austria   Brazil   Chile   Czech Republic   France   Greece
Guatemala   Hungary   Italy   Japan   Poland   Portugal   Singapore
South Korea   Switzerland   Thailand   Turkey   Ukraine   Vietnam

Copyright © 2010 by Oxford University Press, Inc.

Published by Oxford University Press, Inc.
198 Madison Avenue, New York, New York 10016

www.oup.com

Oxford is a registered trademark of Oxford University Press

Library of Congress Cataloging-in-Publication Data

Stephenson, Barry.
Performing the Reformation : public ritual in the city of Luther /
Barry Stephenson.
    p. cm.
Includes bibliographical references and index.
ISBN 978-0-19-973275-3; 978-0-19-973971-4 (pbk.)
1. Fasts and feasts. 2. Fasts and feasts—Germany—Wittenberg
(Saxony-Anhalt). 3. Wittenberg (Saxony-Anhalt, Germany)—
Religious life and customs. 4. Wittenberg (Saxony-Anhalt, Germany)—
Description and travel. I. Title.
BV30.S67 2010
263'.9094318—dc22   2009019138

9 8 7 6 5 4 3 2 1

Printed in the United States of America
on acid-free paper

Acknowledgments

Doug Shantz unwittingly provided the impetus for this project when he told me about a festival in Grimma where each year local residents reenact the story of Katharina von Bora and the other nuns being smuggled out of Nimbschen convent in beer barrels. In short order, I was writing a proposal to study Luther and Reformation-themed festivity, pilgrimage, and tourism. The Social Sciences and Humanities Research Council liked the proposal, and granted me a postdoctoral research fellowship. Ron Grimes agreed to supervise the research; fortunately, our paths crossed in Germany in June 2005, and Ron accompanied me to Wittenberg over the Luther's Wedding festival, running a second video camera and photographing the festivities. His encouragement, support, and confidence in my work kept me moving toward the light, at times quite dim, at the end of the tunnel.

Phyllis Granoff at Yale University provided the opportunity to present and discuss my work with colleagues, as did the Dynamics of Ritual Project at the University of Heidelberg, under the directorship of Axel Michaels. Ute Hüsken (University of Oslo) and I commiserated and helped one another through the problems involved in writing and producing a book with a DVD.

I met many Wittenbergers and visitors to the city who took an interest in my work, and graciously offered up their time and thoughts; their names are listed in the credits on the DVD. If I have missed anyone, my apologies.

Needless to say, if there are errors in the book, they are mine. The interpretations are mine, too. Scholarly analysis, interpretation, and criticism of pubic events may provoke controversy. Sometimes outsiders see things that insiders do not, or have a freedom to say things that insiders lack. I hope I have written book that offers insight into the social, cultural, and religious dynamics of Wittenberg's festival and tourism scene, without running roughshod over the lives of those I represent or the events I discuss.

Monika, Elea, and Kai never tired of hearing festival music and sounds pour through the house as I was editing video, hour after endless hour.

Contents

List of Materials on DVD

Introduction (9:21)
Legend to Portal (6:46)
Wedding Montage (3:46)
Tetzel at the Door (4:38)
The Animators (40:32)
Processing (24:49)
Music (2:37)
Martin (3:11)
Lutherland-Fatherland (19:08)
Worship (38:32)
Extras
    Images of Luther's Wedding, 2005 (PowerPoint)
    Luther Protests (PowerPoint)
    Reformation Day Brochure, 2005 (pdf)
    Luther's Wedding Brochure, 2005 (pdf)
    Selected Websites (pdf)
    Yale Conference Paper, Sensory Overload (pdf)
Note: Extras are accessible by opening the disc in a computer's
DVD-ROM drive. Additional materials for this book are available on
the Ritual Studies Web site: http://ritualstudies.com/oxford-ritual-
studies-series.

List of Illustrations

Performing the Reformation

The important point, so far as the development of my take on things is concerned, is that field research, far from sorting things out, scrambled them further.

—Clifford Geertz, *Available Light*

Introduction

Approaching Lutherland

The life and work of Martin Luther is, as they say, history, and history and theology have been the disciplines of choice for studying the Reformation. Luther's texts (some 120 thick, large volumes), countless texts about Luther's texts, and the historical details of the Reformation have been pored over, praised, criticized, interpreted, and pondered by theologians and historians for nearly five hundred years. The book you hold is, in a way, about the Reformation, but not the Reformation as such, not the event that took place over a number of decades nearly five hundred years ago. Rather, there is a place where Luther and the Reformation are alive and kicking, in the form of public festivity, tourism and pilgrimage, theatre and heritage performance. That place is Lutherland, and at its heart is the city of Wittenberg, Luther's home for thirty-six years, and today a venue for "performing the Reformation."

Luther

In the year 2000, as part of the millennium craze, *Life* magazine published a list of the most influential people of the preceding thousand years. Third on the list, behind Thomas Edison and Christopher Columbus, was Martin Luther (1483–1546). Luther's claim to fame is, of course, his leading role in the Protestant Reformation. The European reform movements of the sixteenth century constituted one of the greatest crises in the history of Christendom. The impact of the Reformation on theology, ritual, politics, commerce, literacy, education, family life, and gender roles was so great that historians typically conceive of the Reformation as a watershed period in Western civilization. The lives of the Reformers mark the transition from a medieval to a modern world; and Luther, if the *Life* magazine ranking is any indication, was the greatest Reformer of them all.[1]

In 1506, Luther turned his back on university studies in law to become a monk in the order of Augustinian Hermits. A year later, he was ordained as a priest. In 1508, Luther's superiors sent him to the town of Wittenberg, located southwest of Berlin, to minister to the community and lecture at the university. In 1512, the university granted Luther his doctorate in theology, and he soon became the head priest of Wittenberg's Stadtkirche St. Marien (St. Mary's Church). In 1515, the Augustinians appointed Luther vicar of eleven regional monasteries. Luther was rising in the ranks, but also headed for a confrontation with church authorities.

In the early sixteenth century, Wittenberg and nearby Torgau were home to the electorate of Saxony, a princely territory of the Holy Roman Empire. As Luther arrived on the scene, calls for social, religious, and political reform were already in the air. The decisive moment came on the eve of All Saints Day in 1517, when Luther, so the story goes, hammered up ninety-five theses against the selling of indulgences on the door of Wittenberg's Schlosskirche (castle church)—the *Thesenanschlag*. John Tetzel (1465–1519), a Dominican monk, had been tramping the roads of the neighboring province of Brandenburg, selling salvation. An indulgence was a purchased document that granted remission of penalties imposed by the church in one's lifetime due to sin. The Catholic Church was, in effect, in possession of a treasury of merit accumulated through the lives of the saints. An individual could purchase a bit of this treasure of good works, thereby circumventing any punishment owed them. By Luther's day, the church had extended indulgences to cover punishments imposed in the afterlife by God himself, the thought of which was a powerful motivator to buy. Sinners gave a bit of extra money to the church, an act that assuaged their fears. The church distributed the good works of the saints in the form of an indulgence document, using the money earned to finance hospitals or crusades or to build cathedrals. By the end of the Middle Ages, professional pardoners, like John Tetzel, were offering unrestricted sale of indulgences, and reformers, like Martin Luther, were taking offense.

When Luther learned that the Medici Pope Leo X was using the income generated from indulgence sales to finance the ongoing construction of St. Peter's Basilica in Rome, he revved up his criticisms of the penitential system of the medieval church: God's grace, the gospel, and faith—not church-granted penance—were the sources of salvation, he claimed. Fellow Reformers printed and circulated Luther's ninety-five theses throughout Germany, and Luther's defiant act of nailing the theses to the church door became, in time, the symbolic foundation stone of the new Protestant faith. Luther emerged as one of the Western world's culture heroes; poor John Tetzel became one of its arch villains, a not-so-shining example of all deemed flawed in medieval church and society. It came as something of a surprise, then, to walk out of Wittenberg's Schlosskirche the morning of Reformation Day to see John Tetzel out in front of the famous Theses Door, selling indulgences—but I am getting ahead of myself.

Lutherland

Sitting in Wittenberg's empty Marktplatz (market square), early morning on the eve of Reformation Sunday, 2004, as I was contemplating Johann Gottfried Schadow's *Luther*, the neoclassical-styled monument honoring the great Reformer that was unveiled on Reformation Day in 1821, four giggling confirmands interrupted my jet-lag-induced slumber by scrambling up on to the monument's base, paper and pens in hand. Talking, laughing, pointing, searching, they turned from their papers to the monument, circumambulating it several times, and scribbling notes. They were writing in an exercise book, the kind you might see members of a school group handling as they make their way through a museum, collecting, copying, and assimilating bits of information from the exhibits. As the confirmands were working on their booklet, two trucks rolled up. The drivers and crew jumped out and set to work unloading tables and chairs, beginning the process of transforming the empty Marktplatz into the "Medieval Market Spectacle" that accompanies each of Wittenberg's two annual Reformation-themed city festivals: Luther's Wedding (Luthers Hochzeit) and Reformation Day (Reformationsfest).[⊙]

Luther's Wedding is a large-scale public festival, inaugurated in 1994, driven in part by efforts to deal with economic and social problems arising from German reunification in 1989. Since the *Wende* of 1989, Wittenberg has turned to developing its considerable cultural resources into tourism capital and receives roughly 350,000 visitors each year.[2] The public performance of the wedding of Martin Luther and Katharina von Bora is the centerpiece of Luther's Wedding, an annual three-day festival held in June. The festival

⊙ See DVD: Introduction.

includes a medieval market; traditional arts, handicrafts, and cuisine; parades and processions, street performers, and concerts; and special worship services, including the opportunity to renew wedding vows in "Luther's church."[3]

Each October, Wittenberg plays host to a Reformation Day festival, a tradition whose roots date to 1617, the year marking the hundredth jubilee of Luther's posting of the ninety-five theses. Reformation Day is part of the Lutheran liturgical calendar, recognized as one of many "lesser festivals" or "commemorations." Like the celebration of Luther's Wedding, a variety of events take place over the three days: worship services, lectures and seminars, special museum displays, confirmation events, concerts and plays, drinking, eating, and shopping. Luther's Wedding draws 100,000 visitors, and Reformation Day draws in excess of 20,000—significant numbers, given that the city's population is less than 50,000 (fig. I.1).

In twenty-four hours, the serenity of the Marktplatz would give way to the excesses of public festivity. The noise and bustle of vendors and shoppers selling and buying; jugglers and magicians performing their acts; artisans producing

FIGURE I.1. The "royal" couple, Martin and Katie, in Wittenberg's Marktplatz during Luther's Wedding, 2005. Johann Gottfried Schadow's *Luther* (1821) stands in front of the old City Hall, overlooking the assembled festival-goers. Photograph by Ronald Grimes.

their crafts and hawking their wares; musicians playing and singing; performers satirizing medieval clerics and monastics; visitors eating sausage, drinking
beer, and mingling; clergy and civic officials in full regalia engaged in the pomp
and circumstance of sermons, speeches, and processions. Jet lag or not, tomorrow the action would begin. As the girls climbed down from Schadow's *Luther*
and wandered off to their next assignment, one of the workers unfurled a large
banner advertising Lutherbier, while his co-workers erected the Lutherbier
stand. Lutherland, I quickly concluded, would be a semotician's dream.

Taking the scene in, inspired by all the work that was going on, I too set to
work. I wrote in my field journal one of the first entries of a project I had tentatively titled "Performing the Reformation": "For those who live here, Wittenberg is home; but I am one of thousands of visitors who pass through the city
each year since the dismantling of the [Berlin] Wall [in 1989] and the fall of the
[communist-ruled] DDR. For me, for these young women going through confirmation, and for those thousands who will soon pour into Wittenberg's old
town to the annual Reformationsfest, Wittenberg is not home. What kind of
place is it then?" A few answers were quick to emerge.

As I watched the confirmands do their museumlike exercises, surrounded
by the streets, buildings, monuments, and churches that were once the haunts
of Martin Luther himself, I was aware of the presence of several actual museums
and heritage homes within a few city blocks; Wittenberg can easily be imagined
as a large open-air museum. The town, along with neighboring Eisleben,
received the imprimatur of a UNESCO World Heritage Site in 1996. Models
and posters displaying the old city in its heyday reinforce the museumlike
character of the old town. City tours are led by guides in heritage costume,
plaques on the buildings name the famous people who lived, studied, or passed
through the city, windows and racks display guidebooks, postcards, DVDs, and
souvenirs—Wittenberg is a location on the global map of heritage tourism.[4]
One kind of place, one kind of visitor: the cultural tourist, in search of history,
authenticity, perhaps edification.

But the confirmands were no ordinary museum goers. They were in Wittenberg for a specific and special reason. They were undergoing a rite of passage that
would grant them full membership in the Evangelical Church.[5] Their elders were
initiating them, confirming them in their faith. Wittenberg is more than museum,
more than a heritage and cultural site—it is also Lutheran (more generally, Protestant) sacred space. Wittenberg is what Mikhail Bakhtin refers to as a *chronotope*.
Chronotopes are "points in the geography of a community where time and space
intersect and fuse. Time takes on flesh and becomes visible for human contemplation; likewise, space becomes charged and responsive to the movements of
time and history and the enduring character of a people. . . . Chronotopes thus

stand as monuments to the community itself, as a symbol of it, [and] as forces operating to shape its members' images of themselves."[6]

Several religiously significant places and objects make Wittenberg a magnet that draws into its force field Lutheran and Protestant visitors, clergy, and officials from around the world. In addition to housing a large Reformation archive, the contemporary Lutherhaus museum is the site where Luther and his wife Katharina von Bora lived, worked, and raised a family. The Schlosskirche (castle church) contains the graves of both Luther and Philipp Melanchthon, and the famous door where Luther posted his theses against indulgences. The Stadtkirche St. Marien is where Luther preached most of his sermons. Protestant theology has long been wary of a Catholic sacramental worldview implicit in pilgrimage practices, yet local and international church-based groups in Wittenberg are actively engaged in promoting and hosting pilgrimage to Wittenberg and the surrounding Lutherland. They sponsor another kind of place: chronotope, sacred site, shrine; and other kinds of visitors: pilgrims, devotees, initiates, clergy in training, and students of religion, like me.

A third way of imagining Wittenberg is as a stage. It has become commonplace in the humanities and social sciences to use performance and dramaturgical metaphors in the study of social behaviors, structures, and processes, but academics are not alone in thinking in terms of performance. The city of Wittenberg Web site and promotional materials refer to the city as "the original dramatic stage of the Reformation."[⊙] The message is clear: Here is where events of world-historic significance took place. If "all the world's a stage," some five hundred years ago high drama took place in Wittenberg, as Luther and his colleagues took on the might of the Catholic Church. The scholars who have produced the rich body of case studies and theorizing of ritual and cultural performances over the past thirty years—Victor Turner, Richard Schechner, Barbara Babcock, Clifford Geertz, Barbara Kirshenblatt-Gimblett, John MacAloon, Edward Schieffelin, Ronald Grimes—do not simply analogize social and ritual action by means of performance. These and other scholars are interested in comparing and exploring the relationship between such genres as theatre, ritual, games, tourism, and festivity, as well as the impact of these on social and cultural life—on religion, politics, media, class, gender, taste, and identity. These writers and scholars are the significant others of my academic life. Their work provides the context, ideas, and methods informing this study, so it is no surprise that sitting in Wittenberg's Marktplatz that chilly October morning, I jotted down some notes titled, "Wittenberg as stage—Wittenberg is a stage."

⊙ A short list of relevant Web sites is available in the "Extras" folder on the DVD, accessible by loading the DVD into a computer, and then opening the disk icon.

We can consider Wittenberg a metaphorical stage—but it is more than that. The preparation for Luther's Wedding, billed as one of Germany's "top-ten summer festivals," involves setting up more than a dozen actual stages. In 2004, residents and a local theatre group literally turned the old city into an open-air stage for the event, Wittenberg auf der Bühne (Wittenberg on Stage). In this theatrical performance of scenes from Wittenberg's past, the city's streets, buildings, and squares became the set pieces on which present-day residents, with the aid of professional actors and directors, were transformed into the notable figures of Reformation-era Wittenberg.[7] Walking the streets were Lucas Cranach, Johannes Tetzel, Katharina von Bora, Frederick the Wise, Albrecht Dürer, Giordano Bruno, Thomas Müntzer, Georg Spalatin, and, of course, Martin Luther. In recent years, Wittenberg has hosted an open-air performance of John Osborne's play *Luther*, utilizing Wittenberg's buildings, streets, and squares in the staging. A new Luther Opera has played in Wittenberg, as have a Luther Oratorio and a Luther Burlesque. In 2008, Wittenberg launched The Luther Decade, kicking off a decade-long series of events and performance to culminate in the five hundredth anniversary of the Reformation in 2017. Stage space calls into existence yet more identities: performers and audiences, not to mention directors, promoters, investors, critics, and, as is said in German, the *Ausgebildete*, social-cultural elites.

Victor Turner describes social processes in terms of patterned, dramatic action, which means that certain places, at certain times, become the ground on which is performed tension-filled or conflict-driven social crisis. The Reformation, or the Wittenberg movement, as it was originally called, was such a crisis. The drama of ritual and performance propelled the Wittenberg movement. There were protests in the streets, mock burnings of the pope, one of history's great trials, public debates, the public burning of the papal bull calling for Luther to recant, and the wedding of a defiant monk and an escaped nun (Luther and Katharina von Bora).

In the past one hundred fifty years, Germany has witnessed more than its fair share of what Turner termed "social dramas." The nineteenth and early twentieth centuries witnessed the rise of the German empire under Bismarck and the ascendancy of the Prussian state. The same era involved the Kulturkampf (culture war) against Catholics, as well as the secularization of society and battles between cultural Protestants and devout Pietists. The fighting of two world wars; the Holocaust; the division of the country into east and west; and the reunification, the Wende, of 1989—these events mark the tumultuous recent history of Germany. The Wende is a social drama that is still playing itself out, as the former East tries to find its footing in the new Germany and the new Europe.

The remembrance, celebration, and propagandizing of Luther have been front and center in German politics, religion, and culture since the man penned his ninety-five theses against the sale of indulgences. Luther has been a renewable resource through which to enact, resist, and process social change, and a touchstone of Lutheran, Protestant, German, and even Western identity. In the course of these social dramas, Wittenberg, as the "city of Luther," has witnessed many main-stage events.

As the crews continued building the Medieval Market Spectacle, I recalled that the National Socialist Party rallied on Reformation Day in Wittenberg's Marktplatz. The Nazis found in Luther's belligerent anti-Jewish writings fuel to fire their crazed ideology and atrocities. Early in his career as a reformer, Luther was sympathetic toward Jews, and even published a tract titled, "Jesus Was a Jew," in an effort to win Jewish converts. When this did not happen, an older, harsher Luther published "On the Jews and Their Lies," a tract that painted Jews with the brush of medieval prejudice and even called for the burning of synagogues to force Jews out of Lutheran territories. The Nazis would later put Luther's writings to use in their pogroms.

The year 1933 was the four hundred fiftieth anniversary of Luther's birth, and the newly installed Nazis, drawing on the legacy of Luther's belligerent anti-Jewish tracts, helped organize and actively participated in Luther's birthday jubilee. Officers of the SA and SS flanked and joined the archbishop and mayor in the requisite procession through Wittenberg's streets, gathering in the Marktplatz, where I now sat. Looking up from my table past the old city hall, I could see the street sign bearing the name Judenstrasse, physically marking the absence of a presence in the heart of this festive city. I tried but failed to imagine what that street's residents must have thought and experienced on Reformation Day, 1933, and I wondered if the word *Judenstrasse* was in the exercise booklets of the confirmands.

Fifty years later, in 1983, the five hundredth anniversary of Luther's birth, a very different kind of Luther celebration took place in Wittenberg. Following the *Festgottesdienst* (festival worship service) on Reformation Day, Friedrich Schorlemmer, pastor of the Stadtkirche (town church), led his flock from the pews through the streets to the Lutherhof, the large, open garden area that fronts the Lutherhaus museum. Timed to echo Luther's protest of institutionalized corruption and irrational authority nearly five centuries earlier, the group, over anvils, literally beat swords into plowshares, an act expressly forbidden by the communist government that ruled East Germany with an iron fist. Residents of Wittenberg, their actions on that night echoing and embodying a historical narrative of religiously motivated protest, played their role in the pro-democracy movement, the Peaceful Revolution, which culminated six years later in the fall of East Germany and the reunification of a divided land.

If Wittenberg was and remains a stage of theatrical performance and symbolic, dramatized action, it is also fast on its way to becoming a Disneyfied space, a combination of Reformation theme park and near-permanent festival center. The gravitas and intensity of the Wende slowly fading from memory, citizens of the former East Germany are getting on with business, and business is brisk in Wittenberg, at least during the tourist season from April to the end of October. Tour buses drop visitors at the Schlosskirche, and pick them up at the other end of town, at the Lutherhaus. In between, you can have your photo taken at Luther's grave, attend a worship service and sing "A Mighty Fortress," and have a Luther or a Katharina von Bora beer with lunch. Afterward, you can buy a pair of red socks with the famous (apocryphal) line uttered at the Diet of Worms, "Here I stand, I can do no other," stitched on the sole. If you stay late, perhaps a dinner theatre with Martin and Katie is in store. The celebration of Luther and the Reformation, once firmly under the control of church and local government, and dominated by ecclesiastical and civil religion, now includes market performances, the aims and interests of which are not necessarily those of faith or the shaping national identity and the politics of the state, but rather the making of revelry, local community, and money.

Graffiti sprayed near the Schlosskirche read *Kapitalismus abschaffen* (do away with capitalism), but Wittenberg's Marktplatz is living up to its name. Luther and the Reformation have become lucrative commodities for a city and a region struggling with nearly two decades of high unemployment (between 20 and 25 percent) and the transition from a communist to a capitalist economy. Once the center of the DDR's chemical industry—in the late 1960s, the government attempted to rename the city by replacing Lutherstadt with Chemischestadt (chemical city)—post-Wende Wittenberg has been transformed into a tourist destination.[8] The old city is the recipient of the tourist's gaze and the tourist's desire to dip into the sea of culture and heritage tourism. Museum, shrine, stage, theme park—the inner, old town of Wittenberg offers a little something for everyone. Gazing back up at the composed yet somewhat defiant Luther of Johann Gottfried Schadow's imagination, I played one of the favorite games in Wittenberg: I wondered what Luther would make of the festival scene that was about to play itself out in his city.

About This Book

This study involves the interpretation of contemporary public ritual associated with the figure of Martin Luther. Its setting is the region known today as Lutherland, a symbolically loaded landscape of heritage homes, churches, squares, monuments, museums, and ritual and performance events. Historically, Luther has been a kind of cipher that maps places and objects to images, narratives, and ideals. The Lutheran tradition is a textual one, but material and performance culture has also played a central role in attempts to shape and understand the meaning and reception of Luther and the Reformation. The meaning of Luther to civil society, culture, and the church has been crafted through particular objects (for example, the Lutherstuhl, Luther's desk chair in the Wartburg castle museum), to whole buildings (the Lutherhaus museum), to an entire city (Lutherstadt Wittenberg) and now, to an entire geographical region (Lutherland).

Geographically, Lutherland is located southwest of Berlin, composed of territory cutting across the modern states of Thuringia and Sachsen-Anhalt. Historically, the region was Luther's stomping grounds, Luther's land, Lutherland. Here we find Eisleben, where the great Reformer was born and died; Mansfeld, the mining community where Luther grew up; Eisenach, where Luther attended grammar school and to whose Wartburg castle he fled in the aftermath of the Diet of Worms; and Erfurt, where Luther attended university and later became a monastic. Torgau, close to Wittenberg, is the burial place of Luther's wife Katharina von Bora and was the seat of the electors of Saxony who supported Luther's work. At the heart of the region is Wittenberg, Luther's home for thirty-six years and birthplace of the German Reformation. This list of cities may locate Luther in geographical space, but Lutherland is no mere container of historically significant sites and events. Lutherland is an event-full medium, a process of place making, a symbolic landscape through and in which particular groups and individuals continue to create meaning out of bits of history, myth, image, and gesture drawn from and tied to the figure of Martin Luther.

The study of Luther and the Reformation is not merely a historical question; nor should students of Protestant culture limit themselves to theological, textual, and ethical approaches. Luther, as the pages in this book and the chapters on the DVD reveal, is still walking the streets of Wittenberg. Since the man penned his ninety-five theses against indulgences, Luther has been a renewable symbolic resource. The historical Luther is both the Luther of the Reformation and the Luther as he has been remembered and represented, ritualized and performed, bought and sold across the centuries.

The methods and theories informing this study are drawn from the fields of ritual studies, performance theory, and symbolic and interpretative anthropology, but I also employ historical methods. The history of Luther festivity is important context for understanding contemporary dynamics. Students of ritual and performance are concerned with describing, understanding, and interpreting the role of embodiment and action in religious, political, and cultural life—a growing counterweight in academia to decades of papers, books, and teaching devoted to discourse and textuality, not to mention textualism, the theorizing of nontextual phenomena through the extended metaphor of the text. Studying ritual and cultural performances involves examining "the embodiment of meanings in social contexts. The study of ritual is not primarily the study of ideas in people's heads or feelings in their hearts but about meanings embodied in posturing and gesturing."[9] An ethnographic approach to Christianity is relatively rare in the field of religious studies, and ethnographic treatments of Protestant culture are rarer still. Lutherland is a site of pilgrimage, public ritual, and heritage and theatrical performances, and the following chapters entail the description, analysis, and interpretation of the meanings of these practices.

On four different occasions over a two-year period, I traveled in Lutherland, visiting, attending, photographing, and filming the places and events that draw hundreds of thousands of visitors each year. In addition to photographic and video documentation, participant observation, and informal conversations along the routes to Luther, I conducted formal interviews with academics, clergy, tourists, pilgrims, performers, actors, and others involved in organizing and producing Lutherland's busy annual event calendar. Classical ethnography involves long-term study; my time in Lutherland more closely resembled excursions or forays into the field, returning home to add to the cache of ethnographic and historical material that has given birth to this book. The timing (and focus) of my visits was shaped by the rhythms and content of the festival calendar. I spent most of my time in the field in Wittenberg before, during, and after its two annual Reformation festivals. Most scholars traveling to Wittenberg do so to study the historical and theological dimensions of the Reformation, making use of the extensive archives that are part of the Lutherhaus museum, and receiving insight and inspiration from Luther's native surroundings. My interests were not historical or archival but ethnographic, though I have utilized historical and textual methods in the course of my research and writing. I witnessed most of the rites and performances discussed in the book at first hand, though I also draw on some retrospective accounts collected in the field, and occasionally on secondary textual, film, and photographic sources.

My fieldwork generated about forty hours of digital video footage, several CDs worth of photographs, a half-dozen high-density minidisks of audio interviews and sounds, a packed field journal, stacks of print literature—posters, postcards, event programs, newspaper clippings, maps, guidebooks—and a few choice souvenirs. As the reader will be aware, this book contains a DVD—but "contain" is the wrong word. The two, text and DVD, are meant to be parts of whole, neither containing the other. The book spins out into the DVD, but much of the multimedia material on the DVD consists of primary data used in the writing of the book. The reader is free, of course, to go about the joint task of reading/viewing as they see fit. The footnotes that appear periodically in the text suggest one option, referring the reader to a particular item on the DVD, a "relaxed link" that suggests "go here now, if you like."'

Following the links into the DVD is a way to add sound, color, and motion to textual description and interpretation of places and events. One aim of combining text and DVD is to utilize advances in digital media technology to bring religion and culture to life. Lived religion—ritual practice, for example—is not simply a matter of assenting to certain beliefs or holding certain values; rather, it is a sensuous activity. Ritual is a practice, a using and forming of the body, a way of bodily knowing and communicating. With video we can see and we can hear lived religion—and if a picture is worth a thousands words, well then, why not?

Yet the DVD materials do more than render the events discussed in the book visually compelling. The production of a DVD was driven by more than the desire to jazz up black marks on white paper. The DVD contains illustrative material and short films, but also data. In picking up this book, you become more than a mere reader. You also become a viewer-observer of the events I observed (or, at least, a record of those events). You can use ethnographic sensibilities and techniques in studying the multimedia materials, a process that may lead to interpretations and ideas at odds with those I develop in and through text and film. Authors are meant to be masters of their craft, but in granting readers access to material collected in the field, the ethnographic process is made more transparent. The combination of book and DVD should offer the reader insight into the relationship between theory, method, and scholarly interpretation. The reader will also find reflection on theoretical and methodological issues relevant to the study of public religion and ritual, including consideration of the use of video in ethnographic research.

Most of the DVD materials are not "raw." Rather, they represent various stages of "cooking"—dishes flavored by decisions about who, what, and how to shoot, by theoretical and methodological assumptions, and, importantly, by the process of editing. In terms of style or genre, the DVD includes a mix of the expository, the observational, and the impressionistic. Can scholars utilize digital video not just for recording data and observations but also for doing their work: explaining, analyzing, interpreting, and theorizing—not through the scholarly paper or the academic book but through the genre and medium of film? Can film stand alone, as Jay Ruby and others have suggested and advocated, as a statement of the academic's discoveries, conclusions, and critiques? Some of the items included here move in this direction, or so I would like to believe. Such a possibility, largely because of the media involved, suggests the scholar-cum-artist, a being rarely sighted in the hallways of academia. I do not consider any of the materials on the DVD "art." Nor do I make any great claims of methodological originality. Ethnographers have long been using a camera for the purposes of research; the past twenty years have witnessed vigorous discussion over the assets and liabilities of "visual anthropology," and there is now a tradition of ethnographic film extending back to the first cameras, some of which borders the domain of the artist, if not crossing over into it. The combining of text and DVD creates something of a new beast, the exact species of which I have yet to identify—but which I hope will not prove too unruly to handle.

I

Opening the Door

The most visited site in all of Lutherland is Wittenberg's Schlosskirche, the castle church. Approximately 80,000 visitors pass through the church each year. The church is a destination of Protestant pilgrims, a venue for heritage tourism, and an important setting for Reformation-themed performances and festivity. Inside the church are the graves of Martin Luther and his colleague Philip Melanchthon (1497–1560). Outside, dominating the façade of the east wall of the church, is the Thesenportal, the Theses Door.

The Theses Door

The door of the Schlosskirche that Luther would have known burned in a fire of 1760. Standing in its place is a set of massive bronze doors installed in 1858, as part of Luther's 375th birthday celebrations (see fig. 1.1). It is fitting that the original door has been lost to the ravages of time. On October 31, 1517, Luther sent written copies of his ninety-five theses to his superiors, Bishop Hieronymus Schulze of Brandenburg and Archbishop Albrecht of Magdeburg. The image of a defiant, rebellious hammering of the theses to the door of the castle church, however, is the stuff of legend, cultivated over the years through visual culture, stories, sermons, biographies, and on stage and screen.⊙

⊙ DVD: Legend to Portal

FIGURE I.I. The Theses Door of Wittenberg's Schlosskirche. Photograph by the author.

Luther's Theses Door symbolically marks the beginning of the Reformation, so it is fitting to begin this study at an auspicious location. But the primary reason for tending to the Theses Door is not so much its place in Reformation history (which is murky, at best), but its ongoing role in the mythologizing, ritualizing, and performing of the Reformation. Given that this book is informed by ethnographic sensibilities, theories, and methods drawn from ritual and performance studies, a church door may seem an unlikely starting point. The Theses Door, however, is a special kind of door—a portal. And a portal is a "locus for architectural symbolism" but it also "elicits ritual action."[1] Sacred architecture is not a static structure but an event-full place. Human hands, interests, and imagination make places, and these, in turn, make us who we are. Cultural geographers and phenomenologists refer to symbolically loaded locales using the notions of *place* and *landscape*, terms that attempt to get at the reciprocal relations between place and identity. Memory is a fickle faculty, and identity is not a given—neither floats freely in the depths of the human psyche. Memory is productive and creative, and identities anchor in specific locations, as Keith Basso has emphasized:

> If place-making is a way of constructing the past, a venerable means of doing human history, it is also a way of constructing social-tradi-tions and, in the process, personal and social identities. We *are*, in a sense, the place-worlds we imagine. . . . Place-making is . . . a form of *cultural* activity, and so, as any anthropologist will tell you, can only be grasped in relation to the ideas and practices with which it is accomplished.[2]

The Theses Door and the act associated with it, the Thesenanschlag (Luther's posting of the ninety-five theses), are prominent landmarks in the landscape of Lutherland. The Theses Door is sacred space for Lutheran and Protestant communities. It is a destination of heritage tourism, and hence a kind of commodity. The door is a cultural artifact, identified by UNESCO as repre-senting a pivotal moment in the course of Western history, politics, and religion. For members of Germany's left-wing protest movement, the Theses Door represents the historical complicity of religion with nationalism, milita-rism, and expansionist politics, and hence in need of an occasional paint bomb-ing. The Theses Door is a symbol, which means its meanings are complex, at times contested, and change over time.

The origin of the story that Luther posted his ninety-five theses originates with his younger colleague, Philip Melanchthon, in a preface Melanchthon wrote to the second volume of Luther's collected works, published after Luther's death, in 1549:

> venal indulgences were [being] promulgated by Tetzel, a friar of the Dominican order and a most audacious sycophant; at the same time, Luther, who was ardent in the pursuit of holiness, being irritated by [Tetzel's] impious and nefarious harangues, published his own

propositions on the subject of indulgences, which are to be found in
the first volume of his works; these he affixed to the church contiguous
to the castle of Wittenberg, on the day before the festival of All Saints,
in the year 1517.

Luther and his fellow Reformers made good use of visual culture for the purposes of propaganda and dissemination of doctrine and teachings. If Luther
indeed made a public display of defying Rome by posting his ninety-five theses,
it is likely that contemporary artists would have depicted the event—yet not a
single item of visual culture produced during Luther's life or in the century following his death documents or depicts the posting. Though the story existed in
a few texts (Melanchthon also mentions the event in a few letters), it was not a
part of Reformation popular culture in the century following Luther's death, an
odd fact given that this is the event said to have launched the Reformation.
Rather, the theme of the Thesenanschlag developed slowly, largely through the
visual culture accompanying Reformation jubilees.

The first representation of the Thesenanschlag dates to 1617, the year of
the first recorded public celebration of Luther's issuing of the ninety-five theses. Among the many items of visual culture produced for the 1617 jubilee in
Wittenberg was a broadsheet relating a dream sequence attributed to Frederick
the Wise, the elector of Saxony who supported Luther's reform. "The editor of
the broadsheet claimed that the story [of Frederick's dream] had been narrated
to Frederick's chaplain, Georg Spalatin, who passed it on to Antonio Musa. . .
who had written it down. The editor . . . claimed to have read this manuscript
in 1591, when it was in the possession of the pastor of Rochlitz, Batholomeus
Schönbach."[3] Such is the invention of tradition. In this 1617 broadsheet image,
Luther writes the ninety-five theses on the doors of Wittenberg's Schlosskirche
with a quill whose reach extends as far as Rome. The end of the quill pierces the
ear of Pope Leo X, who is depicted as a lion backed by clergy and curia. The
Thesenanschlag emerges then as part of the popular mythologizing and celebrating of Luther, mixing prophecy, politics, anti-Catholic polemics, and the
promulgation of civil religion; a year later, the conflagration now known as the
Thirty Years War (1618–1648) would begin.

No coins or medals with Reformation themes struck during Luther's lifetime depict the posting of the theses, nor do those struck for the centennial of
1617. Only in 1717, in conjunction with the bicentennial Reformation celebrations, do medals illustrating the posting begin to appear; yet of the 180 coins and
medals produced, only three depict the posting of the theses. The century from
1717 to 1817 produced approximately 155 Luther coins and medals, yet only three
are theses-related, and two of these three were produced for the 1817 Reformation

celebrations. In the following century, however, a new trend emerges. Between 1817 and 1917, roughly 150 coins and medals with Reformation imagery were struck (a number similar to preceding centuries). Of these, twelve items utilized the theme of the Thesenanschlag, and ten of these twelve were struck for the celebrations of 1917. It is only during the nineteenth and early twentieth centuries that the Thesenanschlag surfaces as an important theme and symbol informing the commemoration and celebration of Martin Luther. In the early nineteenth century, Reformation Day emerges as the date of the Reformation, and Luther as a key figure in the narratives of Enlightenment, nationalism, and Liberalism that characterized the national consciousness of the period.

As the evidence of visual culture reveals, nineteenth- and twentieth-century depictions of the Thesenanschlag cultivate an image of Luther as a heroic figure, a lone individual who took an intrepid step, engaged in the bold deed of publicly defying papal power. The Thesenanschlag was imagined and depicted as an "extraordinarily audacious act which [actually] runs counter to the conservative nature of Luther, particularly at that time of his career."[4] Luther has worn many masks over the years. During the later half of the nineteenth century, Luther became a national hero.

Ritual-Architectural Event

People transform flat, homogenous space into symbolically significant place through a variety of means. Three important vehicles of place making are myth, architectural construction, and performance and ritual. With Luther's Theses Door, object and act, place and performance, story and memory intertwine. Over the years, Luther's Thesenportal has occasioned a variety of rites and performances: commemoration, ceremony, processions, celebration, pilgrimage, tourism, theatre, liturgy, protest, and social drama. These performances, every bit as much as the stable architecture of the Theses Door, have contributed to the meanings, narratives, values, and beliefs that individuals and groups have held and continue to hold with respect to the figure of Martin Luther and the event of the Reformation.

The religionist Lindsay Jones has developed a comprehensive set of heuristic tools for investigating and interpreting sacred architecture. The novel move made by Jones is to focus on events, situations, occasions, and times when sacred architecture comes to life. Rather than "questing after the meanings of buildings per se," Jones calls for interpretations of concrete "situations that bring people and buildings into active interaction"—dynamic occasions that Jones describes as "ritual-architectural events":

Meaning resides neither in the building itself (a physical object) nor in the mind of the beholder (a human subject), but rather in the negotiation or the interactive relation that subsumes both building and beholder—in *the ritual-architectural event* in which buildings and human participants alike are involved. Meaning is not a condition or quality of the building, of the thing itself; meaning arises from situations. The meaning of a building, then, must always be a meaning for some specific one at some specific time in some specific place.[5]

Certain kinds of architecture elicit certain kinds of rites and performances, and Jones maps the relation between place, performance, and ritual enactment in terms of a number of ritual-architectural priorities (table 1.1). These categories

TABLE 1.1 A Morphology of Ritual Architectural Priorities

1. Architecture as Orientation: The Instigation of Ritual-Architectural Events
   A. Homology: Sacred architecture that presents a miniaturized replica of the universe and/or conforms to a celestial archetype
   B. Convention: Sacred architecture that conforms to standardized rules and/or prestigious mythicohistoric precedents
   C. Astronomy: Sacred architecture that is aligned or referenced with respect to celestial bodies or phenomena

2. Architecture as Commemoration: The Center of Ritual-Architectural Events
   A. Divinity: Sacred architecture that commemorates, houses, and/or represents a deity, divine presence, or conception of ultimate reality
   B. Sacred History: sacred architecture that commemorates an important mythical, mythicohistorical, or miraculous episode or circumstance
   C. Politics: Sacred architecture that commemorates, legitimates, or challenges socioeconomic hierarchy and/or temporal authority
   D. The Dead: Sacred architecture that commemorates revered ancestors and/or other deceased individuals or groups

3. Architecture as Ritual Context: The Presentation of Ritual-Architectural Events
   A. Theater: Sacred architecture that provides a stage setting or backdrop for ritual performance
   B. Contemplation: Sacred architecture that serves as a prop or focus for meditation or devotion
   C. Propitiation: Sacred architecture and processes of construction designed to please, appease, and/or manipulate "the sacred" (however variously conceived)
   D. Sanctuary: Sacred architecture that provides a refuge or purity, sacrality, or perfection

From Lindsay Jones, *The Hermeneutics of Sacred Architecture.*

are not mutually exclusive, and most sacred sites serve a number of purposes. With respect to Wittenberg's Thesenportal, several of these priorities are at work. A full interpretation of the Thesenportal must tend to its physical characteristics (architectural symbolism), but also to events the Theses Door occasions (celebration, pilgrimage, public performance) and to its history, to "describing the career of a *specific* architectural work or configuration."[6] The Thesenportal, as we shall see, began its career as both the centerpiece of ritual-architectural events commemorating sacred history and ecclesiastical politics (priorities II B and C), and as a propitious backdrop or setting for such events (III A). The *Thesenportal* is also is part of a sacred building housing "revered ancestors" (II D), provides a setting for diverse rites and performances (III A), and is a "prop" to focus devotion, especially on Reformation Day (III B).

In the course of this study, we will visit Luther's Theses Door several times, examining a variety of ritual-architectural events, both past and present. If the door is a "prop" to focus devotion, it is also place to ground scholarly descriptions and interpretations of the performance of the Reformation. The door opens onto a world of ritual and performance, and these events in turn offer insight into social-cultural dynamics.

Tetzel at the Door⊙

A beggar sits in the middle of the street, cup in hand, pleading his case to the festivalgoers pouring into the city for Reformation Day. Sitting a stone's throw from the famous Thesenportal, he has staked out a spot framed by Wittenberg's majestic Schlosskirche. Twenty thousand people will visit the old center of Wittenberg during the three days of the festival, and many of them will walk by the church and at least cast a glance at the Theses Door. For the beggar, the church with its famous door ought to provide an ideal setting to ply his trade. He has numbers to his advantage today, and history on his side.

For me, an academic trained in the interpretation of the symbols, myths, and rites of religion, the Schlosskirche is a place that generates a wealth of material on which to reflect. An 8 a.m. festival worship service sponsored by the Evangelical Lutheran Church of America (ELCA) has just ended. An hour from now, there will be a second service, the main event of the day, the Festgottesdienst (Festival Worship Service). The large, open plaza of the castle church is abuzz with activity as I mingle, talk with visitors, and film the scene.

⊙ DVD: Tetzel at the Door

For two long weeks leading up to Reformation Day, a lone worker was perched on a scaffold in front of the Theses Door, toothbrush and cleaning solution in hand, delicately removing the effects of a yellow paint bomb thrown at an (in) opportune moment in Wittenberg's festival calendar. The paint bomb was no mere act of random vandalism, but one in a series of anti-Luther protest actions organized by Germany's left-leaning anti-globalization movement in order to cast light on the dark side of Wittenberg's favorite citizen—graffiti as a crime of style, covert occupation of public space, and political dissonance. The man completed his work just in time for the festival opening on Saturday. Now, two days later, the Thesenportal is once again shining and a focus of attention. A camera operator and reporter from ZDF (a national broadcaster) arrive and take the requisite shots of the door and church; they will use these images to frame their report of the day's events. In front of the Theses Door, a few workers are setting up a stage and sound system, which will be used later in the day as part of a confirmation rite with hundreds of young Lutherans. The three American pastors who conducted the morning service are striking a familiar pose, standing in front of the bronze doors for a photograph.

Two of the clergy are members of the ELCA. One is a bishop, the other, program director of the American ELCA Wittenberg Center. The ELCA established the center in partnership with the local German churches in 1999, and one of its roles is to organize pilgrimage and travel-study tours to the area. The third individual, Ross Merkel, is the pastor of St. Paul's Lutheran Church in Oakland, California. Merkel is leading a small group from his congregation on a pilgrimage through Lutherland. Though St. Paul's is on the ELCA church roster, Merkel is no longer ELCA clergy. In 1994, Merkel was defrocked after making public his long-term gay partnership. His congregation, however, has refused to let him go, and their pilgrimage to heart of Lutheran territory is charged with the emotion of a running engagement with church policy over issues of same-sex marriage and the ordination of gay and lesbian clergy.

A small scene in a larger social drama is unfolding this morning. The ELCA bishop who led the morning service was a committee member who sat in judgment on Merkel, casting his vote in favor of dismissal. Tomorrow, on All Saint's Day, Merkel will ascend the raised pulpit in the Schlosskirche and deliver a sermon as part of a communion service the group has planned. Standing over Luther's grave in the place associated with the reformation of the church, what will Merkel say? Will his message be controversial? His demeanor defiant? Will this service alter or reinforce how the ELCA embodies controversial issues of sexuality and marriage? Several of the St. Paul's group wander by, take photographs at the doors, and say hello—I have been spending time with the group the past two days. (I return to a discussion of the St. Paul's group in chapter 7.)

As the congregation disperses, others arrive. A conservative wing of the Lutheran Church in Germany (SELK) is handing out Luther's small catechism and other evangelical literature.[7] Two Jehovah's Witnesses and a lone Hare Krishna are also busy proselytizing—oblivious, it seems, to the fact that this is Luther's city, and Luther's day. A young girl busks with her violin, people are slowly gathering for the Festgottesdienst (festival worship), and the beggar is shouting to those with ears to hear, "remember thesis forty-three." Visitors are milling around the Schlossplatz, taking photos, inspecting the Thesenportal, wandering in and out of the church, socializing, and enjoying the sunshine and unseasonably warm weather. People ought to be in a giving mood, but the beggar is having little luck. Dressed in hooded rags to fit in with the medieval ethos of the festival, the beggar rattles his cup, again calling out, "remember thesis forty-three." It is unlikely that anyone passing by can make the connection—the outcome of four decades of communist government and rampant secularization across Europe. Nor can they shuffle over and read thesis forty-three, since Luther's ninety-five theses are inscribed on the bronze doors in the language of the originals—Latin. I am in the same boat. Though I read Luther's ninety-five theses in preparation for my fieldwork, I certainly cannot recall them by number, and I have little Latin, and less Greek. Like most people here today, I am relatively un-churched, which is something of an odd fact: twenty thousand more or less secular individuals converging on Wittenberg to partake in the Reformation Day festivities. How does the beggar know thesis forty-three?

A university student from nearby Halle, the young man is in Wittenberg playing the role of a beggar, performing his part in the recreation of a medieval world on the verge of tipping into the modern. Promotional materials describe Reformation festivals in Wittenberg as both medieval and Renaissance, drawing on a narrative that takes Luther and the Reformation as the pivot between an old, corrupt, decaying world, and a progressive, renewed social order and faith. The mythic-historical narrative of renewal and reform is enticing in Lutherland. It offers residents of the region the hope that lightning might strike twice, that history may repeat itself, that Wittenberg and the other cities of Luther, drawing on the resources and spirit of their Reformation past, can rebuild the economy, cultural institutions, and a positive sense of identity. Period costuming, heritage performance, historical plays, Renaissance music, a medieval market, traditional arts and crafts—these are the bread and butter of contemporary Reformation-themed tourism and festivity. The beggar has signed on with Heureka, a large firm from nearby Leipzig that supplies performers, stages, children's rides—everything required for a large, open-air medieval-themed festival.

In calling out "remember thesis forty-three," the beggar transports his audience to another place and time, and invites participation in the creation of a fictive world. To give to this beggar in this place on this day is to give as if one were back in Luther's Wittenberg, filled with his spirit of reform, and cognizant of his concern and work for those in need—and that is the genius of the student's begging, for he really is begging. With an unemployment rate of 20 percent in the former East Germany, heritage tourism is vital to the economy of the region. During the summer tourist season, it is common for history students to lead busloads of Americans and Europeans through East Germany's historic sites. Just as tourism, after a decade of rebuilding, was starting to roll, came 9/11, the result being a sharp decline in American tourists and dollars.[8] Many students have taken to earning their keep at Germany's summer festival scene, and playing the role of a medieval beggar in Luther's Wittenberg is a practical, if ludic, strategy.

A five-minute walk from where the beggar sits is Wittenberg's Stadtkirche, or town church, where Luther preached most of his sermons. A large poster hanging in the entrance supplies some context to the beggar's activities here on Reformation Day:

> Your generosity will support our prayers. At the beginning of August,
> we started our special prayers for social justice, and established a
> "community fund." The idea comes from Martin Luther. Martin
> Luther did away with indulgences. Money [that would have otherwise
> gone to purchasing indulgences] was freed up to support the poor,
> the old, the sick of the city. This was the first social safety net of the
> modern world. Social need in Wittenberg is great. . . . Please help
> others help themselves.

Like the poster in the town church, the beggar's call for an act of memory from his audience—"remember thesis forty-three"—is an attempt, he explains, to situate hard times in a foundational principle of Luther's Reformation.

"What is thesis forty-three?" I ask.

"Christians should be taught that one who gives to the poor or lends to the needy, does a better action than if he purchases indulgences."[9]

"Are you Lutheran?"

"No."

"Christian?"

"No."

I have a sense the beggar is feeling slightly embarrassed by my inquiries, so I do not pursue our conversation. The scene is somewhat surreal: a non-Christian beggar citing Luther's theses in front of Luther's Door on Reformation Day to a mix of believers and secular festivalgoers, in the hope that Luther's spirit of charity will encourage some loose change to flow.

Begging is hard work on the best of days, and it has become doubly hard at this moment due to the arrival of another player who is stealing the scene. Brüder Ignatius has arrived. I thank the beggar for his time, and, following the crowd, move closer to the Thesenportal. Assuming the role of his legendary ancestor John Tetzel, Brüder Ignatius has girded his loins and walked into Luther's city, straight to the door whose engraved theses were the product of Luther's outrage, and he has set up shop. Brüder Ignatius is selling indulgences—and everyone wants one. If just one of the buyers had the knowledge of our beggar (or could read Latin), the sound of "remember thesis forty-three" might ring in their ears, and lead them to consider what they are doing; but indulgences are selling like hotcakes—or, to use a more appropriately placed analogy, they are selling like pints of Luther beer.

My short conversation with the beggar taught me that appearances can be deceiving during festival time in Wittenberg, and Brüder Ignatius is not simply cashing in on a good idea. Michael is a twenty-five-year-old kindergarten teacher with a Lutheran church in Leipzig, a faithful Protestant. On the suggestion of his father, he started attending medieval markets and festivals, dressed in the robes of a monk, playing the role of an Ablasshandler—a seller of indulgences. Michael donates the money he collects to his kindergarten. Modeling himself on the figure of John Tetzel, he has mastered some of the villain's famous lines: *Sobald das Geld im Kasten klingt, die Seele aus dem Fegefeuer in den Himmel springt* ("As soon as the coin in the coffer rings, a soul from hell to heaven springs"). The crowd, young and old alike, is eating it up.

As Brüder Ignatius holds court, people crowd around, some tentatively curious about what is going on, others willingly entering into the spirit of the act, playing along, buying their way out of a host of "sins." For a euro or two, Ignatius sells indulgences for hard drinking and gluttony, excessive belching and farting, unfaithfulness in marriage, too much time spent playing computer games or watching television, or for hitting one's spouse; he keeps blank indulgences handy, so he can make up what is required, on the spot.

Our beggar can but frown at this unexpected turn of bad luck. The Theses Door was meant to serve his aims, but Tetzel has possessed it—and it will be several hours before Luther appears on the scene. Knowing the futility of pitting faith in human charity against the desire that our sins be forgiven (or the desire to accumulate kitschy mementoes), the beggar wanders off to find a better location.

Action and Performance

Structuralism is a dominant theoretical paradigm in the humanities and social sciences. Scholars of a structuralist bent utilize the metaphor of built structures (characterized by stability, weightiness, and relative permanence) to think about social-cultural life. In this study, I draw more on dramatistic and performance models than from the tradition of structuralism, a move that is relatively intuitive. The beggar's and Brüder Ignatius's play out front of the Thesenportal is representative of the kinds of activities that constitute the "performing of the Reformation." To treat these performances as representative of social structures is to impose the qualities implied by the structural metaphor (permanence, stability, foundational) on to human action; I want to emphasize matters of expressiveness, embodiment, process, and intention.

A festival, the occasion of Brüder Ignatius's performance, is more like a performance than a structure. Festivals involve costuming, music, theatre, programs, stages, lightning, souvenirs, performers, and audiences. A festival, like theatre, happens, occurs, takes place—and then disappears, only, at some point in the future, to take place again. The temporal character of a festival is puzzling: Its being is inseparable from its presentation, from its performance. A festival is always unique (this year's festival, not last year's or next year's), yet remains the same festival. Paradoxically, the essence of that which exists to be performed is always to be something different, yet somehow the same.

Perhaps the simplest way of characterizing the scene described in "Tetzel at the Door" is through the notion of action. According to Kenneth Burke, "things move, persons act."[10] Burke, in distinguishing between mere motion and purposeful action, emphasizes that deeds are as fundamental to human life as words or ideas. Though we spend much of our time engaged in instinctual or habitual behavior, people also actively work on the cultural or symbolic dimensions of their world; and we do much of this symbolic work through performance and ritual. Burke draws on an age-old way of understanding and imagining human being in the world. Dramatism, the notion that social life is akin to stage drama, has proven itself a fundamental metaphor that informs Western intellectual and aesthetic traditions going back to ancient Greece. Imagining the universe and life as a *theatrum mundi* (theatre of the world) has a long history. "All the world's a stage, And all the men and women merely players," wrote Shakespeare. Centuries later, Erving Goffman would discuss how people, even in the most mundane of situations, are actors, presenting themselves to one another. There "is something fundamentally performative about human being in the world . . . human intentionality, culture and social reality are fundamentally articulated in the world through performance."[11] As a method and a theoretical perspective, dramatism and performance theory draw attention to the role of the expressive, performative, and aesthetic arts in social-cultural life, and emphasizes the metaphor of "life as performance, event, action."

In Burke's dramatism, the verb "to act" covers "any verb, no matter how specific or how general, that has connotations of consciousness or purpose. . . . The basic unit of action would be defined as 'The human body in conscious or purposive motion.'"[12] If the situation happens to be a festival, a liturgical rite, a play, procession, parade, or pilgrimage (the ritual and performance genres discussed in this book)—periodic events that stand in marked contrast to the routines of everyday life—then our actions become highly stylized, decorous, exaggerated, playful, symbolic, and purposeful. Brüder Ignatius was seeking some extra money for the kindergarten (though that is not all he was seeking); the actions of the beggar were to help pay his way through university; the St. Paul's congregation was engaged in deepening their faith.

"Tetzel at the Doors" is an example of heritage performance. Heritage performance involves the use of live actors—we can call them actors even though many of the individuals have had little or no professional training— to portray historical characters, an illusion often achieved primarily through historical dress or costume. Martin Luther leads a tour group through the streets of Wittenberg, or sits at the dining table with you, eating and talking to his wife. The instructor of the local Karate school dresses up like a monk for the Luther's Wedding festival. High school girls become the nuns smuggled out of the convent, one of the remembered narratives of Reformation-era Wittenberg. What are the aims of providing the opportunity for visitors to be led through the streets of Wittenberg by a tour guide dressed in period garb? Or to see Martin and Katharina stroll by arm and arm as you eat your bratwurst? Ideally, the answer is something like this: Living history performance draws the audience into an experience of heritage, an experience of the past that partakes of the authentic, an authenticity that we so often find ourselves desiring in a world of fakery and mediated corporate images. Heritage is a return to local customs and crafts, to regional tastes and products, to the land and seasons, a return that grounds lives in a particular place, countering the placelessness of postmodern culture.

The other side to such arguments involves a radical deconstruction of the notion of authenticity. Overall, scholars have been wary and critical of heritage performance and the production of heritage sites such as Wittenberg. On the one hand, Wittenberg is proof positive that the revitalization of local heritage, traditions, and history can stimulate economic development. But critics of the heritage site phenomenon argue that these gains are purchased at a high price. When culture, so runs the argument, becomes an object to be packaged, bought, and sold, culture is inevitably diluted and local actors become distanced from those very traditions on which the community is founded. Heritage productions, like the Wittenberg festivals, are forms of replication and reproduction, and in our mechanized, mediated age of the copy-commodity, there is a withering of authenticity, a decline of the real, a loss of aura. Roughly 15 percent of Wittenberg's population belongs to the church; far fewer regularly attend. The city and the wider Lutherland region is under economic pressure to, in effect, become "the other"—that is, to become representative of Lutheran, more broadly Protestant, heritage and culture. Wittenberg's Lutheran and Reformation past is being given a monetary value, a process of commoditization that devalues the very rites and material culture of that tradition for the area's local population. Davydd Greenwood made such an argument in the case of local festivals in the Basque region of Spain. Proceeding from a Marxist analysis, Greenwood argued that in transforming local cultural practices into tourist spectacles, "ritual has become a performance for money. The meaning is gone."[13]

My aim in briefly introducing the "tourist impact" critique of the heritage and culture industry is to acknowledge its importance and relevance in the postmodern, global world, but I also want to get it out of the way. The transformations that have taken place in Lutherland since the Wende deserve to be analyzed in terms of processes of what we might call McDonaldization and Disneyfication, processes that have the effect of transforming sites into theme parks, but this is not my aim here; there is something more at work and at play in Wittenberg than the commoditization of culture.[14] Many tourist and heritage researchers "talk about measuring tourist 'impact' on a local culture, language that brings to mind not just destruction (a bomb impacts on a target) but also passivity (the other is always impacted upon)."[15] Festival culture in Wittenberg is anything but passive. The heritage reclamation work that is under way in Wittenberg is not driven merely by economics but also by a genuine interest in revitalizing traditions, building community, and encouraging opportunities for expressive action. As Goethe wrote of Carnival in Italy, it is "a festival that is really not given to the people, but one the people give to themselves."[16] The people in Wittenberg's streets at festival time are not cultural commoditizers but cultural animators.

Burke's view of action reminds us that performance and ritual are neither obsessive nor unconscious forms of behavior, but potentially adaptive and deliberate. Michael's role as an indulgence seller provides him with the oppor-tunity to do more than make some extra money for his church, as he explains: "At first, most people shake their heads or want nothing to do with the church. But through this historical figure that I play, people start talking. Sometimes, I'm really surprised how seriously, how meaningfully, and how long people will talk about the history [of indulgences and the Reformation]. Such an opportu-nity [to talk about Luther with atheists or secularists] is rare."

Michael's play has an allure to it. Through period costuming, role playing, good humor, and a creative reworking of indulgence material, Michael draws people into conversation over issues of interest to him—Luther, the Reforma-tion, the church, and the state of contemporary society. His performance is both profitable and playful. His presence definitely contributed to the festive atmosphere out front of the Theses Door on the morning of Reformation Day—but his intentions are also religious. Michael's Tetzel routine is not simply fun, or simply about making some extra money for his kindergarten, but a thread in the concerted effort of committed Lutherans to rebuild the Evangelical Church. In an ironic twist, his indulgence selling at the contemporary Reformation Day festival is meant to perform a function similar to what Luther intended with the ninety-five theses: to engage people in conversation and debate over social, political, and religious questions.

An approach to ritual and performance that inquires into intentions and motivation must distinguish between purpose and function. Whether the purpose (or intention) of Michael's play resonates with its actual function is a complex question; answering it partly requires considering the reactions from different individuals or groups. Not everyone is pleased with Michael's playful performance of history. Michael first played Brüder Ignatius in 2003, at a festi-val celebrating the eight hundredth anniversary of the small town of Ablass, located a few miles to the south of Wittenberg. When he applied to the city for a permit to work the festival as an Ablasshandler, the Catholic Church attempted to intervene, arguing they had sole rights to sell indulgences. A second concern was that Michael would be wearing the robes of a monk. By law, a person may only wear an official uniform if they hold the office the uniform represents—a law backed up by a 3,000 euro fine. Fortunately for Michael (and an indulgence-hungry public), the law does not apply to historical-themed marketplaces or festivals, so when a suitable festival rolls around, Michael dons his monk's robes. Though Michael is not intentionally satirizing Catholicism, his performance prob-ably perpetuates anti-Catholic stereotypes and sentiments that have long been present in Reformation and Luther festivity. Dressing and playing "Catholic" is a prominent part of Wittenberg's Luther festivals; purpose and function do not always go hand in hand.

The purpose-function distinction (what we intend versus the outcome of our actions) is but one issue or theme in the study of ritual and performance. Another is the connection between play and work. One sense of the verb "to perform" is "to pretend." Michael pretends to be John Tetzel. As Brüder Ignatius, he does not expound, as in a lecture, on Luther's ninety-five theses; rather, he dramatizes part of the Luther story, plays with it, and engages people in the act of buying a fictive indulgence. Much ritual and performance is ludic.[17] Whereas the commonsensical view tends to divorce play and work, theorists of performance and ritual take in interest in the relations between pretending and doing. Performance is understood to be playful and dramatic, but so too is some ritual. Ritual, play, games, theatre—these genres share certain commonalities. They are not entirely driven by a means-end distinction, rather, they are activities valued in and of themselves. When a costumed Martin Luther leads a tour group through the streets of Wittenberg, he is working, but he is also at play. Play, make believe, costuming, role playing—these are defining features of festivals and heritage tourism sites, and regular occurrences out in front of Luther's Door.

2

The Wittenberg Festivals

A number of interrelated features characterize celebration. Celebrations often recall mythological or historical origins, deeds and persons pivotal to religious, regional, national, or other group identities. Celebrations are composed of a mix of ritual and performance genres. Celebrations are public events, and hence tend to be participatory events—the line between audience and participants often blurs, partly because celebrations take place in the streets and in open, public space, rather than in tightly framed spaces (such as a church, theatre, or concert hall). Celebrations are seasonal events; they come around repeatedly, having their own autonomous, cyclical time, punctuating an otherwise homogenous calendar. Celebrations have entertainment value; they are typically joyful, exuberant occasions; and they appeal to all the senses.

A Beer for Martin (I)

On Saturday, October 30, as the bells of Wittenberg's Stadtkirche struck four, the 2004 version of Wittenberg's annual Reformation Day festival kicked off in the Marktplatz. The geographical center of the old town, the Marktplatz is also a focal point for the festivities, host to the "medieval market spectacle." The festival fool and his music-playing, juggling, comic, ironic, tongue-twisting, theatricalizing cohorts called the crowd to order, aided by a short

"Da-Da-Da-DAA!" on a herald trumpet. It was a warm, sunny afternoon. The crowd of 250 or so festivalgoers that had gathered in the Marktplatz was in good spirits, and the spirits—beer and a little wine—were beginning to flow. After a few jokes (satire of clergy and sexual innuendo about monks and nuns), the fool procured himself a beer from a nearby vendor. Balancing the valued brew on his cocked head, the fool weaved his way through the crowd, navigating the uneven cobblestones, chairs, tables, and bodies, returning to the stage tucked away in the corner of the town square.

There the fool waited, beer on head, as his fellow *Spielleute* (players) volunteered a heavy-set, grizzled member of the crowd into their merry band. Hands thrust deep in the pockets of a worn leather bomber jacket, an apprehensive, slightly embarrassed look on his face, the man stepped forward into the middle of the U-shaped circle of onlookers that had formed in front of the stage. As fate (or good planning or good performance) would have it, his name was Martin. The fool, nodding and smiling in approval at the fortuitousness of the man's name, looked up to Schadow's *Luther*, back to Martin the man, and at once equated the two figures with the movement of his hand. Martin the monument was now Martin the man. His task? To down the fool's large mug of beer without coming up for air. Martin lifted the mug, and started to chug. It was over in just a few seconds; the players had chosen well. Martin had indeed been up to the job, and received the crowd's praise by way of rousing applause, helped along with a few more blasts on the trumpet—but the performance was not over.

One of the fool's men turned his trumpet end to end and, holding it to his ear, listened attentively to the stirrings in Martin's belly. Satisfied that all was settling well, the fool then proceeded to spin Martin around like a top. The players bent the poor man over, dizzy from the spinning—not to mention the beer—and listened again, this time with the short end of the trumpet probing the air near the man's backside, the large end funneling fumes back to the player's nose. Martin produced the desired wind—apparently, I can't testify to having heard or smelled it—the crowd cheered, and the fool pronounced the annual Reformationsfest underway. This is not what I had expected—though given my knowledge of the historical Luther it was, I concluded, somehow fitting.

Luther was a genius, a father of modernity, a historical-cultural giant. Luther revolutionized notions about sin and grace and freedom and autonomy. In translating the Bible, he gave birth to the German language; in placing the Book in the hands of the common folk, he wrested interpretive and doctrinal authority from clerics and theologians. He also claimed that if he broke wind in Wittenberg it could be smelled in Rome; he farted at the devil to keep him at bay; and the famed "tower experience," Luther's breakthrough insight that man is justified before God by grace through faith, seems to have been intimately connected with relief from a serious bout of constipation. The man also really enjoyed a good beer. Wittenbergers, I learned that afternoon in the Marktplatz, celebrate Luther warts, farts, and all.

It is said that first impressions are the lasting ones. The contemporary Reformation Day festival consists of much else besides food, drink, shopping, and games in the Marktplatz, but the image of the fool in his black monk's robes, standing with his bald head tilted to one side, delicately balancing a beer with a quizzical grimace on his face has stuck with me. I found the scene comical; comical because the players (Spielleute) are good at what they do, but also because I did not expect such an opening to what I had framed in my mind as a church festival and the rites of civil religion. No contemporary accounts being available, I had, prior to my fieldwork, read some primary source material and secondary research on late-nineteenth- and early-twentieth-century Luther festivity. This early research had not prepared me for mock monks, beer, inverted herald trumpets, and poking fun at Martin.

The opening scene of my first Reformation Day Festival—let us give it a name, "A Beer for Martin"—generated a good laugh. I laughed out of joy over the topsy-turvy carnivalesque festival world I was entering. I laughed at my naive expectations of what the contemporary celebration of Luther and the Reformation might look like—and I laughed, partly out of fear, over whether I would be able make sense of the festivals, the complexity of which was now clear.

The Festivals

October 31, 1517, is a date inscribed in the collective memory of Wittenberg's history, and indeed, the history of Europe and the West. So is November 9, 1989, the day the Berlin Wall, and with it, communism, fell. Germany, a nation divided at the end of the Second World War, was reunited; the punishment for the horrors of the Nazi era was over.[1]

Wittenberg's two annual Reformation-themed festivals are linked to its past, but they take place in the present, a present dominated by the hopes and problems that have accompanied the reunification of Germany.[2] In the post-Wende era, residents of Wittenberg face numerous challenges. The area is plagued by high unemployment and the difficult transition to a twenty-first-century global economy. The repressive legacy of communism has had a negative impact on the development of participatory democracy and an engaged public sphere. Citizens face difficult questions of history and memory in light of East Germany's fascist and communist past; and the region, like other areas in Europe, has seen the rise of right-wing political parties in recent years. There is uncertainty and ambivalence about the place and role of the former East in the new, reunified Germany.

When East Germans poured across the border in November of 1989, they had two primary destinations: the homes of friends and family, and shopping centers. The peaceful revolution was also a consumer revolution, born in part out of the desire to join the modern, global economy, to become a part of affluent society. Wittenberg, like many smaller cities in the former East Germany, however, remains economically depressed. During the communist era, investment in heavy industry made a nearby chemical plant the heart of the local economy, which was modeled on large, state-planned monostructures; few small or medium-sized businesses existed. In 1989, the chemical and mining industries collapsed. These industries, along with the agricultural sector, have rebounded somewhat after a difficult transition to a market economy, but unemployment in the Wittenberg region hovers around 20 percent, and many young people leave the area for jobs and education in larger urban centers. The population has dropped from 68,000 in 1989 to 47,000 in 2008. In less than twenty years, the city lost 20 percent of its population.

Wittenberg's considerable cultural capital is an opportunity to tap the tourism market. Of the sixteen federal German states, Sachsen-Anhalt is near the bottom in overnight stays, one of the key economic indicators in the tourism industry. Wittenberg's annual festivals are the high points in a yearlong calendar of cultural events, an aim of which is to promote tourism and draw overnight visitors to the city. People do not, of course, live by bread alone. The Wittenberg festivals are economic engines, but they are more than that: They play a role in bringing the city and region back to life. The contemporary festivals, as public events, are of and for the public; residents of Wittenberg and the surrounding region make up roughly two-thirds of those attending.

Reformation Day and Luther's Wedding are multidimensional public events. Reformation Day, which falls on October 31, is the smaller of the two, drawing roughly 20,000 visitors. Upward of 100,000 visitors swarm into Wittenberg's old town over the second weekend in June for Luther's Wedding. Reformation Day is a centuries-old tradition; Luther's Wedding is new, inaugurated in 1994. Reformation Day is a church festival and a civic holiday; Luther's Wedding is a *Volksfest* or city festival. These differences aside, the two events bear many similarities. Richard Schechner divides the performance pie into the ideal types of ritual, theatre, play, music, dance, games, and sports. "Together these seven comprise the public performance activity of humans."[3] The Olympic Games, perhaps the grandest of contemporary public rituals, incorporates the range of human performativity. Sports and games are absent in the Reformation Day Festival, though they play a minor role in Luther's Wedding, in the form of contests: log rolling and rooster crowing contests, penny-carnival games, implicit competition among marching bands for the public's eye. Both festivals incorporate ritual, theatre, play, music, and dance.

Wittenberg's annual festivals are integral to the religious, social, political, and economic concerns of the region. They mark the beginning and end of the tourist season; among their other purposes and functions, the festivals fuel the engine of cultural tourism that runs the local economy. Both Reformation Day and Luther's Wedding include a medieval market; traditional arts, handicrafts, and cuisine; parades and processions; street performers and music; buying and selling; concerts and special worship services. A number of groups and institutions organize and promote the festivals, each with their own interests and concerns: regional and local economic development offices; the city of Wittenberg; local community groups and societies; corporate sponsors; local businesses; theatre and performance groups, some specializing in medieval- themed festivals; and church-affiliated groups and centers.

The German Church

Understanding the roles played by various church and faith groups in Wittenberg today requires knowing a bit about the history of Protestantism in the region. Unlike post-Revolutionary America, in post-Reformation Europe church and state were tightly linked. One's religion was not voluntary, but dictated by the circumstances of birth. Following the Peace of Westphalia in 1648, depending on political boundaries, one was born into either a Protestant or Catholic state, and religious dissent was punishable under law. The Protestant church was in turn divided into Lutheran and Calvinist territories. Wittenberg, and surrounding Saxon territory, was Lutheran.

Protestant church history in eastern Germany is a maze of twists and turns. I will pick up the story in the nineteenth century. In the early nineteenth century, Prussia emerged from its humble beginnings as a small state (in what is now Poland) to become a major European power, expanding its territory and influence. The region known today as Lutherland cuts across several states, but it was once enfolded inside the sphere of Prussian influence. Prussian territories were principally Protestant, but comprised a mix of Calvinist and Lutheran communities. In an effort to unite divided princely territories into a modern nation-state, the Prussians, in 1817, formed a Union Church of Lutheran and Reformed parishes in Brandenburg, and most Protestant churches throughout

Prussian territories followed their example. The various *Landeskirchen* (regional or state churches) united as one, giving up the names Lutheran and Reformed to become the Evangelical Church (*Evangelische Kirche*). The term *Evangelisch*, as it is used on the street in Germany, is roughly the equivalent of the English word *Protestant*. Historically, the term derives from an ecumenical union and blending of Lutheran and Calvinist traditions. It is a history with tensions, to which we shall return in chapter 7.

Due to the swift and changing winds of German politics, the Protestant church in Germany has passed through several incarnations. In 2003, at the end of a long process that began with the reunification of Germany in 1989, the older Evangelische Kirche der Union (EKU) of the former DDR became the Union Evangelischer Kirchen (UEK), and then joined with the larger, West German Evangelische Kirche Deutschland (EKD). Wittenberg's two Protestant churches (the Schlosskirche and the Stadtkirche St Marien) are part of the church province of Sachsen, and members of the EKD. Many churches and regions with traditional or geographical ties to the Lutheran Church take Luther's name—for example, Evanglisch Lutherische Kirche in Thüringen. As I write, negotiations are under way to bring these traditionally Lutheran churches into the Lutheran World Federation.

The city's Schlosskirche and Stadtkirche are part of the Evangelical Church province of Saxony. In addition to these two state churches, Wittenberg is home to the Predigerseminar, a pastoral training center for the Evangelical Church. Another center, the Evangelische Akademie, is a ministry and outreach center of the Evangelical Church. The academy hosts continuing education programs oriented toward the lay public and schools, and organizes academic seminars, lectures, and study tours. The Lutherzentrum, founded in 1999, is a nonprofit organization promoting Wittenberg as an intellectual and spiritual meeting place. The center supports local institutions that focus on Luther (the church, museums, historical societies) and organizes religious and cultural heritage programs for tourists, pilgrims, visitors, and scholars. Board members of the center are drawn from the leading members of the Evangelical Church in Saxon-Anhalt, the Lutheran World Federation, and the mayor of the city of Wittenberg. Wittenberg is also home to the Stiftung Leucorea, another of the city's newly renovated centers, located on the site of the old, and once famous, University of Wittenberg. Since 1999, the Leucorea has been the home of the theological institute of the University of Halle-Wittenberg.

In 1996, the Wittenberg English Ministry (WEM) was established, and conducts worship services during the tourist season for English visitors. In 1997, the Evangelical Lutheran Church of America (ELCA) founded a center in Wittenberg, working with closely with the local church and organizing pilgrimage and travel study tours. In June 2007, a four-year-long, 2.7-million-euro restoration project on the former residence of the reformer Johannes Bugenhagen (1485–1558) was completed. The new center houses meeting and exhibit spaces, a gift shop, and a church-café run by Diakonie, the social welfare arm of the Evangelical Church. The goal of the Bugenhagen House is to reflect the presence of the church and community in society.

In spite of all the church activity in Wittenberg, the region reflects the secular nature of Western and Central European society. Since the end of the Second World War, Europe has become increasingly secular, with many people disaffiliating from and indifferent to the life of the church. In the church province of Sachsen, where Wittenberg is located, the Evangelical Church had more than 2.5 million members in 1966, but fewer than 600,000 in 1996. As the church was a site of resistance during the Peaceful Revolution, there was some hope that reunification would alter the fortunes of churches in Lutherland, but this hope remains unfulfilled, with membership during the last decade continuing a slow decline. In 2007, the total population living within the boundaries of the church province of Sachsen was just over 3 million, with 500,000 church members. Declining membership tells only part of the story; of the half million members, a mere 4 percent regularly attend Sunday services. Nearly every statistical category reflecting church participation—membership, attendance, baptisms, confirmations, weddings, funerals—reflects both a numerical decline and an aging church body.[4] It is now the norm in Germany to neither belong to nor actively participate in a church. In Wittenberg, only 15 percent of the population claims church affiliation. Whether the cultivation of Lutheran heritage through festivals, tourism, and performance will lead to increased church participation remains an open question.

In the premodern era, religious culture and festival culture were largely synonymous; the church (Protestant and Catholic) was a central, active player in public festivity. In the nineteenth century, the Prussians fused ecclesiastical and civil religion in part through Luther festivity. Today, Wittenberg's Luther festivals, even though one of them is a church festival, are chiefly occasions for the church to present a face to a distant public, while also attempting to shape the character of the celebration in accord with religious values, narratives, and beliefs.

Reformation Day

Ten years to the day after sending copies of his ninety-five theses to his superiors, on All Saints Day, 1527, Luther and a small group of fellow reformers raised a glass of beer in memory of the tenth anniversary of the "trampling out of indulgences."[5] The celebration of the Reformation had humble beginnings. But already during the man's lifetime the dramatic events of his life were becoming occasions for festivity.

In 1617, the hundredth jubilee of the "trampling," Wittenberg hosted the first Reformation festival. On October 31, a group of university professors, clergy, and students gathered in the Lutherstube, the apartment in the former Augustinian monastery that became the Luther family home. Here, the group sang "Ein Feste Burg ist unser Gott" (A Mighty Fortress is Our God), the famous hymn written by Luther, and then marched in a solemn procession along Collegienstrasse to the Schlosskirche for a special worship service. Reformation Day became an annual festival in Electoral Saxony in 1668. Over time, commemorative practices spread to surrounding lands, and, as Lutherans began to emigrate in the era of colonization, around the globe.

The year 1883, the four hundredth anniversary of Luther's birth, was pivotal, solidifying the place of Reformation Day in both civic and religious life through large public events held in Lutheran territories in Germany and Lutheran communities abroad. In 1883, Luther's Collected Works were published in German, and academic culture became increasingly important to the celebration of the Reformation, though academic lectures and events of the era were characterized by the polemics and rhetoric of German nationalism.

Also in the late nineteenth century, Luther celebrations and Reformation Day came under the influence of secularization and popular culture. Luther festivity, museums, and souvenirs emerged as part of the broader phenomenon of modern tourism. Kaiser Wilhelm II, as part of the 1892 celebrations that marked completion of the renovations to the Schlosskirche, led a procession past the city hall and ended neither at a church nor at a government building, but at the newly opened Lutherhaus museum. One-time monastery and later home to Luther and his wife Katharina von Bora, the new museum was becoming an important social and political institution, and a destination of the growing nineteenth-century phenomenon of cultural and religious tourism. Even North Americans, as the Lutherhaus guestbook reveals, were starting to make the pilgrimage here to gaze on Luther relics. The Lutherhaus was becoming as important to the city as the Rathaus (city hall) or its two houses of God; Reformation festivity was taking steps in the direction of the Volksfest. Wilhelm signed a document signifying commitment to Reformation principles, duty to parents, authorities, and nation, and spoke of the need for religious tolerance. The age of post-Enlightenment Absolutism was then celebrated with a great breakfast buffet: beef tea with asparagus, sole in champagne, beef sirloin steak with vegetables, partridge pate with truffles, lobster, Cornish game hen with fruit salad, peaches, butter and cheese, and desert. After breakfast, the Kaiser led a parade through Wittenberg's streets, with more than twenty wagon-floats and over a thousand people taking part.

Reformation Day and other Luther-inspired festivity, in earlier centuries under the firm grip of ecclesiastical and state control, became popular folk festivals, with a number of events and venues on the program as long as the menu. Concerts, worship services, parades and processions, feasting and drinking, museum exhibits, theatrical productions: A third force joined the mix of public ritual performed in Reformation festivals. Alongside sacred or ecclesiastical rites, and in addition to the rites of civil religion, one could find the performances of the marketplace. Luther was no longer simply a religious reformer and founder of world historical significance, nor was he only a national hero, one of the Fathers of the Fatherland. During the nineteenth century, Luther was commoditized and became the occasion for the production of spectacles designed to leverage political power, but also to woo and wow tourists. The Theses Door and Wittenberg's other memorial sites became tourist attractions in Germany's modernizing, industrial economy.

Traditionally, Reformation Day celebrations were held on October 31, the eve of All Saints' Day. In the twentieth century, many Lutheran churches began to shift Reformation Day to the Sunday before or after October 31, referring to the festival as Reformation Sunday. Most Lutheran churches in Germany have retained the traditional date of celebration, and in the provinces of Lutherland, the day is a state holiday.

Reformation Day is a feast day in the Lutheran liturgical calendar, and no comprehensive study of the larger festival can ignore the festival worship service, the Festgottesdienst, held the morning of October 31. The brochure advertising the contemporary festival in Wittenberg notes that Reformation Day "offers visitors opportunities for spiritual growth and learning. Visitors will have the chance to take part in worship services, some of them conducted in English; to enjoy performances of sacred and choral music; to attend thought-provoking lectures and readings; and to participate in seminars on a wide variety of topics." A photograph of a choirboy is centered on the front page of the brochure. Images of the Cranach altarpiece in the Stadtkirche, Schadow's *Luther* monument, the tower of the Schlosskirche, and the Thesenportal are further visual clues that serve to emphasize the festival's roots as a church festival.

Historically, Reformation Day emerged in the context of the practice of celebrating important figures in the history of the church by giving them a special day in the liturgical calendar. Reformation Day is the only lesser festival of the Evangelical Church not connected to people and events dating back to the New Testament and early church; through the festival, Martin Luther takes his place alongside apostles and saints. For many Lutherans, celebrating Reformation Day in Wittenberg is something special. The city receives roughly 1,000 foreign visitors annually to the festival, and most of these visitors attend for religious reasons, out of the desire to be in Wittenberg, a place of origins, to celebrate the Lutheran tradition.

The festival brochure also includes a reference to "events sponsored by the university community" and a photograph of the Procession of the Academic Senate, one of the major events on the program. The procession is the prelude to a public disputation held on the campus of Wittenberg University. In 2002, the procession and disputation helped mark the five hundredth anniversary of the founding of the University in Wittenberg. Once closely tied to nationalist politics, the Reformation Day festival retains a connection to civil culture through this academic component, as the disputation focuses on topical questions of national, and often international, interest. In 2004, for example, scholars debated the theme of a "culture war,"' and the possibility of coexistence between Islamic and Western societies and worldviews.

Last, but certainly not least, the brochure proclaims that "in addition [to spiritual growth, worship, and learning] visitors will be able . . . to enjoy the atmosphere of late-medieval life set against the backdrop of the historic Wittenberg market square. . . . Medieval markets and wandering minstrels round out the scene, adding authentic historical color and flavor to an already vibrant city." The brochure includes photographs of pipers and masked players, one with a demonic looking bull's head, to illustrate the medieval color and flavor that a visitor can expect to find.

Reformation Day is informed by a historical narrative and liturgical cycles, but the festival itself does not unfold around a narrative line. Rather, the festival consists of worship services and church concerts, interspersed with confirmation events, lectures, special museum programs, and, perhaps most important as far as numbers are concerned, the medieval market spectacle. Reformation Day has neither an official opening nor a closing event. October 31 is a state holiday, an annual echo of the days when church and state spoke with a unified voice. As the festival takes place on the same day each year, the calendar plays a role in determining its size and tenor. When Reformation Day falls on Saturday or Sunday, a larger event is staged; when the holiday falls during the week, a smaller festival is the result.

Of the twenty-four named events on the 2005 Reformation Day program, thirteen were hosted by the church or church-based organizations. On paper, at least, the festival keeps faith with its ecclesiastical origins and history. There are, however, many extra-ecclesiastical events: a Luther dinner-theatre; a brass band concert; hands-on, children-focused activity centers in the Lutherhaus and Cranach museums; Luther beer, socks, and T-shirts. The program invites visitors to a festival of "unrivaled flair" consisting of "religious and academic events, as well as a taste of the cheerful hustle and bustle of medieval life." Ecclesiastical symbols and rites provide the occasion around which are cobbled other interests and performances—commercial, political, and cultural. Whether the ecclesiastical center can bear the weight of the Luther superstructure it is supporting is an open question; and, if it cannot, where is the center of gravity to be found?

Luther's Wedding

Luther's Wedding unfolds around a spine of events related to the historical wedding of Luther and Katharina von Bora, as well as contemporary wedding practices.[⊙] Historically, Luther's writing against celibacy led many monks and nuns to renounce their vows, an act that was punishable by death. At Easter of 1523, von Bora and eleven other nuns fled from Nimbschen convent to Wittenberg. The family of Lucas Cranach aided von Bora, and she and Luther would eventually marry on June 27, 1527, after a two-week engagement. In the nineteenth century, images, books, plays, and souvenirs based on Luther's wedding became popular in Lutheran communities, providing a sedimented tradition upon which the contemporary festival implicitly draws.

The tenor, marketing, and event program for Luther's Wedding are quite different from those of Reformation Day. Luther's Wedding is described as a Stadtfest (city festival). The festival brochure gives a good sense of its nature:

> In five separate venues set in the courtyards, streets, and lanes of the city's medieval center, guests take part in a rich variety of programs and events that would be hard to match anywhere else. . . . Guests will find a festive medieval market of artisans and minstrels offering crafts, arts, and food in the style of the 16th century will enjoy discovering many merchants offering their wares and many purveyors of tasty food and drink. . . . Guests may enjoy the antics of street performers and wandering minstrels and explore the use of old tools and instruments. . . . Wittenberg's civic clubs and societies will set up their historical camps, inviting visitors to experience music, dance, and hearty food and drink. In front of the impressive Renaissance

⊙ DVD: Wedding Montage

City Hall on the town square, the opening takes place on Friday at 5
p.m. Without doubt, the most magnificent event of the weekend is
the festive historical parade in celebration of Luther's Wedding. . . .
Over 1,000 citizens and friends of Wittenberg from near and far
take part, working together to make the parade, which is led by
the newlyweds Martin Luther and Katharina von Bora, into an
unforgettable experience.

In addition to this description, the festival brochure includes a brief historical
account of the wedding of Luther and von Bora. Accompanying photographs
are scenes from past versions of the festival: pipers, musicians, performers,
clubs, marching bands, shots of the parade, and the wedding couple. Nothing
in the brochure identifies the festival as a religious event; Luther is a former
citizen, not a church ancestor.

The festival program is different from that of Reformation Day. For one,
the Luther's Wedding program is forty-six pages long; that for Reformation Day
a three-panel, fold-out brochure, the equivalent of six pages. Several pages of
the wedding program are dedicated to advertising space for local business and
upcoming cultural events in Wittenberg; the Reformation Day program has no
advertising. The organization of the Luther's Wedding program is by day and
location; festival events take place in roughly twenty different locations throughout the old town. As is the case with Reformation Day, Luther's Wedding
includes festival worship services, but these church services take place inside
the larger framework of the festival. The sites, rites, and performances of the
church are in the program as one among many options available to wedding
festivalgoers; in the Reformation Day program, as mentioned, ecclesiastical
events dominate the schedule.

The wedding festival opens on a Friday afternoon, with a procession of the
escaped nuns from the convent of Nimbschen. In the Marktplatz, a crowd of
around 2,000 people watch an opening historical skit—three Hausfraus gossip-
ing, in the course of which they turn their attention to the news of the nuns who
have fled their convent and are heading to Wittenberg for refuge. Outside of the
entrance to the Lutherhaus museum, away from the central Marktplatz, the nuns
(young women of Wittenberg) climb into a horse-drawn wagon. The nuns, led by
flower girls, move up the street toward the city center. Shouting *Horrah, Horrah,
die Nönnen sind da!* (Hooray, Hooray, the nuns are here!), the flower girls
announce the arrival of the nuns in the good city of Wittenberg. The wagon proceeds to the large stage in the Marktplatz, where historically important people
from the Reformation era, played by local residents, are introduced and presented to the crowd. Finally, the nuns move on stage, as the Stadtherald recites

their names; last to appear is Katharina von Bora. "In the morning," announces the Stadtherald, reading from a prepared script, "Doctor Martin Luther will take his bride." The Stadtwache raises the wedding wreath, and the festival is officially under way. The nuns retire for the evening, which is filled primarily with food, drink, music, dance, and plays in various locales throughout the old town.

Saturday morning starts slowly, as people recover from the night before, and prepare for the day. At 1 p.m., the bride is "given away," as Katharina is led by Lucas Cranach and his wife from their home (now the Cranachhaus museum) down to the edge of the old town, where she meets her husband. It is a requirement that both the bride and groom be native Wittenbergers, though it is not unusual for them to have left the city for work elsewhere. Photographs of the wedding couple and larger wedding party (parents, relatives, and dignitaries, both real and performed) are taken in the Lutherhaus museum garden, and in front of the Katarinaportal, as preparations are made for the large wedding *Umzug*, the parade. With over 1,000 participants, the parade is the event of the weekend; it takes more than an hour to complete the loop through old Wittenberg. The streets are packed, several layers deep, with onlookers. Though the parade is said to be led by the wedding couple, their actual location is roughly in the middle. The couple is formally greeted, at 4 p.m. on the main stage in the Marktplatz, and they then move to the garden of the Lutherhaus for a meal and reception, which includes the jokes of Spielleute and Renaissance-era music and dance. The meal is theatricalzied, with the three Hausfraus from the opening ceremony supplying thematic continuity to the day before, seating and serving the head table while performing their roles. Saturday night is devoted to another concert in the Marktplatz, framed as part of the ongoing celebration of the wedding of Martin and Katie.

On Sunday at 4 p.m., the couple meets to cut the wedding cake, and at 5:45 p.m. the couple lead a short procession from the plaza area at the Stadtkirche to the Marktplatz for the closing ceremony, which beings at 6 p.m. Aside from these formal public appearances, the wedding couple make impromptu appearances at various locations over the course of the weekend.

Around this spine of wedding activities—the arrival and welcoming of the nuns, giving away the bride, wedding photographs, the city parade in honor of the couple, the reception, the cake cutting, and closing ceremonies—is cobbled a variety of performative events: music, dance, theatre, lectures, special activities at Wittenberg's museums, worship services, and a great deal of wandering around. Taking in the diverse variety of events, eating, drinking, and shopping are the dominant activities. The festival's overall kinesthetic sense is perambulatory: People wander, socialize, greet friends and family, peruse displays, enjoy a beer in a festive setting, watch street theatre, perhaps have their photograph

taken with the wedding couple. Friday and Saturday nights can become raucous, and considerable time is spent Saturday and Sunday mornings cleaning
up the garbage and bottles left over from the night before. The festival is marked
by the carnivalesque—dressing up, mild forms of symbolic inversion and parody, and, as the partying on Friday and Saturday nights ramps up, license. The
consumption of beer and wine, the large crowd, the music, and movement
through the streets push the festival to the edge of the chaotic, and at the closing ceremony officials take pride in publicly announcing that the festival has
once again been celebrated without major incident.

Framing

Of the various ritual types catalogued by scholars, festivity (or celebration—I
shall use the terms interchangeably) is one of the more difficult rites to study.
How does one go about observing, documenting, and then analyzing, interpreting, and presenting a culturally complex, multidimensional, large-scale
event such as a public festival? An obvious descriptive strategy would be to follow the events on the program. Festivals often follow narrative lines, especially
those that commemorate historical events and persons. But a linear, beginning-
to-end narrative description of a festival would be onerous to write, boring to
read, and practically impossible, since no one person can cover a festival in its
entirety. What is required is a selective presentation of particular scenes,
moments in the life of a festival, informed by both the desire to be faithful to its
complexity and tenor (the aims of comprehensiveness and objectivity), and the
utility of certain scenes to illustrate particular analytical, interpretive, and theoretical interests of the researcher. "Tetzel at the Door" is one such scene; so is
"A Beer for Martin."

I have found it helpful to think about the Wittenberg festivals using an
analytical technique known as framing. Frame analysis began with the work of
Erving Goffman. "I assume," Goffman explains, "that definitions of a situation
are built up in accordance with principles of organization which govern events . . .
and our subjective involvement in them; frame is the word I use to refer to such
of these basic elements as I am able to identify."[6] For example, if you see somebody being attacked on stage in a theatre, the framing of the event—the building, your ticket and seat, the stage set—allows you to recognize the attack as
play or drama. Should the actor be doing actual harm to the other player, it may
take some time for the audience to notice, since fake blood, the sound of breaking bones, cries of pain and the like are understood by the audience to be part
of a good performance. The example is perhaps extreme, but it makes the point

of how powerfully frames can shape our perceptions and understandings of an event. A theatre is literally a framed space, but we also employ gestures, smells, images, concepts, and words in defining a situation. A wink and wry smile before calling a friend an "ass" communicates, "I'm only kidding." Extending one's open hand frames an encounter on the street as cordial and nonthreatening. Frames shape not merely the principles that organize the social world (a handshake rather than, say, a bow) but also our subjective involvement in them (the decorum governing a situation may demand a handshake, even though we may loathe the person we are greeting).

In a word, festivals sprawl, and framing is a way of focusing attention on a few basic elements or themes:

(1) Time. Festivals sprawl across time, usually lasting several days, and their reach typically extends back through the centuries. Festivals take place in real time. But in between the beginning and the end, time is imagined and organized in a variety of ways: a remembered and represented past, a hoped-for future, the rhythms of the tourism cycle, the dates of liturgical calendars, the narratives of sacred history, the history of the specific festival, the event-times on the festival program. Festivals are events; they have a linear, forward temporal flow: they begin, they happen, they end. They also have a circular flow; they come around again, and again, and again. The researcher needs knowledge of historical contexts, must be cognizant of moving in and out of a variety of temporally framed spaces (such as a "medieval" Marktplatz), and must get up early, go to bed late, be on his or her feet all day long, and do this for several days in a row.

(2) Space. Festivals sprawl across space, taking over blocks of streets, flowing into and out of town squares, public buildings, and homes. Festivals utilize space and place in a variety of ways. Festivals often take place at locations made special (even sacred) through a variety of architectural, commemorative, and ritual practices and strategies. Festival sites are often architecturally rich, utilize parades and processions to link together locations, and employ staging (sometimes elaborate) to create a special setting. Because festivals spread out over a large space, they are difficult events to cover. In addition to being on his or her feet for two or three days, full coverage of a large, complex festival demands of the researcher being at two or more places at the same time. This means choices must be made, since key events may happen simultaneously at different locations; moreover, when in one place, the researcher must metaphorically move between or across imagined places (for example, between a contemporary and medieval Marktplatz).

(3) Cultural Domains. Festivals sprawl across cultural domains. Cultural domains are rarely hermetically sealed; in public festivity, the borders between

the arts, religion, politics, and economics tend to bleed into one another, since a variety of individuals and groups bring their own interests and perspectives into the public sphere. Reformation Day is a church festival, but in the Markt-platz, it looks more like a Volksfest. A sermon may praise Luther; the festival fool pokes fun at him. For a hotel owner, the festival is a good opportunity to fill rooms; for the Lucas Cranach society, it is an occasion to promote the local art school and foundation. Even though academics often talk a good interdiscipli-nary game, in practice it is a difficult one to play. Familiarity with the theories, methods, and histories of multiple disciplines or fields demands both time and the willingness to stray across academic borders that are at times vigorously defended.

(4) Senses. Festivals sprawl across the full range of sensory experience. In festivity, sights, smells, sounds, tastes, and touches intermingle, emerge, and fade, make our mouths water and eyes pop, and, when we have reached the point of saturation, send us running in search of quiet shelter. In recent years, scholars working in various disciplines have argued for a more integrated understanding of the interplay of tactile, acoustic, olfactory, gustatory, visual, and kinesthetic senses in shaping personal and group experiences, the embod-ied meanings of ritual practice, and the nature and dynamics of cultural performances. Reformation Day and Luther's Wedding are characterized by sensory intensification, sensory indulgence, and, as a result, sensory overload.

(5) Ritual and performance. Festivals sprawl across ritual and performative genres: carnival, liturgy, civil ceremony, parades and processions, initiation, speeches and theatre, feasting, music, dance, revelry—all these, and more, may make up a festival. Understanding how each of these genres interlock and interweave (or, alternatively, clash and conflict) to produce the conglomeration collectively referred to in colloquial and scholarly speech as a festival is yet another conundrum facing the researcher. Conceived as a rite in and of itself, that is, in its totality, a festival must be greater than the sum of its parts. What binds these parts together? Which rites and performances are primary, deserv-ing of extra attention, and which are secondary? Are certain kinds of rites and performances employed by different social-cultural domains or groups?

(6) Objects. Festivals employ a variety of objects and images: banners, icons, corporate logos, the products of traditional crafts or regional cuisines, relics, even historical figures who become commoditized through imagery or heritage performance. Whereas in everyday life objects are valued primarily for the use value or exchange value, in performance events objects are imbued with symbolic value. Objects are crucial in creating the ambiance and ethos of the festival setting; a festival may even owe its very existence to particular a object (for example, a wine festival).

These six frames are not sacrosanct, but, taken together, they offer a relatively comprehensive set of analytical tools. Although there is a certain arbitrariness to them, they are also intuitive categories; festival organizers and participants often use such frames in planning or interacting with festival events. In analyzing a festival in terms of these frames, beginning with one inevitably leads to reflection on the others, and part of the job is to explore patterns and connections between the various frames.

Frames have an impact on subjective experience and knowledge; people make frames, employ them (often unconsciously), and, if they don't like them, seek to tear them down and create new ones. Framing and frame criticism happens within the Wittenberg festivals, and within academic study. For the field researcher, "frame analysis is the study of boundaries, boundary conditions, and boundary crossings. What it requires of fieldworkers is a rhythm, either physical or conceptual, of moving in and out of some cultural domain . . . while noticing both in themselves and in others what transpires."[7] "A Beer for Martin" is a case in point; in witnessing it, my conceptualization of Wittenberg's festival required adjusting. Framing is not merely a descriptive move; it may also be inherently evaluative. "A Beer for Martin" highlights one important distinction and tension among cultural domains: the church community's and elite culture's understanding and use of Luther versus a popular, carnivalesque symbolization and performance of the man and the events held in his name. This domain tension plays itself out in the style and mood of ritual and performance forms, the symbolic use of objects, the location of enactment, and the organization and use of the senses.

Cultural Domains

It is tempting to bracket out cultural or aesthetic performances such as "A Beer for Martin" on the assumption that they have little to do with religion, but to do so would be a mistake. Religious studies scholars, long closely affiliated with theologians, philologists, and historians, have learned from folklorists, ethnographers, performers, musicologists, and anthropologists that there is more to religion than canonical texts, and that religion is not confined to ecclesiastical spaces. Historically, the reluctance of religionists to make the folksy trek into streets and plazas, not to mention kitchens and gardens, is one reason for the paucity of good descriptions of everyday, ordinary religious life.

A festival is an example of public ritual. Public ritual, as its name states, takes place in public spaces—city streets and squares, churches and museums, stadiums and parks, at heritage sites, in the rooms and grounds of government buildings, the halls and hallways of palaces and galleries. Robert Wuthnow conceptualizes public ritual in the modern era in terms of three interacting social sectors: voluntary organizations (which include the church), the state, and the market. In Wuthnow's model, each of these domains, not just the church, plays a part in "producing the sacred."[8] The church may organize a procession through the streets. A not-for-profit art foundation sponsors an interfaith art exhibit. A representative of the state walks in a procession and is publicly recognized during a worship service. A stand in the festival marketplace specializes in dream catchers, buddhas, and crystals. A theatre company stages a play based on a religious figure or theme.

Clifford Geertz observes that cultural performances such as a public festival are generally a mix of religion, the arts, politics, economics, and that symbolic forms and actions serve many masters. Geertz goes on to note, however, that it is in the "more elaborate and usually more public [cultural performances]" that the observer can witness and investigate a "broad range of moods and motivations on the one hand and . . . metaphysical conceptions on the other"; it is these "full-blown [public] ceremonies" that "shape the spiritual consciousness of a people."[9] In studying religion on the ground, the activities of named religious traditions certainly demand our attention. But a people's "spiritual consciousness" is derived and expressed through both ecclesiastical and extra-ecclesiastical channels.

Crucial to the kind of conceptual model of cultural performances developed by Geertz and Wuthnow are distinctions among ecclesiastical religion, civil religion, and spirituality. Around the 1960s, scholars from different disciplines began studying the religious dimensions of political culture, under the rubric of "civil" or "secular religion." Robert Bellah's study of American civil religion was seminal.[10] Bellah was interested in the way in which God-language is applied to the state and nation: "In God We Trust." Furthermore, the nation-state has its canonical-like texts, times, places, narratives, individuals, and rites and ceremonies that ground, through symbolic and peformative means, the material interests, ultimate purposes, and history of the nation in a kind of transcendent reality. One important facet of civil religion is public ceremony: jubilees, pageants, national holidays, coronations, inaugurations, parades, fairs, and festivals.[11] Since Luther celebrations in nineteenth- and early-twentieth-century Germany were closely implicated in civil religion and the creation of the modern German state, it is worth examining the role of this domain in the contemporary festivals, to see how matters have changed.

Nineteenth- and early-twentieth-century Luther-themed festivity was characterized by a fusion of ecclesiastical and civil religion. Today the trend is toward local heritage, tourism, economic development, and entertainment fueled by the carnivalesque and play, a direction whose religious dimensions are best characterized in terms of spirituality. One definition of religion conceives "one's religion [as] . . . one's way of valuing most intensively and comprehensively," which allows for the fact that people may get and practice their religion outside of named religious traditions.[12] A lover of wisdom or clean air need not be a Taoist or a Muslim or a Lutheran. Thus a distinction is often made between religion and spirituality, the former referring to the institutions, doctrines, beliefs, and practices of specific traditions, the later a more individualistic desire to live a life in harmony with the sacred and in communion with others. Religion and spirituality are not necessarily opposites, but "there is a growing tendency to distinguish sharply" between the two. Many people today consider themselves spiritual but not religious. "Religion is institutional, traditional, and perhaps even moribund, while spirituality is personal, spontaneous, and alive. The current notion of spirituality allows one to espouse a religiosity not identified with the Christian mainstream."[13]

The religion-spirituality distinction should not be overplayed; nor should we be naïve about the oft-assumed apolitical stance of contemporary spirituality; nevertheless, the distinction is an important conceptual tool, particularly in a region like Lutherland, where church attendance hovers around 5 percent, and the tourism industry explicitly seeks to capitalize on "spiritual tourism." For those who hold to a substantive definition of religion (say, religion is going to church, or religion is belief in God), it is a relatively simple matter to argue that German society (indeed, all of Western Europe) is highly secularized; but where religion is under siege, spirituality may flourish. Cultural and aesthetic performances in the Marktplatz are relevant to an individual's spirituality and the character and style of public life. Running a stall that demonstrates the arts and crafts of weaving or glassblowing or metalwork might be considered hobbies, but look closely and one sees that such activities often embody a domestic and aesthetic spirituality. Local *Vereine* (voluntary community associations) are integral to the celebration of Luther, and an individual's contribution to and interaction with the festival is often mediated through participation in community groups, each of which embodies and projects a particular style, set of values, practices, narratives, and beliefs. Finally, in good postmodern fashion, shopping for buddhas in the stalls of the Luther's Wedding festival might well be followed by a Bach Cantata in the Stadtkirche, a cobbling together of things "spiritual" in fashioning one's identity. Religion on the festival grounds sprawls beyond the walls of the church.

One of the first field-based studies of religion written by a scholar trained in religious studies was *Symbol and Conquest* by Ronald Grimes, published in 1976. A study of the Santa Fe Fiesta in New Mexico, this initial foray of a religionist into the methods of field-based anthropology laid the groundwork for an approach to the study of public rites and performances that emphasizes the (often rough and bumpy) intersection of cultural domains. Grimes categorizes the symbols systems and cultural performances of the Santa Fe Fiesta "in terms of their civic, civil, religious, and ethnic qualities," for which he employs the terms *civitas, civilitas, ecclesia*, and *ethnos*.[14] I want to appropriate these categories in analyzing the Wittenberg festivals. The first three are the most relevant to the case of Reformation festivity, though the presence in Wittenberg of American and other Lutherans from around the globe (the dimension of ethnos) is also deserving of attention. *Ecclesia* refers to the rites and symbols of a specific religious tradition—here, to the rites and symbols of the Evangelical Lutheran Church. *Civilitas* refers to symbols, rites and performances directed to matters of state or federal politics, governance, and public policy—to civil or secular religion. *Civitas* refers to symbols and performances aimed at "city-mindedness," at local interests and concerns, and includes the contributions of voluntary organizations as well as those of the marketplace.

We begin with ecclesia.

3

A Mighty Fortress?

The ecclesiastical domain of contemporary Luther festivity is composed of the rites, performances, and public symbols of the various church organizations operating in the city. The main contribution of the church to Wittenberg's festivals takes the form of worship services held in the Schlosskirche and Stadtkirche. The various services are summarized in table 3.1. In this chapter, I focus on two of these services, a Reformation Day Festgottesdienst and a Renewal of Vows service; we will also revisit Luther's Theses Door, since it is a highly visible symbol and celebratory object for the Lutheran community.

Liturgy

The term *rite* refers to distinct, recognized ritual practices, usually enacted at specific times, in special places. If a rite is religious, as opposed to secular, we may speak of *liturgy*. Political ritual and civil religion are often referred to as *ceremony*. Religious traditions organize their ritual practices into systems, and the liturgical system of most religious traditions is based on a central rite. For the Evangelische Kirche, like many other Christian churches, that rite is communion.

Communion in Lutheran and Evangelical churches is based on the saving word of God and the sacraments, and consists of four phases: gathering, word, meal, and sending. The liturgy is opened by

TABLE 3.1 Worship Services held during Wittenberg's Luther Festivals

Group	Reformation Festival	Luther's Wedding
EKD (German)	Festgottesdienst, Oct. 31, 10 a.m. in the Schlosskirche & Stadtkirche	Festgottesdienst, Sunday, 10 a.m, in the Schlosskirche & Stadtkirche
ELCA (American)	English language service, Oct. 31, 8 a.m., Schlosskirche	
WEM (American)		Renewal of vows ceremony, Stadtkirche, Saturday, 6:30 p.m.

calling the community together with a musical prelude, a confession of faith, a greeting, and daily prayer. A series of readings follow. Usually there are two "lessons," drawn from the Old Testament and New Testament Epistles, and a Gospel reading. These readings are interwoven with the singing of a psalm, hymns, a sermon, the recitation of the creed and prayers. Readings are structured according the seasons and festivals of the church year. The service of the meal consists of offerings, thanksgiving, the eating of bread and drinking of wine, and a communion hymn and prayer. The liturgy concludes with a blessing, a final hymn, and a musical postlude.

A full communion liturgy is a periodic affair in Protestant churches. When the service of the Eucharist meal is dropped from the liturgy, the result is a *Gottesdienst* (service of God) or a service of the word, rather than a service of word and sacrament.[1] It is the practice in Wittenberg to hold full communion two times per month. Festival worship is not a full communion liturgy, but a Gottesdienst.

Within the liturgical cycle of the church, the liturgy is adapted to suit the occasion. These occasions may be an ordinary Sunday, principal and lesser festivals, or services that take place in conjunction with passage rites: baptisms, weddings, confirmations, and funerals. In the Christian tradition, in addition to the principal festival of Sunday celebrating the Resurrection and redemptive work of Christ, the church year revolves through a cycle of greater and lesser festivals. The greater festivals encompass the Christ story: Easter, Ascension, Pentecost, Holy Trinity, Christ the King, Nativity, and Epiphany. Interspersed among these are the lesser festivals, which are occasions to celebrate other events in the life of Christ, as well as his presence in the lives of the apostles and saints. In a Christian context, the term *festival*, deriving from the Latin *festum* (feast), refers to a church feast day, which is usually associated with the life of a saint. In everyday speech, a synonymous word for festival is *celebration*, but this word too has its roots in Christianity; *celebration* is another term for the liturgy of the mass. Viewed as a liturgical event, the heart of the Reformation Day festival is the Festgottesdienst, the festival worship service. Luther's Wedding, though not a church festival, neverthe-less includes a Festgottesdienst.

Liturgy is interrogative and declarative; it attempts to answer ultimate questions by stating—in words and gestures, through objects and images, via song and dance—how things are. Liturgy "tries to focus all things through a few things. It does so by 're-presenting' events and event-ualizing structures. Liturgies make events endure, and they make structures 'happen.'"[2] Temporal framing is usually of central importance to liturgy. Liturgy involves paradig-matic words and gestures typically linked to events deemed foundational by a particular tradition: the Jewish Passover, the enlightenment of the Buddha, the gift of the Koran to Muhammad, the Passion of Christ, the protest of Martin Luther. While the celebration of the Reformation makes the memory of a mythico-historical event endure, it also expresses and actualizes foundational principles of the Lutheran tradition and community—liturgy "event-ualizes structures." What does this mean? Consider a female bishop ascending the pulpit in Wittenberg's Schlosskirche to preach a sermon. Ascending the pulpit elevates the word, signifying the importance of the Bible and the sermon; it also embodies the community's attitude toward women's roles. While all branches of Lutheranism place the word at the heart of their theology and faith, not all allow for the ordination of women, and female pastors preaching in "Luther's church" is an act that may clash with the worldview of conservative Lutherans. The LCMS and SELK, unlike the ELCA and the EKD, oppose the ordination of women. Liturgy is an act that puts into force certain beliefs, but also embodies social structures, principles, relationships, values, and attitudes; it is not that ritual simply reflects certain social relations or religious values and beliefs—ritual is itself these very things.

A Reformation Day worship service takes the model of the baseline liturgy and layers it with worship directed at recalling the lives and work of Luther and the Reformers. Luther's Wedding is not a church festival, but festival worship services held during the Wedding are similarly layered; a service of the word is intertwined or layered with the recollection and celebration of the wedding of Martin Luther and Katharina von Bora. Within festival worship, this layering is achieved chiefly through the greeting, readings, and sermon, that is, through verbal content. In analyzing a service of the word, attention to content is impor-tant; but equally important is the embodiment of the word—matters of style, liturgical space and its use, comportment, the sensorium organization.

Liturgy is a social-cultural affair. The fact that liturgy can be described in terms of a general structure points to its long-term stability and normative dimensions. Liturgy appeals to and invokes the past and tradition. That the word *tradition* is often used as a synonym for *religion* means that liturgy is the product of historical development and historical forces that set constraints on rapid changes in form and function. Nevertheless, the specifics informing the enactment of a particular liturgy is dependent on the community and social contexts. Liturgists and anthropologists speak of the inculturation of the liturgy, a notion that points to the fact that liturgical form, despite the inertia and relative stability of tradition, are also subject to the influences and changes within its surrounding cultural milieu. A liturgy may change (or resist change) when it travels to a new country, or when cultural attitudes and values change at home; on the other hand, liturgy may also be a motor for cultural change. Liturgical enactment, in other words, is informed by a dynamic between tradition and change. Tradition makes liturgy reproducible, recognizable, and relatively stable, but because liturgy is something done, because it is an event, it has a dynamic quality as well; somebody may say or do something differently from before.

Insofar as festival worship services conducted in Wittenberg follow a liturgical form shared across Lutheran tradition, they are typical. But they are also unique, and their uniqueness is shaped by local traditions and history, contemporary concerns, and the context of their occurring as part of largely secular, public festivals. Descriptions of liturgy tend to be theologically driven, and so often miss what takes place at the edges and around those acts and words commonly understood as constituting the heart or focus of worship. A more phenomenological and ethnographic approach requires tending to the actualities of particular liturgical enactments.

Festgottesdienst

The 2005 Reformation Day Festgottesdienst in the Schlosskirche was a joint, dual-language service of the EKD and the ELCA.[⊙] Three pastors conducted the service. A bishop of the ELCA, serving as interim director of the ELCA Center Wittenberg, and an EKD pastor handled the greeting and readings. A third EKD pastor, the director of Wittenberg's Predigerseminar (a training institute for clergy), delivered the sermon.

Having attended both regular Sunday services and the Festgottesdienst of Luther's Wedding, my first reaction to the Reformation Day Festgottesdienst was one of surprise: The castle church was filled to bursting. The pews and choir stalls were full, people stood at the back, rubbing shoulders and squirming for room, and a row of people on chairs ringed the apse. The narrow balcony

⊙ DVD: Worship–Festgottesdienst

was crammed with a row of filled chairs, and, in front of the chairs, another row of congregants and onlookers leaned over the stone balcony wall, gazing down at the scene below. (The Festgottesdienst of Luther's Wedding, in contrast, attracts far fewer, even though attendance at the Wedding festival is more than fourfold that of Reformation Day.) Two television camera operators moved slowly through the church during the prelude, shooting both the congregation and the iconic art and architecture of the Schlosskirche. Congregants and visitors were also photographing and videoing the church, family, and friends, as the organist set the tone with the melody of the most famous of all Lutheran hymns, "A Mighty Fortress Is Our God."

In part, the packed church that morning was the result of the annual Lutherspass (literally, "fun with Luther") confirmation program, which brings approximately five hundred young confirmands from around Germany to Wittenberg to celebrate Reformation Day and be confirmed in their faith. The confirmands, parents, chaperones, and other visitors to Wittenberg for the festival helped swell the congregation beyond its ordinary size. There were also three American Lutheran tour groups in Wittenberg that morning—their itineraries timed with Reformation Day—and many of these visitors attended the Festgottesdienst. Though many of the young people attending confirmation were present, the bodies in the pews reflected and confirmed the statistics of an aging church demographic.

Though the church was full, by no means was everyone in attendance a church member. After circling the pews, I made my way to the balcony for a bird's eye view, taking up my precious spot next to an unchurched couple from Wittenberg. They were attending the service as onlookers, not congregants. Although the two were not church members, they thought the occasion merited a visit. Reformation Day is a state holiday and, like attending a Christmas or Thanksgiving church service, the Festgottesdienst is a cultural, not necessarily a confessional, affair. Visitors and residents alike come to the old center of Wittenberg for the festivals, and worship services are one of the events on the festival program. The presence of visitors creates a split of sorts at festival church services between congregants and audience, and this split lends festival worship an air of theatricality. A significant number of those present did not know the words to hymns or the creed (or chose not to sing or recite), nor did they seem to be in step with the flow of the liturgy.

The declarative force of liturgy acquires part of its power from the shared beliefs and worldview of those gathered. In the greeting, the German pastor attempted to create the feeling of *Gemeinschaft* (community) based on a shared understanding of the Reformation as a living movement. "By celebrating together we demonstrate that Reformation Day is not merely a commemoration of events that took place in the sixteenth century, but rather a living, worldwide movement." The American bishop echoed these comments: "Reformation Day is a major festival day here in Lutherstadt Wittenberg, as it is in our churches in the United States of America. We are pleased that you have joined us today for worship." The German word *lebendig* (living, lively) is often used by clergy in festival services to make the distinction between festival worship as *Erinnerung* (commemoration) and worship as an expression and declaration of faith.

Though such a distinction may be a heartfelt part of one's faith, many who attend Luther festivals perceive Luther and the Reformation in historical terms, and Reformation Day in Lutheran churches in North America are typically not the "major" event signaled by the American bishop. The use within the liturgy of the notion of the Reformation as a "living movement" sets up a tension between showing and telling; rather than being a demonstration and declaration of living presence, the comments struck a plaintive chord. Reformation Day worship is liturgy, but also a commemorative occasion. The day is a civic holiday, and attendance at a church service does not necessarily equate to acceptance of the Lutheran faith, as other factors are involved—tradition, aesthetics, historical interests, leisure, and tourism.

Ultimate Sacred Postulates

What the "living movement" claim attempts to convey is the eternal and universal importance to the human community of Luther's Reformation "discovery." In the program for the early morning ELCA Reformation service in the Schlosskirche we read that the "heart of the reform movement was the gospel, the good news that it is by grace through faith that we are justified by God and set free." Salvation by grace through faith is the centerpiece of Lutheran theology, belief, and liturgy. The anthropologist Roy Rappaport calls such liturgical declarations "ultimate sacred postulates," whose job it is to "sanctify . . . [and] certify the entire system of understandings in accordance with which people conduct their lives." Ultimate sacred postulates, which tend to be abstract, generalized, and somewhat disconnected from material realities, provide a foundation to one's view of and action in the world. They ensure that one's values, beliefs, practices, and relationships are not "merely conceptual nor simply explanatory nor even speculative" but "something like an assertion, statement, description or report of the way the world in fact *is*."[3] In a Lutheran Gottesdienst, the weight of this liturgical declaration falls on the reading and hearing of the word.

Lutheran liturgy (especially one without communion) is dominated by the word. The spoken, sung, and preached word are vehicles of expression and praise, but also the means of communicating theological content and matters of belief. In the Festgottesdienst, the traditional notions of sin, grace, and freedom predominated in the spoken word; in addition, scripture was utilized to dramatize the work of Luther and the Reformers in a story of beginnings and origins, with these in turn characterized by the notions of newness and the true church.

On Reformation Day, the biblical texts for reading are Psalm 46, Jeremiah 31:31–34, Romans 3:19–28, and John 8:31–36. Psalm 46 evokes the sense of God as a refuge from a tumultuous world, Jeremiah speaks of a new covenant, Romans speaks to the heart of Lutheran theology (the distinction between works and faith and justification by faith alone), and John to the theme of freedom from sin through true discipleship with Christ. In these readings are distilled Lutheran history, theology, and soteriology—the ultimate sacred postulates of Lutheranism.

The faith-works distinction and salvation by faith emphasized by Luther had an important place in the Festgottesdienst, as seen in the American bishop reading the passage from Romans, a passage of utmost importance to Luther's faith and theology. "Then what becomes of our boasting? It is excluded. On what principle? On the principle of works? No, but on the principle of faith. For we hold that a man is justified by faith apart from works or law" (3:27–28). The Romans passage models the dynamic of question and answer typical of Christian worship: A question is posed, a question of supreme importance to human being, and an answer is given. The Reformation Day liturgy literally speaks to Luther's desire to be free from the burden of sin (his religious or existential question), his discovery of salvation by grace through faith (his answer), and this discovery as the theological basis for reform and, ultimately, a new church (the declaration of the worshiping community). In weaving together a particular theology and historical narrative, the readings (as they are meant to wherever they are read) represented and enacted Lutheran tradition and beliefs to those assembled in the Schlosskriche. The liturgy rendered history (the event called the Reformation) as a reflection of the paradigmatic and timeless, and history becomes foundational and forever; reform (or, less forcefully, renewal) is both behind (in the historical past) and integral (timeless, fundamental) to the life of the church. Focusing on the content of the readings is to paint Reformation Day worship as an illustration of Lutheran doctrine: Behind the ritual enactment stands a theology and set of foundational beliefs, and it is the job of ritual to declare the significance and truth of those beliefs. Ritual does much more than express held beliefs, but the doctrinal dimensions of the Reformation Day liturgy deserve consideration.

Those attending the Festgottesdienst were implicitly asked to affirm (or, at least, to contemplate) a narrative of sin and redemption from sin through the saving work of Christ, yet such notions are not central to the worldview of many people attending the festival, nor to many attending the festival worship service. Though the question was asked (What frees us from sin and justifies us before God?), and the answer given (God's grace through faith in the saving work of Christ), neither was necessarily tended to or carried away by those in attendance. After the service, to stimulate conversation and reflection, I put three simple questions to roughly a dozen people in the large crowd milling about inside and outside the church: Are you a member of the church? If so, do you regularly attend church? What aspect of the service did you like most, and what did you like least? A few of those asked were church members, but only two of the people I spoke with regularly attend church.

Significantly, opinion as to the least enjoyable elements split between the readings and the sermon. One man stated, "The readings are too theological," implying dissonance with his own beliefs. Another observed, "How many [people] really believe in sin anymore? I don't think people are sinners, maybe bad, maybe good, but not sinners. I agree that we need to do more socially, help out those in need, so I agree with that message in the sermon, but social work has always been part of the work of the church." The man's reference to the sermon highlighted the fact that the German sermons in festival worship (the American sermons are somewhat different) tend to refract biblical content and confessional beliefs in a social gospel, emphasizing the need for social responsibility and work in the community. Both the Catholic and Protestant churches continue to play an important role in Germany in administering social welfare services, and people may relate to these moral and social aspects of the church without necessarily connecting to the more doctrinal or theological elements; in other words, moral life does not necessarily require that one hold certain beliefs.

Luther based his theology of grace on a select portion of the New Testament, relying heavily on Paul's letters to the Romans and Galatians. Luther's emphasis on Paul's letters, which contrast a Jewish dependence on law and works with the glad tiding of Christ's love, coupled with the social-historical context of Luther's protest against indulgences, left generations of Lutherans with a rather parochial view of both Judaism and Catholicism. The authors of the books of the Old Testament were not primarily concerned with matters of salvation, and the Pharisees, who did hold to a doctrine of the immortality of the soul, certainly did not teach that salvation required the rigorous fulfillment of all laws and ceremonies. Similarly, the Catholic church at the time of Luther did not yoke redemption to a works-acquired perfection. It is more the case that both Paul and Luther projected their own religious anxieties on to these religious groups within which they were incapable of experiencing salvation, and built a faith around a core notion: salvation by grace through faith.

Historically, one of the defining features of Protestantism has been the centrality of confessions of faith and catechisms, but assent to the theological core of the Lutheran belief system is important to fewer and fewer people in a region that was at one time a Lutheran stronghold. Confessional content remains a significant part of the liturgy, and occasionally plays a role in producing negative reactions: "The readings are too theological." What people do seem hungry for is an aesthetic experience with a spiritual dimension, and the simple location of music in a church is enough to inscribe it with "spirituality."

Ritual and Aesthetic Interests

What my informal conversations and observations during the Festgottesdiesnt lead me to suggest is that the doctrinal and confessional aspects of the service were not of great importance to many in attendance, though the articulation of Lutheran theology and doctrine constituted a good portion of the liturgy. Rather, primarily cultural and aesthetic interests were at play. Overwhelmingly, respondents identified the singing of the hymns in the Schlosskirche as the most enjoyable part of the service, even though some neither knew the hymns nor sang. "I thought the hymns were beautiful." "The choir was beautiful." "For me, the hymns were the best part of the service." One woman enjoyed simply "being here in this church on this day, with all its history." Another noted the "magisterial" ethos of the Schlosskirche as the highlight of the service. The late-Gothic Schlosskirche is an architecturally and visually rich space, and many attending the Festgottesdienst spent the service looking around, soaking up the atmosphere. Although many people related positively to hymns, the historical context, and the architecture of the Schlosskirche, they did not typically connect the experience of worship to confessional belief. This is a conclusion that fits with statistics published by the Evangelical Church.

The attendance figures for various services throughout the church year reveal a very low turnout. Across Germany, only 3.7 percent of church members attend regular Sunday services; 4.6 percent attend Good Friday services, the high point in the church year; 5.1 percent attend Advent. Christmas Eve, in striking contrast, delivers a whopping 36.6 percent of the church community. What puts the people in the pews on Christmas Eve? Not necessarily a confessional faith, but rather fidelity to a religious and cultural tradition, a tradition that embodies a certain practice and aesthetic: the decorated tree, lit candles, gift-giving, time with family, a shared meal, the nativity story, and the hearing of hymns, together, at an evening church service. There is beauty in this tradition.

The kinds of activities pursued within the German Lutheran Church by its members reveal the dominance of aesthetic interests. By far the most sought-after and attended events hosted by the EKD consist of church music. None of the other event-categories identified by the church to define its activities—evangelization, Bible weeks, ecumenical and world mission work, social and political questions, and theological discussions—come close to matching the desire for church music.[4] The aesthetic and broadly cultural contexts of a Christmas service, I suggest, also inform the festival worship services that accompany Wittenberg's annual Luther festivals.

Wittenberg's Reformation heritage sites—its churches, museums, and monuments—host theatre, concerts, and public festivals held through the tourist season from April through October. During the tourist season, the visitors in the church pews in Wittenberg regularly outnumber the local congregation, though the visitors are not typically church members. Overall, church-based religion is in decline across Western Europe. One exception, however, is what the sociologist Grace Davie refers to as the "cathedral church" phenomenon. In historic centers such as Wittenberg, sites that draw significant numbers of tourists, the church remains a center for worship, but also hosts aesthetic and cultural events with broad appeal. Davie notes that historic, cathedral and city-center churches

> still have a place at particular moments in the lives of modern
> Europeans, even though they are no longer able to discipline the
> beliefs and behavior of the great majority of the population. . . .
> [Historic churches] are frequented by regular and irregular worship-
> pers, pilgrims, visitors, and tourists, though the lines between these
> groups frequently blur. The numbers, moreover, are considerable—
> the more so on special occasions, both civic and religious. . . . Looked
> at from the point of view of consumption . . . cathedrals are places
> that offer a distinctive product: traditional liturgy, top-class music,
> and excellence in preaching, all of which take place in a historic and
> often very beautiful building. A visit to a cathedral is an aesthetic
> experience, sought after by a wide variety of people, including those
> for whom membership or commitment presents difficulties. They
> are places where there is no obligation to opt in or to participate in
> communal activities beyond the service itself.

As Wittenberg continues to develop as center for spiritual, cultural, and aesthetic forms of leisure and tourism, the local church will feel the effects, and is likely to continue to move away from its historical roots in confessional belief, emphasizing its aesthetic resources, in particular church music. Didactic, indicative confessions of faith, evangelizing, theology—these are increasingly losing ground to aesthetic and expressive activities. The former evoke little feeling; they seem to be experienced as cerebral, outdated aspects of religion. "The point," argues Davie "is that we *feel* something; we *experience* the sacred, the set apart. The purely cerebral is less appealing. Durkheim was entirely correct in this respect: It is the taking part that matters for late modern populations and the feelings so engendered. If we feel nothing, we are much less likely either to take part in the first place or to continue thereafter."[5]

It is wrong-headed to dichotomize religion and aesthetics. Religion and art are age-old bedfellows. When I discussed distinctions between religion and the arts with the pastor of Wittenberg's Stadtkirche, he was adamant that no sharp line be drawn between the two. Historically, Calvinist streams of Protestantism were wary of the arts, while Lutherans were more accommodating. The arts have a central place in the Lutheran tradition. Luther himself wrote many hymns, adapting popular melodies, and he was shocked at the iconoclasm of some of his fellow Reformers. Lucas Cranach, Luther's friend and colleague, ran a thriving art school in Wittenberg. Perhaps the greatest example of the fusion of art and religion in the Lutheran tradition is the work of Johann Sebastian Bach.

Although art is of fundamental importance to many religious traditions, it would be wrong-headed to recognize no distinction at all. In the modern period, art and religion became conceptually and institutionally distinct domains.[6] We need to imagine a time when the church was the only place where people could find music, drama, visual art, transcendent architecture, story telling, and ritual—activities and genres that speak to our ontological needs and interests. In the modern era, other so-called secular institutions have developed as homes to these interests: the museum, the opera, the concert hall, the theatre, the cinema, the festival grounds, radio and television. One could argue that the great challenge to religion in the modern era—during which time religion increasingly came to be defined in terms of confessional and propositional forms of belief—has not been science but rather art. In the past two hundred years, art has detached itself from an existence bounded by the walls of the church, but the label "art" does not mean that the artistic domain is devoid of religious values and emotions. Owing to the influence of Romanticism, art in German culture often functions as a surrogate or substitute religion, and the arts have a conspicuous presence in Wittenberg. Art evokes emotions, sentiments, and memories. Gregory Bateson conceives art as "part of man's [sic] quest for grace," where grace involves harmony between the unconscious and conscious, intuition and rationality, form and content. "For the attainment of grace, the reasons of the heart must be integrated with the reasons of the reason."[7] Bateson sees in art and ritual such integrative power.

If the aesthetic-confessional distinction I detected in the reception of the Festgottesdienst has merit—and I will return to this question later—there are implications for liturgical practice. In an era and locale of dwindling church attendance and participation, the willingness of the church to serve as host to broadly cultural events is likely to be a measure of its relevance to the larger community. Here, the church faces a certain double bind: The interrogative-declarative theological content of the Festgottesdienst liturgy is largely dissonant from the beliefs of the wider community and the carnival-like ethos of the Luther festivals, yet it is precisely through confessional belief that Lutherans fashion a unique identity. If culture is accommodated by refashioning liturgy in a more aesthetic and less confessional direction, what remains of Lutheranism? On the other hand, if the church holds tightly to its traditional, confessional basis, what will become of the church, which is already in decline?

Dual-Language Services

One of the unusual features of the 2005 Festgottesdienst was the use of both German and English in the spoken word. The use of English in a German church signified the importance and presence of American Lutherans in Wittenberg. Festival time attracts a great number of English speakers to the city (many of whom are religiously motivated), and festival worship always includes the opportunity for English-language services, conducted by both of the ELCA and WEM. In addition. experimenting with dual-language services is an attempt to deal with a linguistically mixed congregation during festival time. For clergy and some congregants, the dual-language service symbolizes and puts into force cooperation between the American and German churches. The former East Germany is now a mission field for North American churches, and the ELCA works in partnership with the EKD with the aim of aiding the revitalization of the German church.

In spite of the best intentions behind the dual-language model, stylistically and aesthetically it introduced awkwardness into the service. Older German-speaking congregants in Wittenberg generally do not know English, and few English-speaking visitors understand German. In a liturgy heavily dependent on the speaking, singing, and hearing of the word, I could see in the faces of those present a certain amount of confusion, frustration, and impatience. Liturgy aspires to evoke and give an answer to the mystery of being, but the back-and-forth between German and English led to a phasing in and out of the liturgical sensibility and experience. If the dual-language model was, as I was told, aimed at projecting "the international flavor of Wittenberg as sacred space to the world's Lutherans," the concrete outcome was a liturgy that felt fragmented, overly complicated, and dissonant with the congregation as a whole.

For some, the use of both German and English was experienced not so much as international cooperation but as a reflection of the position of the German church with respect to the American: It was a sign of dependency as much as partnership, a kind of colonization of the German Lutheran Church in Wittenberg by Americans. German Lutherans spread around the globe during the later half of the nineteenth century, and in the past decade, one group of Lutherans (North Americans with Germanic and Scandinavian roots) is return- ing in significant numbers to visit and establish a presence in the religious home- land. Frustrated about having to listen to a language he did not understand, one congregant, a local man in his fifties, complained about the "American [pastor] in his white robe; we don't need American tourists." German pastors wear black, and the white robe symbolized to this man a false purity or goodness, even a certain arrogance. Of course, Wittenberg does need tourism, especially American tourist dollars, and liturgy is not just about praise—it is also shaped by political, economic, and other social realities. The use of English by the American bishop in the white robes lifted up, to this man, at any rate, not God but an animosity not uncommon among residents of European towns and rural communities that rely heavily on tourism. If dual-language services entail a communion of sorts, they also represent tensions in cultural and economic flows circulating in today's global world. The attitude of many Wittenbergers toward American tourists and presence in Wittenberg, for example, is conditioned by the wide- spread criticism in Germany of the American- and British-led "war on terror." Germany has been a staunch opponent of the foreign policy of the White House of George W. Bush.

Liturgical Space

The use of liturgical space is one way of embodying foundational beliefs and values. The Festgottesdienst was centered on the Schlosskirche's two pulpits. Luther emphasized the saving word of the gospel over what was perceived as the complexities of the Catholic sacramental system, so the preaching, reading, and hearing of God's word became the central ritual action of Lutheranism. As Lutheran church architecture developed, it reflected the new theological direc- tion. The transept, the area that divides the nave (where the congregation sits) from the choir and chancel area (reserved for clergy) in the medieval cruciform church was shortened or removed to emphasize the centrality of space. Pulpits were moved from the chancel into the open space created by modifications to the transept. Lutheran pulpits constructed in the wake of the Reformation were often large and ornate. Protestant pulpits were (and remain) a symbolic register of the importance of the word. One of the special features of Lutheran liturgical space is the combination of altar and pulpit as the focal point of a large, open worship area framed by a circle or semicircle of pews and, in larger churches, balconies.

The Schlosskirche, which was originally built as a Catholic church, retains the more medieval layout of nave, transept, choir, and apse (which holds the altar), but renovations incorporated the Lutheran emphasis on the pulpit. The raised, impressive pulpit of the castle church is given even greater symbolic value by the placement of Luther's grave beneath it, and a raised statue of Luther located at the end of the choir stalls is present to the eye when looking up to the pulpit. For some pastors, climbing the steps to preach over Luther's grave is an awe-inspiring experience: Luther, Melanchthon, and other notables preached right at this spot. On the opposite side of the crossing area is located a much smaller and simple lectern or pulpit, used for the greeting and biblical readings; again, this location, reserved for the reading of the word, is symbolically elevated by the placement of the grave of Philip Melanchthon in front of and his statue behind the pulpit. From these two locations, the word resonates out to the congregation.

Whereas a communion service culminates at the altar, the Festgottesdienst began at the altar, and moved to and culminated in the area marked by the pulpits, graves, and statues of the two great Reformers. Worship began with a congregational hymn, "A Mighty Fortress." Near the end of the hymn, the two pastors made a short procession through the choir area to the altar, for the greeting and reading of Psalm 46, alternating verses in German and English. From this point on, the altar remained in the background, as the focus of the service moved into the crossing area between the nave and choir for the readings and the sermon. In terms of the spatial flow of the liturgy, the opening congregational hymn, which resonated throughout the space, was channeled and focused by the short procession and greeting on to the altar. From the altar, the word was brought forward (through the readings) into the open crossing area, a central space framed front and back by the congregation. Ascending the pulpit for the sermon elevated the word. The final congregational hymn closed the service, releasing the word back to the church body.

The relative erasure of the altar in both services reveals a dissonance between the confessional emphasis in the service on the saving work of Christ and the spatial dynamics of the service. The altar, the physical location of Christ, receded in importance when compared to the use of space framed by Luther and Melanchthon. Perhaps this is appropriate on Reformation Day, but there are both theological and historical questions at stake. One of the three foundations of Luther's theology is *sola scriptura*, "scripture alone." Luther is rightly renowned for the Herculean feat of translating the Bible into German, and Protestantism has invested heavily in the tradition of the text. Yet Lutheranism has not lived by the word alone. Looking out his study window in March of 1532, Luther could see a new construction project on the monastery tower. After Luther married Katharina von Bora in 1525, the former Augustinian monastery was transformed into a family home. But Luther's fame was also having the effect of transforming the house—indeed, the entire city of Wittenberg—into a site for collective commemoration. Luther, ever the curmudgeon, would comment, "If I live yet another year, my poor little room will be no more, and all because I overcame the papacy and 'for which reason a perpetual memorial [*perpetua memoria*] is worthy.'"[8] The end phrase of Luther's remark (uttered at one of his *Table Talks*) was delivered in Latin, and there is an allusion and subtle criticism at play. In Luther's time, *perpetua memoria* was a way of referring to the Eucharist, and Luther's use of the Latin *dignum esset* (to be worthy) is probably an allusion to a Mass response: the celebrant says, "Let us give thanks to the Lord"; the response is: *vere dignum et iustum est* ("it is truly fitting and proper to do so").[9] Luther probably perceived a potential danger or at the very least, a certain irony in his growing cult status. His elevation to the status of culture hero threatened to eclipse the celebration of Christ in the Eucharist, and Luther, it seems, recognized this possibility before he died.

In the contemporary Lutheran Book of Worship we read that a lesser festival "should not be allowed to overshadow Sundays or principal festivals," the modern-day equivalent of Luther's concern. Through the nineteenth and early twentieth centuries, however, this is precisely what happened in Reformation Day and other Luther jubilees and celebrations. Compared with nineteenth-century Reformation Day liturgies, the notion of a heroic Luther has receded into the background, replaced with the seminal theology and faith articulated by the man: salvation by grace through faith. But liturgical space and its use are as important to liturgical enactment as the spoken word, and the Schlosskirche is a monument to Luther and the Reformers. Its symbolism encodes much of the nineteenth-century narrative that was overtly enacted through the spoken word in speeches and sermons. Statues of the great Reformers line the nave; paintings of Luther hang on the walls; Friedrich the Wise and John the Constant kneel in alabaster by the altar, flanking Christ, Peter, and Paul. Friedrich the Wise is also buried in the church, and the Theses Door evokes a narrative of a heroic Luther. At a symbolic level, the church projects the historical fusion of church and state, and the great figures of the Reformation era are literally elevated and placed in locations once reserved for saints, though chiseled with a purposeful defiance and grandeur rather than the melancholic piety of, say, a Saint Francis. If the liturgy is the expression of a "living movement," the church architecture and iconic art is the legacy of a bygone era of liturgical triumphalism, and probably helps instill a historical attitude toward liturgical celebration.

The architecture and rich visual culture of the church, rather than the spoken word, often appeared to be the focus of attention during worship, and I could not help but feel a sense of disjunction between the images and intentions of nineteenth-century German nationalism embedded in the symbolism of the church and the service enacted within its walls. Though the auditory was the dominant sense informing the liturgy, the material, visual culture of the church is also prominent, and for the most part must be assigned to a historical past entangled with difficult memories connected to the era of German nationalism, imperialism, and war. When liturgy takes place in a space that is anachronistic to contemporary political and moral views, and there is nothing in the liturgy to counter, contextualize, or perhaps even critically subvert the symbolism of the space, then attitudes toward that space (of the past, history, heritage, tradition, which may be morally suspect) are likely to carry over to the liturgy as well. The Lutheran Church certainly attempts to deal with the negative legacy of Luther to German history, memory, and identity, but not within the liturgy. Since nineteenth- and early-twentieth-century Reformation Day festival liturgies unabashedly incorporated nationalist and imperial politics, perhaps the apolitical stance of the contemporary Festgottesdienst needs to be rethought. Psalm 46, for example, one of the Reformation Day readings, could certainly be brought to bear on the critical attitudes that exist throughout Germany toward the American-led war on terror and the invasion of Iraq. The historical connection between the Lutheran Church and German imperialism could be made public in the liturgy, the iconography of the Schlosskirche seen through, and the experience and memory of what can happen when military might and religious commitments converge could play a central role, adding a tangible and physically overt lesson to the service.

Embodiment and the Senses

The Lutheran Reformers replaced the rich visual, material, gestural, kinesthetic, and sensual dimensions of Catholic liturgy with a sensually pared-down liturgy. Gone was the open nave, where congregants could move about; pews became a standard church furnishing. Gone was the feel of rose water on the fingertips, the smell of ecclesiastical incense and beeswax, the use of candles.

Icons were removed, as were the bodies and relics of saints. Gone were ornate vestments and the complex gestures involved in the elevation of the host and chalice. It was Luther's view that congregants should "sit still, listen, and reflect," an attitude toward liturgy that severely limits the involvement of the range of human senses and emphasizes the cultivation of interiority.[10]

A Christian liturgy is meant to be an expression of the experience of salvation through the work of Christ. Sunday worship is a celebration, a feast; a festival service is meant to amplify this celebratory mood. Though it was a Festgottesdienst, a festival worship service, the mood of the Reformation Day service was neither exuberant nor especially joyful; rather, its feel was ceremonial. With the presence of festival-goers, the confirmands, the media, and conservative Lutherans handing out evangelical literature at the entrance to the church, the ethos outside was that of a public rally, rather than a prelude to meditative worship. Once inside, there was an officiousness to the service. The dual languages connoted compromise and necessity as much as heartfelt cooperation and fellowship. The alternating between English and German, coupled with the dropping of communion, led to the dominance of the verbal and auditory senses. Kinesthetically, the service was inert—congregants did what Luther advised: They sat still and listened. The creed was recited in a monotone whisper; the readings (which Luther advocated be sung, a practice long done away with) and sermon were uninspired and flat. The choir, not the congregation, carried the hymns. The "voice" felt imperative, rather than interrogative and declarative; the motivation more informed by the force of traditional practices than the feeling of cosmic necessity. The service did not embody the claim that the Reformation is a living movement; rather, it felt hesitant and awkward.[11]

Compared with the plentitude of the senses in the larger festival out in the streets, the worship service came off as one-dimensional. The larger festival emphasizes exteriority, movement, and the use of all the senses. These differences could be understood as complementary ritual forms, the one promoting exteriority, gregariousness, social interaction; the other interiority, quiet meditation, and the nurturing of one's relationship to God. Alternatively, the two can be seen as competing ritual forms, embodying different values and styles of life, an interpretation that I will develop below, and in chapter 6.

Renewal of Vows

The renewal of vows service that takes place on Saturday evening during Luther's Wedding is the creation of the Wittenberg English Ministry (WEM). It has been part of Luther's Wedding since 2002. The service, which takes place in the Stadtkirche, is sparsely attended (fig. 3.1). In 2005, there were approximately twenty-five congregants, predominately American Lutherans in Wittenberg over the festival weekend, though the service was conducted in both English and German. In 2006, more than sixty people took part in an English-language service. The occasion was the tenth anniversary of the WEM, and Keith Loesch, the ministry's founder, led a tour group from his home parish in Virginia to Wittenberg in order to help mark the anniversary with a large, if largely foreign, congregation.⊙

A key aim of the WEM is to provide an explicitly Lutheran confessional context to Luther-themed tourism, festivals, and heritage culture. The renewal of vows ceremony during Luther's Wedding is an opportunity for Christians to attend worship and renew their vows in a place of historic and religious value, and on an occasion of festive celebration. The practice of renewing one's wedding vows is not widespread in Europe or North America, though it is increasing in popularity, often taking place in the context of travel and tourism. The service follows the form of a service of the word described above, shaped with

FIGURE 3.1. Couples gather in front of the Cranach altarpiece in Wittenberg's Stadtkirche for the renewal of vows service, June 2005. Photograph by Ronald Grimes.

⊙ DVD: Worship–WEM service

readings and a sermon that emphasize the importance of the institution of marriage, love between husband and wife, and the marriage of Martin Luther and Katharina von Bora. Luther and "Katie" are held up as role models to the Lutheran community, and the service provides the opportunity for couples to renew their marriage vows.

During the greeting, the congregation responsively reads Psalm 100: "Shout for joy to the Lord, all the earth/ Worship the Lord with gladness/ come before him with joyful songs." The occasion is set up as celebratory, but in both services I attended (in 2005 and 2006), I felt a distinctly ideological undertone; there is more at work in the service than praise and the reaffirmation of vows. The founder of the WEM, Reverend Loetsch, introduced the renewal of vows service in an effort to "uplift the festival," to "take a large beer fest, a party, and inject it with some spirituality, with some connection to Lutheran theology." In other words, the service developed (at least in part) out of the reactions of American Lutherans to the carnivalesque character of Luther's Wedding.

For the wedding festival, two small stages for pipe and drum music are set up just outside the walls of the Stadtkirche. During the renewal of vows service, the drumming, piping, singing, and shouting outside is so loud that it pours through the walls of the church. If the service aims to "uplift" the festival, the festive sounds of street celebration threaten to drown out the attempt. One of the most popular New Testament readings at weddings, and part of the renewal service, is 1 Corinthians 13, the well-known meditation on and celebration of love. The first line reads, "If I speak in the tongues of men and of angels but have not love, I am a noisy gong or a clanging symbol." During the sermon, as the music and noise from outside became obvious competitors to the action inside, the American pastor commented, "I was thinking while you were reading the Corinthians section about [the] gonging symbols that are outside of our [sic] church here. A little added emphasis for the Holy Scripture." A good-natured laugh rippled through the congregation, but the "gonging symbols" comment did not diffuse a palpable tension.

A few minutes later, during the middle of the sermon, the outside noise once again became a nuisance. The sermon was on the theme of how the good news of the gospel is the answer to dealing with whatever "crosses one's path." With the noise from outside obviously crossing the path of the service, the pastor fell into implicitly pitting the church and faith against the festive celebrations. "The church is a refuge, is a place where we can come and spend time with God and say to him, 'Help me deal with the rest of the world that crosses my path every single day. [A world which] is loud and full of debauchery, and full of kinds of temptations out there that cross my path every single day." The wedding festival does indeed become raucous, but characterizing it in terms of debauchery, synonyms for which include wickedness, corruption, depravity, and sin, would be considered laughable and overly puritanical by the vast majority attending the festival, including most German Lutherans. The comment set up the small group worshiping in the church as a bulwark against a sea of corruption outside. The tone of the service became defensive, as the outside noise continued to interfere with worship. The extra-ecclesiastical celebrating outside could have been framed in terms of Psalm 100—people shouting for joy, praising with joyful songs—but it was not.

Martin and Katie: Gendered Roles

As if concerns about overindulgence, license, and the pagan roots of the contemporary carnivalesque were not enough, the fact that the rowdy, medieval ethos of the festival is occasioned by the marriage of Luther and von Bora is also a sore point. Many of Luther's contemporaries perceived his marriage to Katharina von Bora as a scandal: a monk marrying a nun in an era whose sexual ethics were defined by centuries of equating the spiritual life with sexual asceticism, virginity, and purity. The Reformation was not merely a theological or political revolution but also a sexual one. Luther and other Reformers directly attacked the practice and theology of clerical celibacy; they also sought the reformation of marriage and sexual life in general, which they saw as being plagued by adultery and licentiousness. For the Reformers, an institutionally imposed celibate life for clergy was not an expression of a higher spirituality than that achievable through marriage. On the contrary, Luther was cognizant of the power of the sex drive and argued that imposed celibacy, far from elevating one spiritually, more often than not led to a descent into fornication. As Johannes Bugenhagen, Luther's contemporary, quipped, "Faith, not virginity, fills Paradise."

The Reformer's preaching against celibacy spread to monasteries and nunneries, and many monks and nuns began to leave, or rather flee, since flight from a convent at the time was an act punishable by death. In 1523, Luther aided the escape to Wittenberg of twelve nuns from the nearby Nimbschen cloister.[12] Two years later, on June 13, 1525, he would marry one of them, Katharina von Bora. Clerical marriage became a prominent part of the Reformation, and marriage became the backbone of the social order and ethics.

Over the centuries, the marriage of Luther and his Katie has been amplified symbolically through visual culture, the publication of diaries and letters, and given dramatic treatment in plays and films. Within Lutheranism, the couple became an exemplary model of the ideal parsonage, of married life, and gender roles. Luther was the active father, husband, doctor, theologian, and pastor; Katie, the dutiful, committed, supportive housewife and mother. Memory and narratives of their relationship fit well the saying "behind every good man is a good woman." In the nineteenth century, the same period that witnessed the use of Luther for political purposes with the fusion of church and state under the kaisers, the domestic and private side of Luther's life became the subject of considerable attention. The discourse of "Fatherland" in nineteenth-century German culture wove together the ecclesiastical, political, and domestic domains through reference to Luther as father of the church, the nation, and the family.

In the past twenty years, many Christian churches and denominations have struggled with—and some have split over—three thorny interrelated issues: the ordination of women, the ordination of gays and lesbians, and same-sex marriage. Recently, the issue of same-sex marriage has received a great deal of public attention, and caused acrimony in many a church. Within Lutheranism, the marriage of Martin and Katie has played an important role in shaping traditional views on sexuality and gender. The couple can easily become a rallying symbol for socially and theologically conservative forces within the church to resist the encroachment of thorny social changes into the ecclesiastical domain.

With respect to these contentious issues, the ELCA has moved farther to the left than has the LCMS. The LCMS does not ordain women, certainly not gays or lesbians, and same-sex marriage is an anathema. The ELCA does ordain women, but will not ordain openly gay and lesbian clergy. Clergy are expected to be either in a heterosexual marriage or celibate; gay or lesbian clergy, if they keep quiet about the fact, generally retain their positions. On the question of same-sex marriage, the ELCA allows for same-sex blessings, but does not endorse clergy performing wedding rites. The position of the German Lutheran Church (EKD) on these questions is similar to that of the ELCA.[13]

Given the intensity of contemporary debate within the church surrounding these issues of sexuality, a worship service aimed at the reaffirmation of a couple's wedding vows performs double duty, becoming an occasion to reaffirm traditional views of both marriage and sexual ethics. The marriage of Martin Luther and Katharina von Bora is not merely an occasion for a "large party" but, at least for some Lutherans, fundamental to their faith and identity; to fail to give the wedding proper respect and a religious context is to demean a set of values and way of life that many Lutherans feel exemplified by the wedding and marriage of Luther and von Bora.

The prayer and the lessons in the renewal service carried a subtext that bears on the issue of same-sex marriage:

> Heavenly father, we rejoice in the great love by which you join husbands and wives in marriage and enable them to live out their life together in care and nurture for each other and their children. On this weekend when we celebrate the marriage of Dr. Martin Luther and Katharina von Bora we praise you for their life-long love and for their commitment to you and to each other, and for the example they set for families throughout the world. Help us to value our own marriages and to grow in love and faithfulness to our spouse that we may be blessed in our life together, provide healthy examples of marriage to our children, and contribute to the well-being of community life in all the places where we live. Make us one in our marriages, dear Father, even as You are one with Jesus Christ and the Holy Spirit, one God, now and forever."

God joins "husbands and wives [men and women] in marriage," Martin and Katie set "the example for families throughout the world," and, emulating them, husbands and wives will "provide healthy examples of marriage to our children." An inference here is that Martin and Katie are a healthy example of marriage not simply because of their love for one another but because they embody traditional, heterosexual marriage.

The ethos of the service reflected traditional, some might say patriarchal, expressions of gender roles. In the first lesson, from Ephesians, the congregation heard how "wives [must] submit to your husbands as to the Lord. For the husband is the head of the wife as Christ is the head of the church, his body, of which he is the savior. Now as the church submits to Christ, so also wives should submit to their husbands in everything." Theological gerrymandering can re-interpret such passages more in keeping with contemporary attitudes that value greater gender equality, but couples at the liberal end of the moral spectrum would likely not choose such a passage for their wedding. The reading of Ephesians continued, quoting Matthew 19, "'For this reason a man will leave his father and mother and be united to his wife, and the two will become one flesh.' This is a profound mystery—but I am talking about Christ and the church." Matthew 19:4–6 was the Gospel reading, a reiteration of the theme of heterosexual marriage. "Jesus answered, 'Have you not read that he who made them from the beginning made them male and female, and said, 'For this reason a man shall leave his father and mother and be joined to his wife, and the two shall become one flesh'? So they are no longer two but one flesh. What therefore God has joined together, let not man put asunder."

Such passages validate heterosexual marriage as natural and God-given. The union of a man and a woman is a mystery, the analogical equivalent of the union of Christ and the church. God joins not simply a couple in marriage but grounds an institution and an understanding of proper gender roles and sexuality. While those present at the service were celebrating and reaffirming marriage, the service was also an example of what Judith Butler calls the "performance of gender." Butler argues that there "is no gender identity behind the expressions of gender . . . identity is performatively constituted by the very 'expressions' that are said to be its results."[14] In other words, the "naturalness" of the heterosexual declarations in the renewal of vows service is not the result of being God-given (an expression of a universal essence), but rather a pervasive cultural configuration of gender, so pervasive that it seems entirely natural.

My framing the renewal of vows service in terms of the issue of gender performance and same-sex marriage may seem overly critical to some readers, perhaps even insensitive to those who participated in the service. My interpretation here could be criticized as turning the worship service into the enactment of ideology, whereas it was principally an opportunity for loving couples to reaffirm what they hold dear. To understand ritual we need participatory empathy, but also critical distance. Heterosexual marriage, shaped by ideals surrounding children and family life, has long been an officially (and unofficially) approved way of life. Heterosexual marriage is a shared ethical ideal; for some, it is also a religious ideal. People are confirmed and sustained in living a way of life that receives a socially recognized stamp of approval. In a heterosexual marriage with two children, there were parts of the renewal service to which I could closely relate. Secularized Protestant men who in waves left the pulpits for the university lectern through the nineteenth and twentieth centuries modeled the intertwining of Luther's work as pastor, university professor, and student of religion with his domestic life with wife and children. Luther as scholar-husband-father is a model that I have, in many ways, unintentionally emulated.

My sensitivity to the question of gender performance in the service has been shaped by my education, by the public attention given of late to same-sex marriage, and by having to deal with matters of homosexuality and lesbianism within my immediate and extended family. I also spent time in Lutherland with a congregation of American Lutherans, many of whom are gay and lesbian. Germany legalized same-sex marriage in 2001, as have many other Western democracies, at either the national or the state level. The modern state no longer sees fit to endorse a specific form of marriage, a decision with which I agree. Many people experience this loss of official confirmation as a threat to a cherished way of life; when heterosexual marriage is closely intertwined with religious discourse and practices, challenges to its hegemony are often experienced in terms of a falling away from God, and as leading to corruption within society.

The significance of the renewal of vows service with respect to these questions is that it takes place in Wittenberg, conducted by an America Lutheran body that is far more conservative than the local and national church body. Like a feedback loop, the expression and embodiment of heterosexual marriage through the service in "Luther's church" (a place of authority), grounds traditional views with the weight of history. As an official of the WEM plainly stated to me, "Conservative Lutheran groups come [to Wittenberg] very interested in such questions [as same-sex marriage, and the ordination of women, gays, and lesbians], and [while here] they reaffirm the position of the LCMS on these questions." When a gay or lesbian Lutheran couple shows up one day at the renewal of vows service with the intention of renewing their wedding vows, the differences among the various Lutheran groups operating in Wittenberg will be put to the test.

The Door as Ecclesiastical Symbol

In chapter 1, I introduced Lindsay Jones's notion of the ritual-architectural event as an analytical tool for examining the various dimensions of Luther's Theses Door. As commemorative architecture, the Theses Door is implicated in notions of divinity and sacred history (priorities II A and B), as well as having a ritual context of contemplation (priority III B). The Theses Door "commemorates, houses, and/or represents a deity, divine presence, or conception of ultimate reality . . . commemorates an important mythical, mythicohistorical, or miraculous episode or circumstance . . . and serves as a prop or focus for meditation or devotion."[15]

The Theses Door is a celebratory object, the material focus of the Reformation Day festival. Built by church and emperor in the nineteenth century, the Theses Door is one of the set pieces that turned Wittenberg into a staging ground for Luther-themed jubilees and celebrations. Victor Turner notes, "[religious] celebrations [typically] have mythical 'plots,' and are based on narratives of divine intervention in human affairs. Celebratory objects may remind participants of those myths, and of the primal energies they re-present (that is, make present again to the senses, changing the symbol into what is symbolized)." In Turner's symbolic anthropology, celebratory objects communicate meanings through their visible and tangible qualities, as well as condense and encode those aspects of religion and culture that a society or group construe and value as being fundamental to their identity, or especially representative of their beliefs. When objects such as the Theses Door of Wittenberg's castle church, "are recognized as being culturally specific symbols to be decoded," and when they are furthermore "set in their proper celebratory context," the meanings and messages they suggest are multiplied and magnified. Symbols may "represent ideas, objects, events, relationships, 'truths' not immediately present to the observer, or even intangible or invisible thoughts and conceptions."[16]

In Turner's model, there are three steps involved in the interpretation of symbols. An *exegetical* approach calls for explanation or interpretation, whether from a layperson's point of view or informed by specialized knowledge of history, theology, or theories. An *operational* approach to symbolic meaning emphasizes how an object is used, the observation of attitudes that may be publicly displayed toward an object, how an object is handled or treated. To generate a full interpretation of celebratory objects we must "view them in action, in movement, in becoming, as essentially involved in process. Much of an object's 'meaning' is equated with its use: we must observe what a celebrating group does, not merely what it says." A third kind of symbolic meaning, one associated with structuralism, Turner refers to as *positional* meaning, the relationship of a particular symbol to other symbols.[17]

Symbols point or refer beyond themselves—to ideas, values, meanings, stories, acts, other symbols. Symbols are always symbols for someone; they mean different things to different people and groups. Symbols are evocative. Symbols are "multivalent," and "multivocal"; they are linked to other symbols and cultural processes, and their meaning is dependent upon context.[18] There is no way to establish a one-to-one correspondence between symbol and meaning. Symbolic analysis has more to do with texturing, contextualizing, and thickening than establishing univocal meaning. In the following sections, I take an exegetical and operational approach to the symbolic dimensions of the Theses Door, limiting the discussion to the ecclesiastical domain; later, I will add further interpretive perspectives.

Exegesis

In 1995, UNESCO added the Luther memorials in Eisleben and Wittenberg to its list of World Heritage sites. "As authentic settings of decisive events in the Reformation or in the life of Martin Luther, the memorials in Eisleben and Wittenberg have an outstanding significance for the political, cultural, and spiritual life of the western world that extends far beyond the German borders." UNESCO documents on the memorials refer to the Thesenportal as the place where "Luther launched the Reformation by nailing his 95 Propositions to the north door of the Castle Church in Wittenberg." This is an exegetical meaning given to the Theses Door by an important cultural institution with a global reach.[19]

Similarly, the most common exegetical meaning given to the Thesenportal by visitors to Wittenberg is that the door brings them face-to-face with history. Standing at the portal, individuals are transported back to a pivotal event in the history of Western religion and civilization. "Here is where it all happened," one person told me, and this is a very typical remark. Whether we ask individuals traveling to Wittenberg, read the documents of those institutions promoting travel and pilgrimage to the city, or witness the variety of ritual and performance events occasioned by the door, the chief exegetical understanding of the Thesenportal is connected to a remembered "history" of the Reformation, informed by the language and feeling of authenticity.

An important interpretive move in an exegesis of the Thesenportal is to replace primary references to "history" with "myth" or "narrative." As Turner has pointed out, a layperson often understands or explains symbolic material or objects through their "role or place within a religious myth or heroic tale"; typically, "analysis stops at myth."[20] In common parlance, the word *myth* is often equated with lies or untruth and can be wielded as a weapon to implicitly denigrate someone's beliefs. This is not how I am using the term. *Myth* may be used normatively, but it is also a descriptive term. As I use it here, *myth* refers to culturally important images and narratives that establish convictions concerning fundamental conceptions of the world and our life in it. When used descriptively, the crucial factor in fashioning a response to myth is not the question of belief. The pressing point about myth is whether we consider it normative and constitutive of our sense of self—whether we take it as a basis for orientation, value, and action in the world.

For Lutherans and Protestants traveling to Wittenberg, the door is a symbol linked to a canonical, foundational myth. Outside of a specifically religious context, the *Thesentür* (thesis door) connotes the Western practice of conceptualizing history in terms of three defining periods—the ancient, the medieval, and the modern. Visitors to Wittenberg, whether they are pilgrims or travelers, explicitly or implicitly relate to the Theses Door in terms of a story of the origins of the modern world. There is nothing in the explicit architecture of the Theses Door that depicts the story of the heroic struggle of a lone individual against the power of a mighty, corrupt Catholic Church. Nevertheless, most visitors I spoke with (informal conversations out front of the doors with Germans and some Americans visiting the city on Reformation Day) identified the Theses Door as the place where Luther posted the ninety-five theses. Some knew that these were not the original church doors, but later replacements; a few noted that Luther may not have actually posted his theses; but visitors with such historical knowledge and interests were rare. When asked what the door represented or symbolized, the majority gave a version of the story of Luther's battle with the corruptions of the Catholic Church, and most connected the spot with Luther's protest against the selling of indulgences.

Historically, the story of the Thesenanschlag (Luther's posting of the ninety-five theses) has been mediated through images, texts, sermons, folklore, and plays. In the contemporary setting, we must add to these traditional media many others: travel guidebooks and literature, city tours, documentary and feature-length films, photographs, Web sites, and performances such as that of Brüder Ignatius. Most people interested in travel to Wittenberg have had their expectations molded by such media. The latest cinematic version of the Luther story (*Luther*, 2003) portrays a defiant, heroic Luther (played by Joseph Fiennes) challenging church corruption by hammering his theses to the door of Wittenberg's Schlosskirche. Action at the door during festivals tends to confirm in visitors narratives of the heroic Luther. The performance of Brüder Ignatius implicitly invoked the myth of the heroic Luther. One of the functions of heritage performance is pedagogic. Young people are drawn to such performances of the past, and parents or elders often supply an exegesis of the scene being witnessed. In the case of "Tetzel at the Doors," parents tell their children the canonical story of Luther's protest against the might of the Catholic Church.

Individuals who self-identify as Lutheran or Protestant typically add a layer of theological interpretation to the Theses Door, associating it with Luther's discovery of salvation by grace through faith. At times, this theology is also intertwined with anti-Catholic polemics. In discussing the significance of the site with a Lutheran husband and wife from Minnesota, for example, I learned that Luther thought the Catholic Church was a "giant blood-sucking worm."

"I read in my guidebook that Luther called the Catholic Church a 'giant blood sucking worm.'"

"Do you think he was right?"

"Back then, it was true, with indulgences and the emphasis placed on works, like pilgrimage. The Catholic Church has been blessed lately with strong leaders who understand [the importance of] grace. But if Luther's church [*sic*] hadn't been there over the years, there would have been nothing to pull the Catholics back [in line] with the truth of our faith. He forced them to think about grace."

The two-ton door is understood to be a bulwark against theological error, part of the "mighty fortress" proclaiming a gospel of grace, and emblematic of Luther's heroic battle with the Catholic Church. The term *Thesenanschlag* connotes such meanings.

The noun *Thesenanschlag* derives from the German verb *anschlagen*, which principally means "to hang up," or "to fix or fasten," as in hanging (or hammering) up a poster or picture on a wall. The German verb has rich connotations: to strike, to change one's tune, to give tongue, to take aim, to take a stand—all of which is suggestive of defiant, convicted action. To be Protestant means to protest. But to protest what?

The influential Lutheran theologian Paul Tillich sees in Luther's protest against indulgences both the working and the articulation of a universal principle, which Tillich terms the "Protestant Principle" or "prophetic principle." Human beings, argues Tillich, have a tendency to conflate human powers, institutions, and ideologies with the divine. When people confuse what is finite, limited, and conditioned for what is infinite, transcendent, and absolute, they make gods out of God. When life is not informed or grounded in a transcendent call to be holy, an unconditional moral imperative to raise oneself up to a higher level of being, then deceit, conceit, and corruption are sure to follow. It is criticism and protest of this conflation of human powers, interest, and institutions with the sacred that Tillich perceives in Luther's ninety-five theses.[21] Informing Luther's protest is the freely given grace of God—anything less would be a merely human response.

Luther's mythologized hanging/hammering of the ninety-five theses embodies protest, but it also resonates with the image of Christ hammered to and hung from a cross. The Thesenanschlag and the crucifixion are both symbols of grace and salvation, and this connection is embedded in the design of the portal. Above the bronze doors is a painting of Luther and Melanchthon at the scene of the crucifixion. The two men and the savior are alone, in the foreground. Behind them is the river Elbe. The skyline of the city of Wittenberg rises on the far shore; the castle church and town church dominate the horizon. The men are on their knees; a calm, steadfast Luther looking upward to the dying Christ, Melanchthon casts a contemplative gaze at the ground. Each holds a text—Luther, an open Bible, his translation, no doubt; Melanchthon, a copy of the Augsburg Confessions. The crucified Savior's head is fallen to his right shoulder, toward the kneeling Luther, his loincloth flowing outward to both sides in a gentle breeze. A bridge connects the two shores, and a naturalistic sky is replaced with gold illumination.

By placing Luther and Melanchthon at the scene of the crucifixion, it is implied that the Reformation, Lutheran theology, and confessions of faith have their beginnings at Golgotha. Though Luther's protest and work was the act of an individual, the architectural symbolism of the Thesenportal incorporates the generative power of trans-human forces. The painting emplots the Reformation story in the Christ story, and a connection is established between Christ the father of the church and Luther and Melanchthon as the fathers of the Lutheran Church.[22]

Door symbolism has always had a central place in Christianity. John 10:9, for example, has Christ pronouncing: "I am the door. By me, if any man enter in, he shall be saved: and he shall go in and go out, and shall find pastures." Revelations employs door imagery to evoke a sense of the coming Kingdom: "I know thy works: behold, I have set before thee an open door, and no man can shut it: for thou hast a little strength, and hast kept my word, and hast not denied my name" (Rev. 3:8). "After this I looked, and, behold, a door was opened in heaven: and the first voice which I heard was as it were of a trumpet talking with me; which said, Come up hither, and I will shew thee things which must be hereafter" (Rev. 4:1). Moreover, the color bronze in biblical symbolism typically refers to judgment and sacrificial death. The sacrificial altar where the lamb was slain is brazen (Num. 21:9; 2 Cor. 5:21), and bronze (or copper) characterizes the sacrificial death of Christ: "His feet were like bronze glowing in a furnace, and his voice was like the sound of rushing waters" (Rev. 1:15). Luther's life was filled with dramatic events. Luther, for example, publicly burned the papal bull calling for him to retract his views. That the legendary Thesenanschlag emerged as the chief symbol of Luther and the Reformation is probably due to the biblical images of Christ as the door to salvation, and the nailing of Christ to the cross.

If a characteristically Lutheran theology of grace is reflected in the symbolism of the Thesentür and the "event" of the Thesenanschlag, this symbolism is not without irony or paradox. The kaisers who built the door undoubtedly modeled it on the great bronze doors of the Renaissance. The doors designed and crafted by Ghiberti for the Baptistery in Florence signified the rise of that city as a center of not just the arts but of political and economic power. The Medici were patrons of artists, many of whom put their talents in the service of the church. The echoes of this fusion of church, state, and culture would linger into the era of the German Kaiserreich, as commemorative monuments to Luther drew on and mimicked the power of monumental forms of art and architecture employed during the Renaissance. That the Evangelical Church would place such an investment in the temporal power of the state is not necessarily contradicted by Luther's theology, but it does offend Tillich's elaboration of Luther's emphasis on justification by grace through faith; the ecclesiastical politics that created the Theses Door could not be further from Tillich's Protestant Principle.

None of the visitors I spoke with in the Schlossplatz on Reformation Day connected the These Door to the rebuilding of the Schlosskirche during the nineteenth century. This social-historical context is not part of the consensus-remembered "history" of the door, and therefore not part of its meaning. I have participated in three guided city tours of Wittenberg. In each, it was mentioned that the portal was a gift of Frederick Wilhelm IV, and one guide was quite adamant in making the point that the Thesenanschlag was not a historical event. Nevertheless, the door, even if not historically "authentic," is generally imagined in relation to a presumed authentic act—the heroic Thesenanschlag—not in relation to the creation of Germany as a nation-state in the nineteenth century.

In Turner's model, the exegetical meaning of symbols can be further broken down into a "normative" and "oretic" pole. At the normative pole is found an "anchoring celebratory symbol [that] 'stands for' or 'signifies' a number of aspects of the moral, social, and political order." The Theses Door, created during the nineteenth century, was meant to be such an anchoring symbol. Contemporary Reformation celebration, tourism, and pilgrimage draw on the legacy of the *Heldenmythos*, the hero myth, that grew up around Luther through the nineteenth century. Standing out front of the Theses Door, people remember and see performed Luther as good bürger of the city and doctor of the university, the story of indulgences, John Tetzel, and a corrupt church. They do not see Kaiser Wilhelm, the interweaving of religion and politics, the social construction of place. Perhaps performances of civil religion in nineteenth and early twentieth centuries should have a place in Reformation-themed festivity, heritage performances, and theatre in Wittenberg.

Operational Uses

As a relatively immobile church door, it is tempting to interpret the symbolism of the Thesenportal in structuralist terms, in relation to some larger, more fundamental, and presumably stable structure, such as the church or society. Turner's operational hermeneutic requires us to tend to how symbolic material is used, to what people do with a symbol, to the attitudes and emotions held and expressed in relation to it. As Lindsay Jones has emphasized, sacred architecture need not be understood in terms of the principal metaphor of structure—rather, a sacred building is an eventful place. Unlike a smaller, portable object, the Theses Door is not handled, but operational considerations are still relevant.

Normally, an iron gate cordons off, protects, and elevates the status of the Thesenportal (see figure 1.1). One way in which the Theses Door is used is to not use it, or rather, to use it only on a single, special occasion—Reformation Day. On Reformation Day, the gate is opened and the Thesentür can be approached, up close. Not only is the protective gate opened but the door itself opens. Reformation Day worship services attract large crowds, so on this day the portal is granted its primary function as a church door, taking some of the burden off the smaller entrance near the church tower. The door marks the threshold between profane and sacred space, opening and closing as the congregation and visitors enter and exit the church, an annual respite from its otherwise still silence as a purely commemorative object. The opening of the Thesenportal marks a point in the liturgical calendar, is a public statement about the religious and social importance of recollecting tradition and heritage, and creates a pathway in which past and present meet in the act of projecting a future.

The counter pole to the normative dimension of a symbol is its oretic or sensory quality. The Thesentür is opaque, massive, weighty, solid, part of a castle complex, a "Mighty Fortress." On the one hand, the physical properties of the door connote permanence and stability; on the other, when the door swings open, appetite, desire, feeling, and process are suggested. Though Reformation Day celebrations may reinforce structure, they may also call into being the public airing of grievances and the articulation of new "theses" for debate. Through the 1980s, for example, prodemocracy and prounification forces within the East German society used Reformation festivals in Wittenberg as a forum to stimulate public debate. In 1983, which was a major jubilee year (the four hundredth anniversary of Luther's birth) the church in Wittenberg organized a *Disputationsgottesdienst*—a public discussion of theses posted on the door of the Schlosskirche in the context of a festival worship service. Debate and criticism is deliberately structured into the official schedule of the Reformation festival, in the form of a public disputation on a topical question or theme. The potential of and for antistructure, in other words, is a part of the normative structure and use of the doors.

The second major use of the Thesenportal is in relation to processions and the staging of other kinds of performances. The Thesenportal supplies a setting or stage for ecclesiastical rites, but also for what Jones calls "Theatre: Pomp, Procession, and Pageant" (priority III A). "In their affect, theatrically presented architectural events are those that work . . . to make an impression, to influence, touch, impress, sway, and persuade the assembled audiences and participants." An example of this priority is the procession of the confirmands.

The Procession of the Confirmands

The ecclesiastical and theatrical are fused in the procession of the confirmands, held annually in Wittenberg since the inaugural event in on Reformation Day, 2000.⊙ *Lutherpass* or *Lutherspass* is the name given to the two-day meeting. The

⊙ DVD: Processing–Confirmands

German *Pass* means "passport," but it also refers to a road or path through a mountain range, a mountain pass. *Spass* means fun. And so, *Luther(s)pass* is a passport to Luther (a passport granting full entry and participation in the Lutheran Church) through fun with Luther. The culmination of Luther(s)pass is a procession of the confirmands to the Thesenportal, which begins at the Stadtkirche St. Marien, as its bells ring at noon.

On Reformation Day in 2005, the boisterous cohort, more than five hundred in number, ages thirteen to fifteen, most of them German, but some from Scandinavia and the United States, walked from the Stadtkirche, the Town Church (often referred to as Luther's church), past the profane Marktplatz, with its beer and sausage and kitsch, down Collegienstrasse, on to Scholssstrasse. None other than Martin Luther himself led them, shouting to everyone in earshot, "Welcome these young people into our church. They show that our church is strong, and that our church lives." A mix of curious (at times disdainful) looks from shoppers and café goers followed the confirmands along the length of their route. Singing "Prince of Peace and Lord of Lords, Glory, Halleluiah," they attempted to cut a wake of the sacred into a sea of secular festivity. The processants carried banners and sang popular evangelical hymns, as they passed shoppers, the outdoor tables of busy cafes, stuffed Nemos, dream catchers, beer stands, carved buddhas, T-shirts, and Luther memorabilia.

The confirmands have a periodic, small group presence in the old city during Reformationsfest, but for the procession they fill the streets en masse, walking from Luther's church to Luther's doors. The mustering point for the confirmands, the Schlosskirche, is well chosen. Here is the door on which Luther nailed the ninety-five theses. Inside are the graves of Luther and Melanchthon; and when you are under siege—church attendance across Germany is between 5 and 10 percent—a castle is a wise choice as a rallying point. The Schlosskirche projects solidity; its spire, power and a note of defiance. This is the church, the city, the faith that Luther built, and Luther is front and center in this rite of confirmation.

The confirmands filed into the Schlossplatz, singing and joking with one another, and then, Luther, played by the *Kirchenmeister* (building manager) of Wittenberg's town church, was called on stage. "The ninety-five theses of Luther stand behind us in bronze . . . there to read, and many of them still valid today—or, Herr Luther, how do you see it?" Luther's message to this new cohort of church members was short, and to the point: "That is definitely the case. The church must continuously be renewed, through fresh, young spirits, like you." A roar of applause rippled through the crowd. Standing in front of his doors, Luther delivered one last message before the confirmands begin heading home. He added a "ninety-sixth thesis" to the others inscribed behind him in bronze: "A

Christian must be a cheerful person. And so I hope that you found joy here, joy in the Lord God, joy in one another–and *friends*. And this I say too: it is better to loose one's possessions than one's friends. And therefore stay true to one another."

The age and practice of confirmation has varied over the years and across denominations. Luther abolished the rite of confirmation as a sacramental act required for salvation, but the practice of confirming youth into the church through catechism and a public profession of faith has remained part of Lutheran tradition, but only barely. In 1954, in the wake of the worker's uprising, the government of the DDR initiated policies aimed at curbing the social-political influence of the church. The state began to encroach on the traditional territory of the church, restricting the right of religious education in schools and forbidding the meeting of some church youth groups. The government also instituted a *Jugendweihe*, a youth dedication ceremony, to replace the traditional church rite of confirmation. The new ceremony was explicitly atheistic, promoted a Marxist ideology, and the church refused to accept members of the state youth movement for confirmation. By the time of the Wende, in 1989, nearly 90 percent of German fourteen-year-olds attended the Jugendweihe. Though technically voluntary, the coming-of-age ceremony was in practice a necessity if one was to have hopes of professional, political, or economic success in the former DDR. The Wende ended antagonisms between the church and the communist state, but the Jugendweihe has continued, though participation has declined to around 50 percent. Those orchestrating the present-day confirmation event understand the procession of the confirmands to the Thesentür in the context of the state suppression of religion, and the need for the church to regain an instrumental role in initiating young people into adulthood.

The procession of the confirmands on Reformation Sunday emphasizes what is common to all processions, namely, being seen and bearing witness; it is also an annual act of territoriality. Twenty thousand people cram into the old town of Wittenberg on Reformation Day, an area just a few blocks wide and a mile long, and most of them are not there to sing "A Mighty Fortress" and worship in Luther's church. Rather, they come to drink beer and eat, to buy their kids a wooden sword and ice cream, to listen to music, to hang out, to attend a lecture or exhibit, to talk and gawk. Luther is the occasion, not the focus of festivity; worship is not the celebratory center of gravity. By bringing together a large cohort of initiates on Reformation Day and marching them through the city, the church employs the power of numbers to resist the secularization and commoditization of Luther and the festival. The confirmands literally occupy public space during the course of the weekend; in so doing they claim it as sacred space, Lutheran space, their space, their inheritance. The beginning and end points of the procession are churches, and the route traversed by the initiates passes the central Marktplatz; public space is thereby framed on either side by ecclesiastical space.

The procession to the Theses Door, led by Luther, allows for a certain direct participation in sacred history (priority II B). The formal title of the procession is "Aktion der Konfirmanden an der Thesentür der Schlosskirche," a title that echoes Luther's famous action. Holding confirmation in Wittenberg on Reformation Day and processing from the Stadtkirche to the Thesenportal enfolds a number of different scenarios: a biological coming of age, a rite of passage, and a mythical act of foundations. One set of messages is: At a certain age (adolescence), a person is granted certain rights (full participation in the church through communion), and now bears the responsibility to help renew the church. The procession enfolds two scenarios: The day on which a person enters the church is the day on which Martin Luther founded the church.

Classical rites-of-passage theory maps initiation in terms of a three-stage process of separation, transition-liminality, and return. This model fits the confirmation events quite well. The confirmands leave their respective homes and come together as a cohort in a sacred place of historical and mythological significance. Elders communicate sacra to the initiates through workshops and theologically informed tours of the city's historical and religious sites. Group identity and fellowship is built through dance, theatre, music, and worship services. The procession begins the process of return, presenting the church's new members to the public as they gather at Thesenportal.

Ritual enactments are embodied. "Posture and gesture, though micro-units in a ritual enactment or ritual tradition, assume considerable importance, because they encode both intended and unintended meanings—meanings 'transmitted' as well as meanings 'given off.'" Posture and gesture refer to "physical comportment . . . but also to one's attitude."[23] Like most processions, this one is linear. But in moving from the church where Luther preached to the church where the Reformation began, a metaphorical circularity is introduced. In going forward in their new life in the Evangelical Church, the confirmands travel back to the beginning. The movement of the procession connotes process. Individual confirmands move forward to a new status in the church, while the large group procession literally puts and displays the church "on the move." The processants give the church a presence at a festival in danger of losing its liturgical basis; they also embody the church in terms of movement, youth, vitality, exuberance, and beginnings. Their walk to the Thesenportal as the final act of Luther(s)pass signifies the importance of tradition and heritage to a church body struggling to renew itself.

The door lends the confirmation rite an aura of import. The Thesenportal is architecturally impressive. UNESCO has stamped it as a place of world historic significance. The endless round of festivals, plays, and concerts make the Theses Door a center of culture. The procession of the confirmands to the portal inscribes onto the bronze doors the values, narratives, and images embodied in the procession: the value of friendship, a narrative of origins and renewal, an image of a jovial Dr. Martin Luther, the notion that the church has a vital role to play in social-political life. The Theses Door in turn validates these values, narratives, and images, giving them weight, tactility, a physical location and origin, and a sense of permanence.

4

Martin Luther, German Hero

In this chapter, I deal with the cultural domain of civilitas, the civil dimensions of contemporary Luther festivity. The term *civil religion* typically refers to the mythologizing of history and the use of public ceremony and iconic architecture for the purposes of creating and maintaining state power and a collective, national identity. Ritual is typically identified with religion, but there is a rich literature detailing the centrality of ritual to political life.[1] In considering the civil dimensions of present-day Lutherland, historical context is important, since the figure of Luther was pivotal in the emergence of modern Germany in the nineteenth century as a politically and militarily powerful nation-state.

In Europe and North America during the eighteenth and nineteenth centuries, state nationalisms began to take on the socially integrative role once played by traditional forms of religion. Historical narratives (myths), monumental buildings and statuary (sacred places), legendary figures (founders and heroes), charters and constitutions (sacred texts), public ceremonies (rituals), and civil holidays (liturgical cycles) worked in unison to form a collective set of beliefs, values, and identity structures associated with the nation. This new nationally oriented worldview supplanted older confessional models. One of the aims of the Enlightenment philosophes was to break the hold of confessional identity structures, and reorient collective identity around national symbols. An individual would no longer be principally a Lutheran, a Calvinist, or a Catholic, but a German, a Frenchman, an Englishman, an American. Such efforts were only partly successful, and confessional and national identities in Europe and the Americas intertwined in complex ways.

Modern civil religion was the creation of political and intellectual elites, aided by forms of popular culture and ecclesiastical institutions. In Germany, Martin Luther played a role analogous to that of Washington, Jefferson, and Lincoln. Like Lincoln, Luther was the heroic figure whose efforts laid the groundwork for the creation of the modern German state. Like Lincoln, Luther was one of the common folk who rose to greatness, and whose life and work forged a new nation. Throughout the nineteenth century, the Prussian monarchy worked closely with the Evangelical Church, intertwining sympathies for a new, unified German nation, monarchical government, and the traditional practices, values, and beliefs of Lutheranism.[2] In 1817, the fledging Prussian state formed a Union Church out of the various Reformed and Lutheran Landeskirchen that dotted Prussian territory, part of the effort to unite diverse religious, political, and cultural regions into a nation. Monumental statuary, the restoration of important architectural sites, and public festivals commemorating the eminent people, accomplishments, and events in Germany's past were important tools in the rise of Germany as a nation-state and European power. Among those people, places, and events to figure prominently in the new Germany were Luther, Wittenberg, and the Thesenanschlag.

Luther and the German State

Royal progresses . . . locate the society's center and affirm its connection with transcendent things by stamping a territory with ritual signs of dominance. When kings journey around the country side, making appearances, attending fetes, conferring honors, exchanging gifts, or defying rivals, they mark it, like some wolf or tiger spreading his scent through his territory, as almost physically part of them.

—Clifford Geertz, *Local Knowledge*

On May 12, 1806, the neoclassical sculptor Johann Gottfried Schadow began a six-week trip through Lutherland. His aim was to discover the genius and essence of Martin Luther. The newly founded Literary Fatherland Society of the principality of Mansfeld (the province in which Luther was born), the Berlin Academy of Art, and the Prussian king (Friedrich Wilhelm III, 1770–1840) had commissioned Schadow to produce a monument honoring Luther, and his trip was undertaken to gather impressions from which he could draw in designing his work. Schadow's route passed through Eisleben, Mansfeld, Erfurt, Eisenach, Torgau, and Wittenberg. Schadow's travels of 1806 were a pilgrimage of sorts, the prototype of contemporary Reformation pilgrimage and heritage tourism.

Even before setting out, Schadow had formed a powerful image of the Luther he sought to fashion in stone. "The people no longer know the man. What greatness! What valor! What a hero! He has become my hero; I am inwardly filled with veneration for him. With profound love I am working on his image, and I worship this work of mine." Eleven years later, in 1817, with a symbolic first strike of the hammer, Schadow set the monument's foundation stone in Wittenberg's Marktplatz on the second day of the annual Reformation Day festival. The monument was completed and unveiled exactly four years later. During the Reformationsfest of 1821, on the evening of October 31, to the fanfare of trumpets and the rush of pounding drums, Schadow's *Luther* was revealed to the public. The newly created hero of the embryonic German nation struck a progressive, convicted, slightly defiant pose, holding fast to his Bible, illuminated in the Wittenberg night by dozens of torches surrounding the monument's base.[3]

In nineteenth-century Western Europe, "historical monuments and civic spaces as didactic artifacts were treated with curatorial reverence. They were visualized best if seen as isolated ornaments; jewels of the city to be place in scenographic arrangements and icongraphically composed to civilize and elevate the aesthetic tastes and morals of an aspiring urban elite. This was an architecture or ceremonial power whose monuments spoke of exemplary deeds, national unity, and industrial glory."[4] Through the nineteenth century, Prussian kings deliberately charted a course of marking Wittenberg as a symbolically significant place in the landscape of the modern German nation. Frederick Wilhelm IV (1795–1861), upon taking the throne, announced his plans for the Schlosskirche, which had suffered extensive damage in 1760 (during the Seven Years War) and again during the Napoleonic Wars of 1813–1814: "If it is no longer possible to restore the church to its original state, then I will focus on the Theses Door. This Door is a monument to Reformation history. Let us renew them in kind, poured in ore, and, just as Luther attached his 95 Theses, engrave the Theses on the Door in gold."[5]

If Luther hammered up the ninety-five theses, then there had to be a door— a door whose stature and import was equal to the world-transforming act of the great Reformer. In 1858, Friedrich's wishes were fulfilled, and the bronze Thesenportal was installed in a ceremony on Reformation Day, the year coinciding with Luther's 375th birthday. Kaiser Wilhelm I (1797–1888) and Kaiser Wilhelm II (1859–1941) would pursue Friedrich's vision for the city of Wittenberg, seeing to the production of large statues of Luther and Melanchthon in the Marktplatz, the conversion of Luther's former home into a museum (the

Lutherhalle or Lutherhaus, opened in 1883), and further costly renovations to the Schlosskirche, which were completed in 1892. Under the Kaisers, Wittenberg became hallowed, ceremonial ground. The very name of the Schlosskirche (castle church) reflects the interweaving of church and state. Inside the church are the graves of Luther and fellow reformer Philip Melanchthon, as well as the rulers of Saxony in Luther's day, Frederick the Wise and John the Constant. The vaulted Gothic-styled roof, the statuary honoring Luther and other reformers, stained glass windows, a large stone altar framed by a vestibule of alabaster monuments to Sachsen royalty, medallions and coats of arms lining the nave—the church exudes a palatial grandeur befitting the final resting place of great reformers and Sachsen nobility.

The Theses Door and Schadow's *Luther* project a set of values, a mythologized history, and conjoin two social domains: religion and politics. Schadow's *Luther*, located in the Marktplatz, places Luther in public space. Beside him is a statue of Melanchthon, installed in 1865. Behind the two men is the Rathaus, the city hall. The view and approach to these two fathers is framed (backed, supported) by a civic building—Luther and Melanchthon, church reformers, are also fathers of civil society. Through the production of monumental architecture, Luther was no longer simply the chief ancestor of the German Evangelical Church and growing Lutheran congregations around the globe; he was fast on his way to becoming a father figure capable of uniting a religiously and politically divided family of princely territories. When Schadow's *Luther* was unveiled, for the first time in history a public monument in Germany had been dedicated not to a ruler or a general but to a preacher, a doctor of the university, a theologian, a husband and father, a commoner—the son of miner from the small town of Mansfeld.

Wittenberg's iconic architecture created the setting for the pomp of civil ceremony and the rhetoric and gravitas of liturgy. Kaiser Wilhelm II spared no expense in making the 1892 Reformationsfest something to remember. The highest officials from the Evangelical Church attended, as did members of the German parliament. Kaiser Wilhelm II personally invited the queens of England and Holland and the kings of Denmark and Sweden. The kaiser made his way in a procession from Wittenberg's train station to the Schlosskirche, taking his throne on a large stage built for the occasion and positioned with a view to the Thesenportal.

After listening to numerous speeches and sermons, the kaiser gave permission for the key ceremony to begin.[⊙] The architect of the portal came forward carrying the golden key on a cushion. The kaiser stepped down, and,

⊙ DVD: Legend to Portal

in front of the doors given to the church by his ancestor, Frederick IV, with Germany's and Europe's political, economic, and religious elite looking on, passed the key on to the president of the Evangelical Church, who received it with hyperbolic deference: "Your Highness, greatest of kaisers and kings, most merciful gentleman! With deep reverence and thanks I take the key from your noble hands."[6] The Schlosskirche was the church that Luther built; through the 1892 celebration, it became the emperor's, too. Religion and politics were fused in a normative symbolic object and myth: the Thesenportal/Thesenanschlag.

Looking through the bibliographic record, we find that it was common practice through the nineteenth and early twentieth centuries to collect and publish sermons delivered on the occasion of Luther jubilees, something not done to mark, say, Easter or Christmas worship services. Festivals were described as *Tage der geprochende Wortes*, literally, "days of the spoken word." The sermon was the high point of the celebration. In these Prussian-era sermons, Luther is invoked as a foundational figure of both church and state, as theology, belief, mythic-history, gesture, and nationalist politics intertwine.

In 1917, to consider one festival occasion, with the nation mired in war, Wittenberg celebrated the four hundredth jubilee of the Reformation. Speeches, processions, sermons, and other events were inscribed with the sentiments of nationalism and the tones of militarism, and the celebrations were dominated by ecclesiastical events. On the morning of October 31, people gathered in front of the Katharina Portal at the Lutherhaus. An opening address was followed by a procession, in which catechumens led seminary students, university faculty, clergy, and church and government dignitaries from the Lutherhaus to the Schlosskirche. A second service followed in the Stadtkirche, and a third large gathering was held in the *Grosse Hoersaal* (large lecture hall) of the Lutherhaus museum. A children's worship service was also held in the Stadtkirche. The sermon preached to the gathered children captures the sense of the heroic Luther:

> Dear children, you all understand, and every one of you can explain,
> the significance of this day. This is the day on which, 400 years ago,
> our Dr. Martin Luther posted his 95 theses on the door of the
> Schlosskirche; the day on which, as our Kaiser once said, right here
> in Wittenberg, that "the greatest of all Germans performed the great
> liberating deed for the whole world; the awakening sound of his ham-
> mer resonated over German lands." Today is the birthday of our dear
> Evangelical Church, the day on which its foundations were laid; it is
> also the day on which began a new era, when one man, our Dr.
> Luther, guided by God's spirit, cleansed the temple of God from the

buyers and sellers, who set up their worldly indulgences coffers in the house of the Lord and sold God's grace for money."[7]

Luther is front and center as heroic figure in this sermon. His great deed is emphasized; the hand of God himself guides Luther's work. The echo of Luther's hammer enfolds "German lands" as a unified nation; Luther's importance to a new world order buttresses the German nationalism of the day. The Catholic Church is criticized, perhaps even demonized. The Luther story is enfolded in the Christ story, the defiant reformer "cleansing the temple," as did Jesus.

Nineteenth- and early-twentieth-century Reformation monuments and festivity are examples of what Eric Hobsbawm calls the "invention of tradition." One of the features of the rise of the nation-state in Germany and elsewhere during the nineteenth century was the use of ceremonial occasions to "inculcate certain values and norms of behavior by repetition, which automatically implies continuity with the past."[8] Nineteenth-century Prussia created a Luther who was seen as the originator and carrier of "Prussian" values: order, discipline, sense of duty to family, nation, and God. Luther was depicted as a progressive genius, a rugged individual, a dutiful friend, and supporter of the aristocracy—these were building blocks of the new nation, a nation whose very newness was masked by linking its origins to a selective remembering of four centuries of Lutheran and Reformation heritage.

While the Prussian nobility was involved in ecclesiastical politics, Lutheran theologians and ministers, even those of the school of "liberal theology" were engaging in nationalist politics. Adolf von Harnack (1851–1930), to take but one example, writing at the close of the nineteenth century, claimed "Protestantism and Germanness belong together indivisibly. Just as the Reformation saved the German Reich in the sixteenth century, so today the Reformation is still the Reich's strongest power, continuing principle, and highest goal."[9] Protestantism was touted as the unique world-historical contribution of the German Volk to Christianity, as religion, ethnicity, and the fortunes of the nation-state merged. At every turn—monuments, architecture, texts, sermons, theologies, processions, ceremonies, liturgies, museums—Luther was transformed into the founder and figurehead of German nationalism and religion.

German Hero?

If at the turn of the twentieth century Luther was the paragon of German greatness, by the turn of the twenty-first he had become, to say the least, a troubled character. In the 1960s, looking back through a half century devastated by two world wars and the horrors of the Holocaust, hard questions about the historical Luther and the complicity of the Protestant and Catholic churches with the Second and Third reichs challenged previously unquestionable assumptions about a heroic Luther.

Already in 1945, Thomas Mann, speaking before the United States Congress at the end of Second World War, addressing the question of German war guilt, supplied the impetus and direction for post-Holocaust Luther scholarship:

> Luther was a liberating hero—but in the German style, for he knew nothing of liberty. I am not speaking now of the liberty of the Christian but of political liberty, the liberty of the citizen—this liberty not only left him cold, but its impulses and demands were deeply repugnant to him. . . . Luther hated the peasant revolt which . . . if successful, would have given a happier turn to German history, a turn toward liberty. . . . He told the princes that they could now gain the kingdom of heaven by slaughtering the peasant beasts. Luther, the German man of the people, bears a good share of responsibility for the sad ending of this first attempt at a German revolution.

Mann was referring to Luther's tract of 1525, *Against the Murderous, Thieving Hordes of Peasants*, in which Luther wrote:

> Whosoever can, should smite, strangle, and stab, secretly or publicly, and should remember that there is nothing more poisonous, pernicious, and devilish than a rebellious man . . . the Gospel does not make goods common, except in the case of those who do of their own free will what the apostles and disciples did in Acts IV. They did not demand, as do our insane peasants in their raging, that the goods of others—of a Pilate and a Herod—should be common, but only their own goods. Our peasants, however, would have other men's goods common, and keep their own goods for themselves. Fine Christians these! I think there is not a devil left in hell; they have all gone into the peasants.

Luther's political views encouraged the compliance of the Lutheran Church with a monarchical and authoritarian German state. In the communist DDR, historiography emphasized Luther's siding with state power in the brutal suppression of the Peasants' War, marking him as an opponent of the ideological aims of socialism: the emancipation of labor and the improvements of the conditions of the working class. Even more disturbing than Luther's penchant for authoritarian state power were the postwar revelations of Luther's anti-Semitic diatribes. Tracts such as Luther's *On the Jews and Their Lies* (1543) supplied the

Nazis with fuel for their ideological fires. W. H. Auden, writing five years before Mann's address, made explicit the Luther-Nazi connection:

> Accurate scholarship can
> Unearth the whole offence
> From Luther until now
> That has driven a culture mad
> Find what occurred at Linz
> What huge imago made
> A psychopathic god:
> I and the public know
> What all schoolchildren learn,
> Those to whom evil is done
> Do evil in return.[10]

Hitler was born in Linz, and returned in 1938 for the annexation of Austria. He was the "psychopathic god" who, raised on a culture of anti-Semitism, knew what "all school children learn"—that the Jews are an evil race that has done evil to Germany, and must, therefore, face "evil in return."

A line of argument that directly links Hitler to Luther radically oversimplifies complex social-historical processes. Still, when Luther's attempts at converting Jews failed, an older Luther tapped a reservoir of anti-Jewish sentiment and let fly a torrent of words that will forever haunt his achievements. He deserves to be quoted at length:

> What shall we Christians do with this rejected and condemned people, the Jews? Since they live among us, we dare not tolerate their conduct, now that we are aware of their lying and reviling and blaspheming. If we do, we become sharers in their lies, cursing and blasphemy. Thus we cannot extinguish the unquenchable fire of divine wrath, of which the prophets speak, nor can we convert the Jews. With prayer and the fear of God we must practice a sharp mercy to see whether we might save at least a few from the glowing flames. . . . I shall give you my sincere advice: First, to set fire to their synagogues or schools and to bury and cover with dirt whatever will not burn, so that no man will ever again see a stone or cinder of them. . . . Second, I advise that their houses also be razed and destroyed. For they pursue in them the same aims as in their synagogues. Instead they might be lodged under a roof or in a barn, like the gypsies. . . . Third, I advise that all their prayer books and Talmudic writings, in which such idolatry, lies, cursing, and blasphemy

are taught, be taken from them. Fourth, I advise that their rabbis be
forbidden to teach henceforth on pain of loss of life and limb. . . .
Fifth, I advise that safe-conduct on the highways be abolished
completely for the Jews. For they have no business in the countryside,
since they are not lords, officials, tradesmen, or the like. Let them stay
at home. . . . Sixth, I advise that usury be prohibited to them, and that
all cash and treasure of silver and gold be taken from them and put
aside for safekeeping. . . . Seventh, I recommend putting a flail, an ax,
a hoe, a spade, a distaff, or a spindle into the hands of young, strong
Jews and Jewesses and letting them earn their bread in the sweat of
their brow, as was imposed on the children of Adam (Gen. 3 :19). . . .
The judgment of Christ . . . declares that they are venomous, bitter,
vindictive, tricky serpents, assassins, and children of the devil who
sting and work harm stealthily wherever they cannot do it openly. . . .
I wish and I ask that our rulers who have Jewish subjects exercise a
sharp mercy toward these wretched people, as suggested above, to see
whether this might not help (though it is doubtful). They must act
like a good physician who, when gangrene has set proceeds without
mercy to cut, saw, and burn flesh, veins, bone, and marrow. Such a
procedure must also be followed in this instance. Burn down their
synagogues, forbid all that I enumerated earlier, force them to work,
and deal harshly with them, as Moses did in the wilderness, slaying
three thousand lest the whole people perish. They surely do not know
what they are doing; moreover, as people possessed, they do not wish
to know it, hear it, or learn it. Therefore it would be wrong to be
merciful and confirm them in their conduct. If this does not help we
must drive them out like mad dogs, so that we do not become
partakers of their abominable blasphemy and all the their other vices
and thus merit God's wrath and be damned with them. I have done
my duty. Now let everyone see to his. I am exonerated.

For many generations of Lutherans, Luther's anti-Semitism was an embarrass-
ment, and his pleas to burn synagogues were quietly ignored.[11] But with the rise
of the Nazis to power, and in the wake of the atrocities they committed, it is impossible to read Luther's tract without noticing the similarities between his polemics
and the atrocities committed in Nazi-era Germany. On Kristallnacht, the night of
November 9, 1938, more than one hundred synagogues across Germany, along
with Jewish-owned shops and homes, were burned and vandalized.

Of special relevance here is the Nazi involvement in Luther celebrations.
The role played by Luther's anti-Jewish tracts in the rise of the racist ideology

and horrific atrocities of National Socialism is a hotly debated matter. What is certain, however, is that the Nazis made use of Luther for their own purposes, including playing an active role in planning and participating in the Luthertag festivals of 1933, celebrating the four hundred fiftieth anniversary of Luther's birth. Hitler's appointment as chancellor early in 1933 was well timed to take advantage of Luthertag festivities. Wilhelm Frick, a high-level Nazi party member, took part in celebrations in Wittenberg in November. Frick spoke of Luther's "ruthless will to truthfulness," his "inner modesty," and "uncompromising belief." "Broad segments of the Nazi party participated in Luther Day across Germany," and the rhetoric, proffered by Nazis and non-Nazis alike and embodied in processions through the streets, was one of Luther's contribution to the reawakening of the German Volk, represented by the rise to power of the National Socialist Party.[12]

The opposition of Lutheran pastors such as Dietrich Bohnhoffer and Martin Niemöller to Hitler's Third Reich is often and rightly praised. But memory of their courageous work has tended to obscure the widespread complicity of the Evangelical Church with the aims of National Socialism. In 1934, for example, Lutheran bishops unanimously affirmed loyalty to the National Socialist government, and condemned "all intrigues of criticism of the state, nation, and movement which might endanger the Third Reich. . . . We admonish all members of our church to stand with us in intercession for and fidelity to the Führer." Most did precisely that. "Churchmen hoped for the rebirth of the German people, nationalistically and religiously. Many expected that the new national movement was going to mean the salvation and renewal of the church. Others claimed that there could be no true national renewal without the accompanying depth and support of a religious revival. And Luther could point the way to such religious and national renewal, as was apparent in a rash of articles and books with titles such as 'Luther and the State' or 'Luther and the Volk.'"[13]

The historical and religious reasons that led to near-unanimous church support for the Nazi movement are complex. The Treaty of Versailles, which forced Germany to assume total war guilt, was deeply resented. Socialism and communism, powerful cultural forces at the time, were seen as promoting a godless society, which helped push the church to the right. Conservative Lutherans perceived the Weimar Republic, a modernizing force, as a threat. Protestant territories, especially in the north, had sympathies for strong, central government. German culture had deep sympathies for the notions of a mythical German Volk and its attachment to German land. In academia, scholars working outside of the Lutheran tradition were challenging the uniqueness and status of Luther's theology. The Catholic Heinrich Denifle had published a work arguing for Luther's close continuity with Romanist theology, and Rabbi Reinhold Lewin's study of Luther's vile attitudes toward Jews was acclaimed by Catholics, liberal Protestants, and secularists. Moreover, the milieu of liberal Protestantism in the 1930s was increasingly critical of Luther. In the climate of the German defeat, it appeared to conservative, nationalist Lutherans that their perceived enemies of Germany—liberals, most Catholics, Jews, and Social Democrats, all supporters of the new Republic—were also the enemies of Luther.

Since the 1960s, a decade that witnessed the beginning of the Cold War and the building of the Berlin Wall, Luther has been the subject of thoroughgoing critique, especially by Germany's liberal left. The use of Luther to encourage state absolutism and imperialist sympathies in the nineteenth century and then to validate the horrific pogroms of Hitler's Germany has demanded the attention of academics, politicians, activists, the church, and the general public. The consensus is that within Luther's writings are hooks of such size and strength for the politicization of the man to have caught hold. Luther was but one of many factors that contributed to the German anti-Semitism incarnated in the Third Reich, but in a post-Holocaust world, Luther's stature as culture hero has been destabilized, as Germans continue to deal with difficult questions of cultural memory.

And not just Germans. As Lutheran pilgrims travel to Lutherland, an encounter with the shadow of Luther's genius is often in the cards. In fact, in the ELCA center's programs, Luther's connection to the Holocaust is explicitly present, as I discussed with the center's director, Twila Shock:

> "I notice there is discussion of anti-Semitism in Luther's writings and their legacy is in your programs. Does it ever happen that someone comes and experiences a crisis of faith. . . . Does a visit to Wittenberg ever question, or offend, or shatter one's faith? Because [some of] your programs build these difficult questions [of Luther's anti-Semitism] in."
> "Perhaps 'offend' is not the word I would like to use, but in a certain way we would like that to happen. If you look at the radical nature of God's grace, as Luther was trying to proclaim it, it is bound to offend someone. Because it is I think far more open than any of us would like to believe, it includes our own worst enemy. And I think coming out of our puritanical experience in the United States—I'm speaking just about a certain group of our people but . . . I think when your worldview or faith is shattered or challenged, you are still accompanied by other people who bolster you up on that day you go to Buchenwald and are confronted with the darker side of the face of humanity and know that perhaps you would have participated as

well. So we want that to happen. . . . But you [also] want to be able to
put people back together; otherwise it is no longer pastoral. . . . You've
been to Wittenberg, you've sung 'A Mighty Fortress,' you've gotten all
revved up over being in Wittenberg, and then you go to Buchenwald.
And you discover that Luther had—not anti-Semitic, but anti-Jewish
writings—and you realize that your own heritage was used as a tool
to victimize an entire race of people. So in that context we do a service
of confession and absolution where we also use our church's procla-
mation to the Jewish community. So we try rather than [engage in
self-flagellation] or trying to ignore it, we try to open it up. And then
try to proclaim a word of grace."

Luther is the father of the church, but also a scar on Lutheran identity.

In spite of Luther's contributions and connections with a troubled past, the
man remains a figure closely identified with German genius and greatness. In
November of 2003, the national broadcaster ZDF (Zweites Deutsches Fernse-
hen) asked Germans to vote for the greatest German of all time. The event was
called "Our Best" (Unser Besten) and when the votes were tallied, Luther stood
in second place, behind Conrad Adenauer, West Germany's first chancellor following the Second World War. ZDF invited a prominent intellectual or public
figure to sponsor a candidate, and Luther's sponsor, pastor Margot Kässmann,
offered the following in favor of voting for Luther: "For me, it is obvious that
Martin Luther is the greatest German. He shaped our language, our culture, and
with his theological insights he authored world history and opened the door to
the modern world. When he stood before the judgment at Worms and said, 'Here
I stand, I can do no other,' he demonstrated the courage, decisiveness, and clarity
that we are in need of today."[14] Kässmann captured the sentiments of other commentators who focused on what are typically seen as Luther's remarkable achievements: his creation of modern German through the translation of the Bible; his
protest against institutional corruption; his embodiment of heroic values.

Memory of Luther, in other words, moves in two contradictory directions:
Luther is both a heroic figure and someone whose thought and actions seeded
the ground for a totalitarian state and anti-Semitism. How is this tension
handled in contemporary Luther festivity?

Renaissance Man, Good Bürger

Luther walks the streets of Wittenberg during both Luther's Wedding and Reformation Day. A resident or former resident of Wittenberg is selected each year

to play Luther in the Wedding festival, and Bernhard Naumann, the Kirchen-meister (building manager) of Wittenberg's Stadtkirche, performs Luther during Reformation Day. These performances involve period dress, ambling through the streets, informally conversing with the public, and posing for photographs.

During the Wedding festival, neither Luther nor his Katie says very much. The *Stadtherold* (town crier) presents Katie to the crowd in the Marktplatz on Friday afternoon; she wears the robes of a nun, but says nothing. Luther first appears on Saturday morning, walking and waving with his Katie, now transformed into a bride, during the Wedding Umzug, the city parade. The couple sit together at the dinner table later that afternoon, but say nothing; they simply eat, and enjoy performances of Renaissance-era music and dance. On Sunday, they cut the wedding cake, but say nothing; they lead a procession to the stage in the Marktplatz Sunday afternoon, but again say nothing. Their presence is thoroughly iconic.

In these performances, we see a jovial "Dr. Martinus," the doctor of the University and Renaissance man who gave birth to the German language and the cherished value of the right of individual conscience before irrational, institutionalized authority. He is composed, pleasant, a good *Bürger* (citizen) of Wittenberg. His doings over the weekend revolve around cultural and aesthetic activities: eating fine meals, enjoying music, walking the streets, soaking up the festive atmosphere, serving as a mobile mannequin for a photograph-hungry public. The historical man of action turns out to be relatively passive; the reformer with a streak of belligerence is at peace with the world; the medieval man who shouted and threw ink pots at the devil is thoroughly modern; the vengeful, bitter Luther who wrote scathing attacks on Jews never peeks out from beneath an aura of dignified warmth.

Nothing the couple does during the Wedding festival could be construed as political—certainly not in any nationalist sense. Neither is the wedding couple directly involved in any ecclesiastical events or settings. The performance of the Reformation during the Wedding festival has more to do with civic than civil or ecclesiastical religiosity. Civil religion is associated with nation, politics, and government, civic religion with city-mindedness, renewal, self-esteem, local issues, economic development, aesthetics, entertainment, and culture. The same is true of the performance of Luther during the Reformation festival. Here, Luther becomes more of an ecclesiastical figure, and slightly more performative, involved with confirmation events, leading the procession of confirmands, and publically exhorting the new members to help renew the church.[⊙]

⊙ DVD: Processing—Confirmands

But Naumann's performance during Reformation Day does not entail any overtly political dimensions. Civil religion in the contemporary Wittenberg festivals is a far cry from what it once was. It is well nigh impossible to imagine politicians today using Luther as a figurehead for the nation: There is simply too much history, and Germany is too secular and pluralistic for Luther to again be elevated to the status of a "father." Culturally, Luther retains his place in the pantheon of German luminaries, but politically the connection between Luther-land and Fatherland has been all but broken.

Listening to Luther

A regular feature of both Luther's Wedding and Reformation Day is a public lecture by Friedrich Schorlemmer. We might call these historical lectures, since they typically deal with Wittenberg's Reformation past. But they are also informed by contemporary social and political concerns, and aim to retrieve elements of Luther's thought and practice, and bring these to bear on contemporary life. Schorlemmer is a prominent citizen and resident of Wittenberg. As the pastor of the Stadtkirche during the 1980s, he played an important role in the protest movements that culminated in the Wende. He now works with Wittenberg's Evangelische Akademie. The organization is responsible for hosting cultural and academic events, and works to build lines of communication between the Evangelical Church and the public.

A Schorlemmer lecture is one of the listed events of Luther's Wedding. Timed to coincide with Reformation Day is a Luther-themed academic conference, listed as part of the official Reformation Day celebrations, and hosted by the Evangelische Akademie and the Luther Memorials Foundation (Luthergedenkstatten). Themed with the conference and taking place on Reformation Day is a Schorlemmer lecture in the Lutherhaus; the later event is titled *Luther lessen* (reading Luther). Given that Luther was a leader in his community, working tirelessly for social reform and religious-political change, Schorlemmer, more than a costumed Luther in the Marktplatz, could be considered the contemporary face of Luther in Wittenberg. Articulate, passionate, and committed to rebuilding and revitalizing both the church and an active public sphere in post-Wende Germany, Schorlemmer commands attention: When he speaks, people listen.

In 2005, for Luther's Wedding, Schorlemmer delivered a lecture to a packed audience in the beautifully renovated hall of the Cranachhof. The theme was "Luther and State Violence." He began his lecture by spinning a host of contradictory images that attach themselves to the name of Martin Luther: "Martin Luther: a lackey of the nobility, a miserable Jew-hater, one who ate Catholics with pleasure, a persistent malevolent spirit, and a horrible divider of the church. Is this not so? Martin Luther: bringer of freedom, a linguistic genius, social caregiver . . . prophet of his time, amazing hermeneut, and so on." Schorlemmer went on to outline Luther's attitude toward violence. Luther, he lectured, advocated that individuals must listen to their conscience and speak out against oppression, especially if the power of state authority is against Christ. Luther had warned Saxon nobility, for example, that if the needs of the peasants were not met, they would undoubtedly "rise up one day, and it will be your own fault." Luther, Schorlemmer continued, supported the demands of the peasants, but not their ultimate resort to violence. "One must carry the fight with words, but the fist must hold still; this is our order," he quoted Luther. Physical resistance, violent insurrection was off limits; a defiant speaking of the truth to power a necessity.

These same words of Luther are quoted in the Lutherhaus museum, prominently displayed in extra large font in one of the exhibits. They were written in 1524, addressed to Thomas Müntzer, in an effort to diffuse tensions driving the peasants' uprising. When the peasants did not relent, however, Luther came down hard on the rebellion. In 1525, in his tract titled *Against the Murdering, Thieving Hordes of Peasants*, Luther argued that violence must be met with violence:

> For rebellion is not simple murder, but is like a great fire, which
> attacks and lays waste a whole land. Thus rebellion brings with it a
> land full of murder and bloodshed, makes widows and orphans, and
> turns everything upside down, like the greatest disaster. Therefore let
> everyone who can, smite, slay and stab, secretly or openly, remembering
> that nothing can be more poisonous, hurtful or devilish than a rebel.
> It is just as when one must kill a mad dog; if you do not strike him,
> he will strike you, and a whole land with you.

The image of Luther crafted by Schorlemmer runs at odds with those by Thomas Mann and W. H. Auden cited earlier, and with the passage cited above. The belligerent Luther of *On the Jews and Their Lies*, or the *Against the Peasants* did not make an appearance in Schorlemmer's lecture. The transmission of tradition is selective. Clearly Schorlemmer was drawing on elements of Luther's thought, life, and work in order to cultivate a vigilant, truth-speaking public—individuals willing to stand up to state violence, but unwilling to engage in it. A context informing his lecture is the American-led "war on terror."

Another event that turns the mood of frivolity within the larger festival toward matters of gravitas is the procession of the academic senate and civic officials during Reformation Day celebrations.$^{\odot}$ Formal debate was part of the medieval university system. In Paris, Bologna, and Wittenberg a highly formalized system of public debate was central to university life. Some debates included processions of university, church, and civic officials through the city's streets. Debate, which emphasized the use of reason, proficiency in rhetoric, and the skillful use of body language and gesture, came to rival the formal lecture as the chief instrument of university education. The literary products of debate are the genres of dialogue and the disputation; the medieval master of these was Peter Abelard, exemplified in works such as *Dialogue between a Philosopher, a Jew, and a Christian*, and *Sic et Non* (Yes and No). Luther inherited this tradition, and wrote his ninety-five theses in the spirit and culture of public debate and disputation.

There is no convincing evidence that Luther posted his theses on the church door, or that scholars debated his theses at the University of Wittenberg. Later, once the theses were published and were being widely discussed, Luther did formally debate. In 1518, his monastic order, the Augustinian Hermits, invited Luther to debate his new theology in Heidelberg. A year later, one of Luther's older university colleagues, Andreas Carlstadt, arranged a debate with the prominent theologian and strident critic of Luther, Johann Eck. Carlstadt, Melanchthon, and Luther, followed by two hundred students (some carrying spears should events turn violent), made the trip from Wittenberg to Leipzig for the debate, held on July 16, 1519. When Carlstadt began losing ground against Eck, Luther, who had gone with the intent of merely listening, jumped into the fray, and Eck and Luther went toe to toe. It was a defining moment in Luther's career as a Reformer, in part because Eck goaded Luther into publicly sympathizing with the Czech Jan Hus, who had been burned at the stake in 1415 for his heretical views.

In the procession of the Senate during Reformation Day there are echoes of this tradition in which academics publicly debate questions of import, and specifically an echo of Luther's intellectual and moral challenge, embodied and symbolized in the theses and the legends and images of the Thesenanschlag. The Senate of the University of Wittenberg, the mayor, city councilors, and their families gather inside the foyer of the old Rathaus, the old city hall that backs the central Marktplatz. The crowd waits, cameras at the ready. In 2005, after a rather length delay, the Senate and city council emerged to face an audience who had grown somewhat impatient. With time on their hands and a restless public, the performers on the small stage in the Marktplatz adjacent to the city hall improvised a skit, satirizing the pomp and ceremony of the

⊙ DVD: Processing—Senate

moment. The crowd cheered the performers on, and when the elite group finally took its place on the Rathaus steps they were greeted with a mix of genuine and mock applause. Fortunately for the fate of the procession, the band quickly took control, trumpets and drums easily drowning out what few jeers were still being thrown. Little did the group know what awaited them further down the street.

Slowly, with a dignified air befitting their station, the processants, cameraman in tow, passed between and by the statues of the two great Reformers, and turned not right to the Schlosskirche, following the confessional route of the confirmands, but left toward the Lecorea and the campus of the University Halle-Wittenberg. Halfway to their destination, the procession was ignominiously forced to the edge of the street, which had been blocked by the crowd that had gathered to watch a South American band perform. A bit further on, several people sitting at a streetside table, enjoying their beer and sunshine, jumped to mock attention as the Senate passed. "Oh, here come the important people," they chided, and added salutes and mock bows to drive their point home. The Senate did not acknowledge the barbs, did not break ranks, and carried on to the university.

The procession was the prelude to a disputation on the question of a culture war between the West and Islam. After all, Luther was a doctor. To celebrate Luther is to engage in academic debate, even if this means questioning Luther. Like Scholemmer's lecture earlier in the year during Luther's Wedding, the debate focused on the meaning and legacy of Luther to contemporary politics and global affairs, shaped as these are by imperialism and state power, and mired in violent conflict—conflict driven or exacerbated by the fusion of religion and politics. There is sense in which Luther remains important to civil religion in Germany. Indeed, the inclusion of public lectures, the Senate procession, and formal debate in Luther festivity is paradigmatic of Germany's contemporary process of embodying a national identity and culture. In light of the horrors of the past, acts of memory and the necessity of vigilant questioning of state and religious power have been elevated to a sacred duty. A persistent national theme in Germany is questioning, remembering, and debating matters of Holocaust guilt and memory.

In the reunified Germany, debate over the Holocaust crystallized in the fall of 1998. The context was comments made by the esteemed author Martin Walser, in his acceptance speech of the Peace Prize, handed out annually by the German Book Trade at its fair in Frankfurt. Walser was critical of constant references in the public sphere to German Holocaust crimes as a "permanent representation of our shame." Moreover, he lamented that Holocaust memory entailed the "instrumentalization of our shame for current purposes," a form of "negative nationalism" disseminated by "intellectuals" and "opinion soldiers." The Holocaust, he claimed, was being used for political purposes; with special interest groups holding the nation "at moral gunpoint" as a "means of intimidation deployable at any time" in order to label and find guilty "all Germans." Any sense of national pride and self-satisfaction is immediately and effectively "thwarted" by reference to the Holocaust, by use of the "Auschwitz cudgel." The audience of 1,200 influential politicians, artists, media owners, and business people rose to give Walser a standing ovation—all save three, one of whom was Friedrich Schorlemmer. The other two were Ignatz Bublis, head of the Central Council of Jews in Germany, and his wife. Bublis and Walser carried out a heated debate in the press, a debate that still resonates through Germany, as the country continues the long, difficult process of memory work and the creation of a new national identity, one that acknowledges crimes of the past but is not forever hamstrung by "negative nationalism."[15]

The debate over Germany's Nazi past—the rather placid term *debate* completely fails to capture the tangled knot of emotions surrounding the issue—is generally carried on in what Jürgen Habermas referred to as the public sphere: print journals, editorials, book reviews, conferences. Alongside this largely textual and linguistic sphere are the contributions of theatre, cinema, and television programs, museum exhibits and memorials, and public events, such as Walser's Peace Award speech. Germany's war guilt has been a persistent topic in schools, the media, literature, the media, and academia. Each region in Germany approaches and refracts these difficult memories through the particulars of local history. In and around Wittenberg, this means dealing with Luther's anti-Jewish tracts and his sympathies for authoritarian power. Lifting this side of Luther into the light of day is especially relevant, given the region's efforts to use Luther as an economic and cultural resource.

Festivity and other events in Wittenberg include exhibits, lectures, seminars, or conferences dealing with the region's war history, and questions of memory, power, and representation (fig. 4.1). The Lutherzentrum, which promotes Luther-related research and cultural events, for example, sponsored a traveling exhibit titled "The Jews of the Luthertown Wittenberg in the Third Reich." The exhibit deals with the treatment and fate of Wittenberg's Jews in the Nazi era. Such exhibits, lectures, and conferences, though part of the annual event calendar and open to the public, are not public in the same sense that a parade is public. The events are generally inside; people sit and listen or quietly walk through an exhibit. They are hosted by academic institutions, or by church organizations such as the Evangelishe Akademie. A difficulty is that these efforts at pursuing the historical Luther and his connection to the atrocities of the Nazi era (or state nationalism and imperialism, or the violence of the Peasants' War), are terribly at odds with how Luther and the Reformation is produced, consumed, and interpreted by the production of festivals and tourist spectacles. Contemporary Reformation festivity does make a place for questioning and talking back to Luther. But the troubling of the figure of Luther tends to take place behind closed doors—in public spaces, to be sure, but not in the open-air theatrical or festive performances, nor in liturgical spaces and rites. Religious and cultural leaders in Wittenberg, through exhibits, conferences, and lectures, vigilantly pursue the deconstruction of Luther as German hero, but the iconic sites of Wittenberg and the relatively benign images and

FIGURE 4.1. A poster for a conference in Wittenberg, illustrating the current interest in questions of cultural memory and creating a usable past. Photograph by Ronald Grimes.

performance of the man in the streets during festival time have not been touched by this mood of negation and symbolic stripping.

Paintbombs and Protest

As the happy couple cut the wedding cake in 2005, it was difficult for me to ignore the fact that this use of Luther and Katharina to promote civic pride, economic development, and cultural renewal took place on Judenstrasse, and that in 1933, SS officers and Nazi party officials lined Wittenberg's streets and attended Luthertag celebrations. Is there a fundamental tension or contradiction in using Luther to promote social renewal and civic identity, when it is this same man who contributed to the horrors against which renewal efforts, acts of memory, and religious, regional, and national identities will continue to be measured? Questions surrounding Luther's posthumous involvement with Germany's troubled twentieth century do not go unasked during Wittenberg's festivals, but they do not take place in Wittenberg's streets—at least, not officially.

Joseph Pieper, in his widely read study of festivity, emphasizes the importance of praise, laughter, joy, and exuberance to public celebration. Clearly, festivals are meant to be joyous occasions. Festivals ascend to a mood of collective celebration through what Ronald Grimes calls superstructuring, which involves "magnifying and turning a culture's good, virtuous, and proper side to public view." When festivals are informed by traditions of European Carnival, with its penchant for satire, parody, and grotesque realism, superstructuring is tempered by deconstructing. "Deconstructing a celebration means turning the public view toward the under, down, dark, unstructured, or emergent side of culture." While a mood of ritual and symbolic ascension is prominent within Luther festivity in Wittenberg, deconstruction, a "mode of negation, of symbolic stripping," is also at work.[16] In the wake of two world wars, the Holocaust, and the cold war, the figure of Luther and events celebrating his genius carry an inherent ambivalence. Luther is a cultural and religious resource informing Lutheran and regional piety, festive revelry, and civic pride, but he is also something of a scar on Lutheran and German identity, a fact that reared its head in 2005.

Again, we return to Luther's Thesenportal, and further develop the "operational uses" to which this celebratory object has been put. One of Lindsay Jones's ritual-architectural priorities is politics. The rubric directs attention the "role of architecture and ritual . . . in relation to the exercise of . . . governmental force and authority but also . . . to the perpetuation (or subversion) of any sort of social or economic hierarchy."[17] One of the ironies of the Theses Door is that although it calls to mind Luther's protest of temporal authority, the portal was designed and used to legitimate the temporal authority of the Kaiserreich. An understanding of the operational use of celebratory objects requires tending to the attitudes and emotions evoked by those objects. In the case of Luther, places such as the Theses Door can become charged with memories and conflicts the likes of which it is difficult, if not impossible, for many North Americans to comprehend.

The complex history of the portal as a setting for both ecclesiastical and political rites, the ubiquitous presence of the camera and media, and the power of the church to attract large numbers of tourists—these features make the large open plaza in front of the Schlosskirche a natural stage for protest. If the Theses Door is used to encourage group identity among young Lutherans, it is also used by those who oppose the current revitalization of Luther (principally through films, media, festivals, and tourism) as one of Germany great historical figures. In May of 2005, shortly before the annual Luther's Wedding festival, many of the heritage sites of Wittenberg were sprayed with graffiti. Wittenberg residents awoke one morning to find a leaflet, supposedly from the NPD (Nationaldemokratische Partei Deutschlands), the right-wing, neo-Nazi party in Germany, announcing a rally in Wittenberg. The leaflet called for a "national procession" in Wittenberg's Marktplatz, in the context of Luther's importance to questions of national identity and the welfare of Germany's youth. According to Jörg, who is involved in anti-Luther demonstrations and who is a consultant with Projektwerkstatt, a left-leaning direct action and protest organization, the leaflet probably

FIGURE 4.2. Graffiti sprayed near the Schlosskirche prior to the Luther's Wedding festival, June 2005. The "thesis" translates, roughly, as "Upend Luther's Wedding." Photograph by the author.

did not come from the NPD. "My hunch is that people who are critical of Luther put out the leaflet to call attention to the fact that the Nazis (and Hitler himself) found much in Luther to praise; they saw themselves as fulfilling Luther's [anti-Semitic] ideas." In the decades after the Second World War, Luther became a troubled figure, as historians, politicians, and theologians weighed his legacy in light of the horrors of two world wars. In the post-Holocaust era, Luther's anti-Jewish tracts in particular have been a stumbling block in the search for a useable history in Germany. Luther railed against the "Jews and Their Lies," and "the terrible tragedy of the relationship between Jews and Christians in world history can be studied in concentrated form in the history of this one man."[18]

The release of the motion picture *Luther* in October of 2003 probably influenced Luther's high ranking in the ZDF poll of Germany's "best." The film was much anticipated, and a box office success in Germany. It also generated a good deal of critical discussion, even protest. The subtitle used in the German release, "he changed the world forever," and the phrase prominent on advertisements for the film, "a story of German heroism," reflect the manner in which the film depicts Luther in continuity with the nineteenth-century Heldenmythos. Several groups organized demonstrations at cinemas showing the films, and these demonstrations led to further actions at Luther and Reformation festivals and in the various "cities of Luther," including Wittenberg (fig. 4.2).

As Jörg explained:

> the contents of the film about Luther were a catastrophe of historical blindness. Luther's role in the history of religion, even more so in the history of Germany and the changes from the Middle Ages to the modern period are generally seen in a positive light. I see it differently. . . . [Luther's] ideas and works functioned to resist trends toward greater freedom; his support for the nobility against the peasants is relatively well known. He also blocked humanistic and anticlerical currents. His comments about women, the disabled, and Jews are completely unacceptable. At any rate, I'm not criticizing Luther; he's long dead. I am critical of the functionaries of the church, filmmakers, and the politicians and media people who laud the man as an image or hero on which to base national identity.

Luther is a metaphorical portal into a hornet's nest of emotion around questions of memory in German society. Like the actual portal identified with the man, Luther is a figure of "considerable ambivalence, attracting dangerous, as well as beneficent forces." The legend of the Thesenanschlag created the Thesenportal, and now the door itself is one of the places that Luther's critics come to challenge the legend.

In state elections in Saxony in September of 2004, the neo-fascist NPD received 9.2 percent of the vote, just 0.5 percent less than the leading Social Democrats. New Right parties also made gains in state elections in Thuringia, and in elections for the European parliament. (The cities in which Luther lived and worked are found in Thuringia and Saxony.) Through the 1990s, the federal government made several unsuccessful attempts to ban Neuerecht (New Right) parties such as the NPD. Far-right ideologies are gaining footholds in schools, are being articulated by an increasing number of educated professionals and politicians, disseminated through Web sites, CDs, and rallies, and are slowly migrating from the fringe to the mainstream; the 2004 elections were something of a wake-up call for antifascist groups in Germany.

One of the key principles and aims of the New Right in Germany is the establishment of a *Volksgemeinschaft*, "a mythical society of the German people."[19] Historically, Luther was instrumentalized for precisely such purposes. "Immediately after 1945 the Reformer Martin Luther, and with him often German Lutheranism in general, were seen in certain circles as one of the spiritual roots of national-socialism. Luther had helped, so his critics argued, to prepare the mentality structures, especially the servility towards the state, which had resulted in the creation of the Third Reich."[20] Such critical sentiments still exist, and are not without reasoned justification. In the context of rising neofascism, especially in the heartland of Lutherland, protesters such as Jörg are concerned over public events and media that uncritically elevate Luther to the status of historical or legendary hero, without remembering the dark side of one of the land's favorite sons.

On May 18, 2005, Jörg and few others from a small theatre group descended on Wittenberg for a street theatre event in front of the Theses Door. The performance was called "Channeling with the Dead: Today, Martin Luther."⊙ As often happens in Wittenberg, Luther was brought back to life through performance—but this performance did not portray the man as hero but rather as an anti-Semite, a political conservative and reactionary, and a bigot. Through a loudspeaker, Dr. Luther was asked a series of questions, responding with answers drawn from his published works. Needless to say, through a selective handling of the sources, he was not depicted in a favorable light, as Jörg comments: "Passersby got interested. They thought we had to something to do with the graffiti and paint-bombs . . . and wanted to talk with us. Many of them stood there and just shook their heads over the bullshit that Luther spewed out."

⊙ DVD: Extras—Protest

It is difficult to imagine such performances becoming an integral part of the official festival-theatre-tourism scene in Wittenberg. But in their absence, the Thesenportal is sure to continue to attract graffiti and paint bombs, sprayed and thrown to the challenge the Heldenmythos that continues to surround the figure of Martin Luther.

5

Sociability, Conviviality

On the cover of the Luther's Wedding program is a digitally modified copy of Peter Brueghel's 1658 painting, *Peasant Dance*. The image is also used for large posters advertising the festival (fig. 5.1). The scene depicted is one of festive merrymaking; villagers dance, play music, socialize, kiss. Superimposed on the image, centered on the background horizon, is Wittenberg's Schlosskirche. (Similarly, on the front of the Reformation Day festival program are two images: one a Lucas Cranach painting of a stately Luther, the other a photograph of a group of three "medieval" musicians: the minstrels and clowns are back in the streets during an ecclesiastical feast.) There are four features of this image that suggest lines of inquiry to follow in this and the following chapter, which deal with the social-cultural domain of civitas. As I described it earlier, *civitas* refers to symbols and performances aimed at city-mindedness and at local interests and concerns; it includes the contributions of voluntary organizations as well as those of the marketplace.

First, the poster reveals that the Luther's Wedding festival is of and for the people, the Volk, rather than the church and clergy, or the state and politicians: Luther's Wedding is a Volksfest. Residents of Wittenberg and the surrounding region make up roughly two-thirds of those attending Luther's Wedding. The domain of civitas dominates Luther's Wedding and rivals the ecclesiastical origins and contexts of Reformation Day. Various groups and institutions play their role in festival planning and

FIGURE 5.1. Poster advertising Luther's Wedding. Wittenberg's Schlosskirche is superimposed on Pieter Brueghel's *Peasant Dance* (1658). The text refers to the festival as "Wittenberg's city festival," described as "one of the best city festivals in Germany, on the original dramatic stage of the Reformation." The festival's major sponsors are identified at bottom. Photograph by the author.

enactment in Wittenberg. Alongside the large, visible institutions—the Luther Museum Foundation, the University of Halle-Wittenberg, the Evangelische Akademie, the Lucas Cranach Foundation and Art School, the local church community—are Wittenberg's many clubs and societies: marching bands, theatre and dance troupes, naturalists, farmer's organizations, artists and craftsmen, heritage and cultural societies. Most of Wittenberg's local Vereine (community associations) have emerged since 1990, and they contribute a great deal to the festivals; they are responsible for setting up and operating historical-themed stands and displays.

Second, Brueghel's painting points to the atmosphere and style of the contemporary festivals, a mix of conviviality and the carnivalesque. *Conviviality* is a term I borrow from the philosopher and social critic Ivan Illich, who is concerned with how human tools and institutions limit or encourage convivial relations. Festivals are tools created and employed to achieve a number different ends—economic development, for example. But to the extent that a festive celebration is convivial, that it promotes what the German sociologist Georg Simmel called sociability, it becomes an end unto itself, not a means to some further end. Conviviality is a baseline of sorts. Festive celebration is a manifestation of the impulses to socialize, feast, and play—aspects of life that are irreducible to supposedly more fundamental functions or goals. The villagers dancing, playing music, and socializing in Brueghel's painting are not doing so for any reason other than that these are things people enjoy.

Third, the poster includes an implicit narrative. In adding Wittenberg's Schlosskirche to Brueghel's painting, festival organizers and festival-goers draw on cultural resources of the past to imagine and create the present. Brueghel is well known for his depictions of the so-called Little Tradition, the daily life, ritual, and festive events of the lower classes of early-modern-era Europe. Festival culture in Wittenberg takes as its model the festive, popular culture of Brueghel's day, and recreates it. Ritual creativity is at work in Wittenberg, and there is a self-conscious attempt to reach back to forms of public festivity that existed at the time of the Reformation (or, at least, the contemporary imagination of such practices). There is a story embedded in the poster, and one of my aims is to lift it out.

Finally, it is important to reflect on the setting in Brueghel's painting, which has implications for understanding changes taking place in what is often called the public sphere. One of the stated goals of the Wittenberg Kulturverein, an arm of the municipal government that oversees the organization of the festivals and other cultural events, is to develop *Bürgerschaftliches* engagement, community participation. Wittenberg's festivals cultivate vibrant sociability. The celebrations take place in the streets, market squares, and courtyards of the old city—outside, in spaces openly public, rather than inside, in spaces associated with particular cultural spheres and specialized institutions, interests, and statuses.

The *Festumzug*

Rather than attempt to describe the immense variety of sociable activities, events, and performances that make up the Wittenberg's Luther festivals, I will focus on an exemplary one, the Luther's Wedding parade, the *Festumzug*.[○] The parade is a preeminent example of festive display in Wittenberg. Held on Saturday afternoon at 2 p.m., the parade marks the halfway point of the festival. The parade is referred to as the *historichse Festumzug* the historical festival parade. Costuming, artifacts, music, and dance locate the event in an imagined past, in Reformation-era Wittenberg. Participating in the parade are kindergarteners, schoolchildren, teens, adults, and seniors, representing a variety of local groups and interests: schools, music, dance, and theatre clubs, Wittenberg's many Vereine, civic and university officials. Though most people in the parade are from Wittenberg and the surrounding area, the inclusion of groups from partner cities and heritage and tourism organizations from around Europe—Germany, Italy, Denmark, and Belgium—mark the event as an international affair.

The Umzug is described as the *Hohenpunkt* (high point) of the festivities. A full one-third of a commercially produced DVD of the Wedding in 2007 is devoted to the parade, which in real time takes up two hours of a three-day event. The German national tourist office refers to the Umzug as the "pinnacle" of the festival. Local television crews film the parade; newspapers print photographs on the front page, and devote a good deal of column space to covering the parade. A cast of a thousand walks the two kilometer route from the gate of the Lutherhof, looping around the old town to the Marktplatz, and then back the Lutherhof. Up to 40,000 spectators line the streets—a number just a few thousand less than Wittenberg's population. Everyone, it seems, does love a parade. And what do the onlookers see?

The structure of the Umzug varies little from year to year. In 2005, the parade was composed of nineteen different groups, the members costumed in early-sixteenth-century attire. The various groups represent both historical figures and local organizations and institutions; often, individuals who hold the corresponding or similar position in contemporary Wittenberg play the

○ DVD: Processing—Parade

historical role. The "noble mayor Anton Niemegk," as he is described in the festival program and over two loudspeakers announcing the parade to the onlookers, is played by the Wittenberg's current mayor (since 1994) Eckhard Naumann. Niemegk was from a prominent Wittenberg family and was mayor from 1521 to 1525. The mayor in the historical parade, then, is indeed the mayor. Following the mayor walks a group of historical Wittenberg's *Handwerker und Mesiter*, (trades people, masters, apprentices) played by their contemporary equivalents and local small-business owners. Then come Reformation-era farmers from the Wittenberg area, represented by farmers, and then "citizens and nobility" played by today's prominent, politically and economically influential citizens. And so on. Lucas Cranach is played by a member of the Lucas Cranach Foundation; the historical Luther's university colleagues by professors and students from the Leucorea (the Wittenberg campus of the University Halle-Wittenberg); the medieval Spielleute are played by Spielleute. There are exceptions to this mirroring of past and present—for example, the nuns who fled the convent along with Katharina von Bora are played not but real nuns but by students from Martin Luther High School (at least the theme of virginity is mirrored). Martin and his Katie are played by residents or former residents of Wittenberg. Many of the groups in the parade are *Eingetragener Vereine*, registered community associations with the legal status of a corporation, among them marching bands, dance clubs, the "historical city police," the "Friends of Luther," and "the workers of Katharina." Interspersed in the parade are the antics of Spielleute, pipe and drum bands, and a few commercial entries: an Ur-Krostitzer beer wagon (one of the festival's major sponsors); a carriage advertising itself for rent for weddings; and a float, in the form of Spanish galleon, sponsored by a hotel and restaurant from nearby Wörlitz, and called, somewhat bizarrely, "Columbus's Discovery of the New World."

Parades are chiefly about display, and the Umzug is the residents of the city and region showing themselves to one another. This might seem obvious, but it is important. The parade allows various individuals and community groups to display themselves to one another. The Umzug, like the larger festival, is a magnet; the parade makes Wittenberg—for a short time, at any rate—the place to be. There is a saying in German: *sehen und gesehen werden*, "to see and to be seen." Wittenberg at festival time is such a place. The colors come out, flags and banners are hung, costumes are dusted off and spruced up, stages are put together, parade floats are built, flyers are printed, fancy cakes are baked, the streets are given an extra sweeping, and the walls a fresh coat of paint. Whether it is the procession of the Academic Senate that takes place during Reformation Day, or the rooster-crowing contest held during Luther's Wedding, or the various processions, display is central to both festivals. One definition of performance has it as the "showing of a doing."[1] At festival time, individuals and groups put their doings on display.

A relevant social-historical context in which to situate the Wedding Umzug is the radically constricted and tightly controlled public sphere of the communist DDR. State-organized parades were an important feature of political life in East Germany. Workers, youth, and sport groups would pass by a podium of party officials, carrying banners and listening to an audio track from a loudspeaker extolling the virtues of the state. Participation was organized by place of work or school, so it was easy to identify those who did not participate. The projected symbolism was a relationship of unity, loyalty, and equality between rulers and workers, wedded to a secularized sense of divine mission. But the tight proscriptions on the form and content of the parade, coupled with intense pressures to conform and participate, meant that claims of unity and harmony were largely the product of stage-managed illusion, photographed, filmed, recorded, and then repackaged and distributed through the mass media.

It is worth noting who does not appear in the contemporary Luther's Wedding Umzug: no police, no military or paramilitary groups (other than fictional medieval knights and the historical "city police"), no state officials representing a more central, hierarchical authority, no political parties, and no formal group representing the church. While some of the Vereine carry flags, the emblems of state and even municipal government are conspicuous by their absence. The didactic, ideological dimensions of military and state parades are not present in the Umzug. Rather, an event (a wedding) is celebrated, an event that allows the entire community to contribute. The parade is dominated by clubs and societies, the satirical clowning of fools, marching bands, and the quasi-royal couple Martin and Katie, framed by their entourage of "historical" folk from the Reformation era. Kinetic, colorful, slightly chaotic, filled with music, dance, performance, and art, eclectic and open to broad participation, the parade is a far cry from those conducted in the era of the DDR.

The prelude to the Umzug takes place Friday afternoon, in the Marktplatz, as the nuns and Katharina are presented on stage to the crowd. The beginning of the festival is formally marked with the raising of a large wedding wreath (about a meter and a half in diameter) up a six-meter-high pole. On Sunday afternoon, the wreath is lowered, brining the festival to a close. A smaller version of the pole and wreath, the *Hochzeitkranz*, is carried by attendants to Katharina in the Umzug, trailing behind the couple. The symbolism is relatively clear, and perhaps fitting for a wedding of two virgins, a monk and a nun.

Just as family and friends gather for a wedding, the entire city gathers for the wedding of its most famous citizen and his wife, represented by a hometown boy and girl. The virtues and themes associated with a wedding—bonding, fertility, gift giving, making new relations, the promise of new life, collective feasting, music, and dance—are transferred to the city's residents as a whole. And just as large weddings have various sideshows, interests, and perhaps even arguments occasioned by but tangentially related to the actual wedding couple, so too at Luther's Wedding. Some in attendance are there not principally for the couple, nor what they symbolize, but drawn to the spectacle of it all.

Though the historical wedding was a small-scale, quiet affair, its ritual reenactment is a blowout to which everyone comes: the butcher, the baker, the candlestick maker, the electors of Saxony and their tailor, a group of medieval knights, peasant farmers, university professors, "guests from near and far," even a witch, pulled along by hooded axmen leading her to the flames, and heckled by erotic, dancing female spirits. The organizers of the Umzug make room for diverse groups, and this in turn gives the doings of those groups public visibility, public legitimacy, and public value. Unlike the top-down parades of the DDR era, which emphasized and valorized a single theme—the importance of the worker and his or her relation to the goals and mission of the state—the Umzug is bottom-up and emphasizes play, aesthetics, and diversity. Though the workaday world is represented—farmers, for example, parade—local leisure and aesthetic interests dominate.

The entries of the Lucas Cranach Foundation exemplify these aesthetic interests. The 2005 entry consisted of a living-bronzed Cranach, surrounded by members of the Cranach Foundation and Art School, carrying prints of Cranach's work, and banners that read "Lucas, where are you?" and "Cranach–500 Years in Wittenberg" (fig. 5.2). The aim of the entry was to raise awareness about one of the city's great historical figures, about the work of the Cranach Foundation and Art School, and to aid fundraising for a Cranach monument. (The monument would indeed be installed in the Cranachhof in the fall of 2006.) Their 2006 entry was similarly dynamic: A float carried one of the school's members, who stood at a large canvas, playing a the role of Lucas Cranach in the process of creating one of his best-known works, *Adam and Eve*. As the parade moved through the streets, Cranach's *Adam and Eve* took shape. The Cranach entries symbolize and enact the processual dynamics of the Umzug and the larger festival. The parade is bears witness to a community in the process of displaying, re-creating, and validating itself; a community on the move, being reborn, the new life symbolized by Adam and Eve.

For most of the Luther's Wedding festival, the public moves to stations or locations of interest: this stage, that building, one of Wittenberg's many courtyards. Few festival-goers take in the entire diversity of the festival; rather, they pick and choose what interests them. The Umzug mobilizes the groups and actors who otherwise perform in relatively bounded, fixed locations; the festival

FIGURE 5.2. Members of the Cranach Foundation and Art School parade through Wittenberg's streets. Photograph by Ronald Grimes.

crowd stops moving and the actors themselves move, thus providing the opportunity to present everyone to everyone. Unlike a procession, which is linear and culminates at a sacred or special location, the Umzug route is circular, around the boundaries of the old town, marking it as special. Some parades go through a space; this one goes around a space, literally and symbolically creating the locale, the arena, the game board of Luther-themed festivity and performance via circumambulation.[2] It is not a destination that is important, but a communal place. This circumambulation with the diverse cast of characters symbolizes a valuing of the community as a whole and a public recognition that the beating heart or center of Wittenberg's future cultural and economic vitality is also its geographical center. The old town is where the community circles the wagons; the old town, in the face of economic threats and processes of cultural revitalization, is where Wittenbergers are making their stand.

Sociability

It is tempting to view the parade an expression of social class. As a rough approximation, members from various social status positions play their respective

historical counterparts. In some ways, the festival does articulate social structure, which is not unusual, since every society has some form of hierarchical
relations. From another perspective, the eclectic action of the festival is in
keeping with the spirit of postmodernity. The variety of music alone over the
course of Luther's Wedding is enough to blur any sense of being in a place
with a bounded ethnic or regional identity.$^{\odot}$ Although Lutherland as a tourist
space is relatively homogenous, the festivals, which cater largely to the locale
population, revel in heterogeneity. The cosmopolitan style of both festivals is
somewhat surprising, given Wittenberg's small size. A more interpretively
useful notion than class, structure, or the postmodern, however, is that of
sociability.

The Umzug is but one of many examples in Wittenberg at festival time of
what Xavier Costa refers to "festive sociability." By this Costa means public
events, preeminently festive events, that include "humor, play, communal eating, sociable work, satiric criticisms, parades, etc. . . . Participants mobilize
their bodies to music and they present them in costumes and fancy dress in a
joyful manifestation of emotions displaying their festive identity and deeply
rooted tradition." Costa further emphasizes the importance of art, play, and
reflexivity to festive sociability.[3]

Following the Wedding Umzug, the principal actors of Luther's Wedding—
the wedding couple and those individuals playing historically significant figures from Luther's circle—gather at the wedding table set-up in the courtyard
of the Lutherhaus for a meal. About three hundred onlookers, family, friends,
and visitors, sit and watch them eat, and are entertained by Renaissance music
and dance, and the follies of Spielleute. Later that night, young people dance to
Calypso music at the concert in the Marktplatz. The next day, the Cranach
Foundation serves coffee and cakes to the sounds of a pianist playing everything from Bach and Nora Jones, in a gallery of the Cranach museum housing
an interfaith art exhibit. Visitors amble through the streets, watch a blacksmith
demonstrate his trade, visit with friends and family over a beer, and watch a
piece of street theatre. All this is festive sociability.

In the modern era, the idea of sociability has its roots in Enlightenment
thought. The Enlightenment philosophers struggled with the tension in human
life between the desire and needs of individual autonomy and the demands of
community life, collectivities, and social institutions. A radical individualist
stream of modern thought developed an anthropology in which people are considered by nature solitary, egotistical beings; such views are challenged by both

$\odot$ DVD: Music

humanist thought and the worldview of many traditional religions. The "political demand for autonomy" writes Tztevan Todorov, need not be based on "an
anthropological doctrine of 'atomism.'"[4] We do not become most fully ourselves by accessing the deep recesses of our thoughts and feelings, but in and
through interaction with the people with whom we live. Autonomy and interdependence are not mutually exclusive, but the bases of human life.

At the beginning of the twentieth century, the German sociologist Georg
Simmel emphasized the importance of sociability. For Simmel, men and
women are social animals. There is a drive or impulse to sociability in people,
wrote Simmel: "To be sure, it is for the sake of special needs and interests that
men unite in economic associations or blood fraternities, in cult societies or
robber bands. But above and beyond their special content, all these associations are accompanied by a feeling for, by a satisfaction in, the very fact that
one is associated with others and that the solitariness of the individual is
resolved into togetherness, a union with others." Simmel's discussion of a
drive to transcend a skin-encapsulated ego through "union" and a "resolu-
tion" of the individual into a larger collectivity should give us pause. The
fascist and totalitarian regimes of the twentieth century sought to resolve
individuality in larger collectivities. Moreover, the period witnessed the creation of institutions that seemed to swallow the autonomy of the individual,
turning people into cogs in the wheels of industry or bureaucracy. If we look
more closely at Simmel's thought, however, we see that his notion of sociability emphasizes play, fun, affections, and democracy. "The vitality of real individuals, in their sensitivities and attractions, in the fullness of their impulses
and convictions . . . shows itself in the flow of a lightly amusing play."[5]
Playfulness and the freedom to play are necessary to the kind of union that
interested Simmel.

Another term for sociability is conviviality. The word *convivial* comes from
the Latin *convivium*, meaning "banquet." In the Oxford English Dictionary, the
adjective *convivial* is defined as, "Fond of feasting and good company, disposed
to enjoy festive society; festive, jovial." Asking why we are disposed to such
activity is like asking why kittens play; whatever survival value play has, it is also
clear that play is an activity animals enjoy, that they take delight in. Some ritual
theory aims to explain or account for ritual from the outside. But convivial festivity is a matter of fact; it may be a means to other ends, but it is also its own
end. The notion of sociability and conviviality grant festive celebration its own
integrity and validity; it need not be explained on terms other than its own. The
Latin *convive* is both noun and verb; "a feast," and "to feast together." One can
eat alone, but not feast or banquet alone. The Latin roots of the word hit
bedrock: *cum* and *vive*—"with life" or "to live."

Richard Schechner has discussed the carnival-like playfulness of chimpan-zee behavior known as *kanjo*, first described by R. L. Garner at the turn of the twentieth century:

> One of the most remarkable of all the social habits of the chimpanzee
> is the *kanjo*, as it is called in the native tongue. The word . . . implies . . .
> the idea of "carnival." It is believed that more than one family takes
> part in these festivities. Here and there in the jungle is found a small
> spot of sonorous earth. It is irregular in shape and about two feet
> across. The surface is of clay and is . . . superimposed upon a kind of
> peat bed, which, being porous, acts as a resonance cavity and
> intensifies the sound. This constitutes a kind of drum. It yields rather
> a dead sound, but this is of considerable volume. This queer drum is
> thus made by the chimpanzees. . . . After the drum is quite dry, the
> chimpanzees assemble by night in great numbers and the carnival
> begins. One or two of them beat violently on this dry clay, while others
> jump up and down in a wild and grotesque manner. Some of them
> utter long, rolling sounds, as if trying to sing. When one tires of
> beating the drum, another relieves him, and in this fashion the
> festivities continue for hours. I know of nothing like this in the social
> system of any other animal, but what it signifies or what its origin was
> is quite beyond my knowledge. They do not indulge in this *kanjo* in all
> parts of their domain, nor does it occur at regular intervals.[6]

Schechner comments that in Garner's description are the formal properties of festive celebration: "Aren't these [chimpanzee] 'carnivals' prototypes of celebra-tory, theatrical events? Their qualities are worth noting: 1) a gathering of bands—not individuals—who are neither living with nor total strangers to each other; 2) the sharing of food . . . 3) singing, dancing (rhythmic movement, drumming: entertainment; 4) use of a place that is not 'home' for any group as the grounds for the gathering."[7] Festive celebration involves a periodic gather-ing of a group, in a marked-off space and time for the purposes of play, engag-ing in aesthetic activity, sharing food, exchanging gifts, stories, songs, and then dispersal.

Sociability and conviviality point beyond the typical sociological concern over social structure to matters of individual and group expression, perform-ance, and play. Johan Huizinga rejects efforts to reduce play to something more fundamental, such as the establishing of social hierarchy or biological func-tionalism. Biological attempts to explain play have included "the discharging of superabundant energy, of relaxation after exertion, of training for the demands of life, of compensating for unfulfilled longings." Each of these, argues

Huizinga, misses the fun of play; its expressiveness, its performativity, "its profoundly aesthetic quality."[8]

One could argue, of course, that sociable behavior maintains the solidarities and hierarchies of a group, but we could just as well say that festive celebration is fundamental to human being. Moreover, in the absence of periodic festive gathering, a society or social structure is very likely to be pathological, unhealthy, dysfunctional, unsustainable, and not a whole lot of fun. As Bakhtin put it: "the official feasts of the Middle Ages, whether ecclesiastical, feudal, or sponsored by the state, did not lead people out of the existing world order and created no second life. . . . The tone of the official feast was monolithically serious and . . . the element of laughter was alien to it. . . . But . . . true festive character was indestructible; it had to be tolerated and even legalized outside the official sphere and had to be turned over to the popular sphere of the marketplace."[9] The festive social is irrepressible, indestructible, which is to say, fundamental, bedrock, a foundation. It lies deep in the bones, and deep in social life. So it is no surprise, after several centuries of relative success by church and state at suppressing it, the festive social is back at play in the streets of Wittenberg, a story I will consider more fully in the next chapter.

Creating a Festival

The year 1993 marked the seven hundredth anniversary of the founding of the city of Wittenberg, a perfect occasion to build community in the years following the Wende. Three hundred residents from Bretten (located in western Germany) traveled to Wittenberg to aid in the celebration. Bretten has a rich and complex festival tradition, its origins dating back to 1504. The city's Peter and Paul Festival attracts about 80,000 visitors each July, and is a prime example of Germany's "medieval" fair and festival scene. With the aid of the contingent from Bretten, the anniversary celebrations were a rip-roaring success, and Wittenbergers began wondering whether and how another similar celebration could be held. The idea was to hold an annual city festival, but it needed to have a theme, something to make it compelling and evocative.

Johannes Wincklemann, director of the Wittenberg Kulturverein, explains the origins of Luther's Wedding: "We discovered there was a small group of employees, working at the Lutherhaus museum, who had, since 1986, been holding a small museum fest, designed around the celebration of Luther's Wedding. These were small festivals, in the garden area, with music, food, and *Schauspieler* (players)." The idea emerged that a city festival could be created around the theme of the public celebration of Luther's wedding:

[We asked ourselves], Can we do this again? A monk marrying a nun? What will our Catholic brothers and sisters think? The significance of the wedding has long been debated; the Peasants' War was raging at the time. In the following centuries people have argued over and bad-mouthed his [Luther's] wedding. It is not so easy to bring Luther in to the streets. You can bad-mouth him, you can make satirical comedies about him; the discussion was intense. We didn't want to misuse Luther, but rather celebrate; and against celebration Luther had nothing to say. . . . We were partly concerned about what Catholics might say–a monk marrying a nun. But it worked so well in 1994, people were not upset at all but rather inspired and really enthusiastic.

Once the idea gained momentum, Wincklemann and others began gener-ating the roles or groups that would surround the central event—a wedding parade. Out of these groups emerged Wittenberg's Vereine, modeled in part on those from Bretten. Bretten, for example, has a large, active *Bauernverien* (farm-er's association), and a farmer's association was established in Wittenberg. In the first four or five years following the Wende, residents of Wittenberg estab-lished numerous associations, but they emerged in the context of the Wedding Festival. Some men, to take one example, started a Carnival association follow-ing the Wende; but because Carnival was not part of the region's history, it was not taken too seriously, and was principally a drinking club. As Luther's Wed-ding developed, as those involved in the Carnival association saw the potential of the festival, they transformed themselves into the *Historische Stadtwache*, the "historical city police" of Luther's day. New costumes were made, the drinking was tempered, and the association developed a role, in the context of the city's many historical-themed events throughout the year. The group has around twenty-five or thirty active members, including women and children, and another dozen or so "friends," affiliated members. In 2008 the Stadtwache celebrated its tenth anniversary. "It really is amazing," says Wincklemann, "what this festival or this theme has accomplished. We now have a public cul-ture, a Vereine culture. We would have established this in other ways, but not in the historical sense. If you have a Verein you want to celebrate together, you want to experience together, do something together. To be together, to develop projects, to achieve goals you've set—and here it is, the Stadtfest."

Festive Joy

Festivals transpire across a range of emotions: expressive joy, exuberance, and frolicking fun are typical; look closely and frustration, anxiety, boredom, and group tensions, if not outright conflict, may rear their heads. In the words of one influential theorist, "to celebrate a festival means: to live out, for some special occasion, and in some uncommon manner, the universal assent to the world as a whole."[10] In this model, a festival is akin to a giant tuning fork struck by the hand of God, an instrument whose waves, through resonant, sympathetic vibrations, tune the individual into the realities of cosmic order, sacred presence, and social harmony. A festival can create and strengthen bonds between individuals, build bridges across social classes and groups, and connect a people to that which is felt to be sacred; but festivity can also work to loosen these ties, or manifest the different, at times competing, interests and values of social groups. They can also be boring, and even have an underbelly of despair.

Wittenberg's festivals are indeed sociable occasions, and, for the most part, good fun. One of my first conversations in Wittenberg, however, revealed a side of festival life rarely considered. It was with a man who operates a garlic bread stand. I emphasize the word *operates*—he was not the owner, but an employee of the firm Knöblibrot. He arrived in Wittenberg the day before Luther's Wedding to set up his stand in the Marktplatz; I shared a beer with the man that evening, and he talked candidly about his life. He spoke of being away from his family, of feelings of depression and of low self-esteem nurtured by his inability to find work as an electrician (for which he was trained). Alone on the road in Germany through the summer and again over Christmas, usually in England, selling garlic bread at various fairs and markets, surrounded by people enjoying themselves and having fun with the friends and family, led him to view festivals not as occasions of joy but of severe disappointment and frustration. Like Christmas time, which occasions a higher-than-average suicide rate, the festive nature of celebration is for some people a double-edged sword.

Locality

One function of the Umzug is the creation of locality, a sense of being from and belonging to a particular place, part of which involves knowing the stories of who has come before. Linking the present to a remembered past of cultural greatness (Reformation-era Wittenberg) develops local knowledge, esteem, and pride in one's self, traditions, and city.

The Wedding Umzug is an occasion to creatively rework and transmit tradition. Children tug at their mother's sleeve, asking, "Now who is that?" and receive a short explanation of Luther's disguising himself as Junker Jörg, during his flight to Wartburg Castle to escape arrest. Two commentators, microphone

and script in hand, are in the streets, moving in and out of the parade, announcing the groups and identifying the actors, enfolding bits of history around the
flow of bodies, and even asking various participants in the parade for their
thoughts. Luther himself can proudly announce to the crowd, "it is a beautiful
parade you have thrown for our wedding," and Katie thanks everyone for coming. In addition to waving to family members or friends that walk by, the audience engages in discussions of history, storytelling, even interpretation. Asking
someone in the street what they made of the second-to-last entry, "The Discovery of the New World," a float representing a Spanish galleon with a heroic
image of Columbus tacked to the bow, I received the following reply: "It's the
New World, and progress, and Luther brought a new world too. They are both
important cultural figures." The transmitted tradition in the parade wraps
Luther in playful, aesthetic, festive celebration, identifies the great man as a
resident and citizen, but also draws on bits of the standard Luther story, the
heroic, young man Luther who leaves behind a dead world to create a new one:
a German Columbus whose work helped create and define the modern world.

As the anthropologist Arjun Appadurai notes, "even in the most intimate,
spatially confined, geographically isolated situations, locality must be maintained against various kinds of odds."[11] In contemporary Wittenberg, these
odds include the relative loss of the defining, if limiting, narratives and ideologies of socialism, the opening of the east to the economic and cultural flows of
a global world, the exodus of young people in search of education and work,
and the legacy and histories of fascism and the Stasi. Locality, for Appadurai, is
a relational, phenomenological quality having to do with matters of agency,
sociality, and reproducibility. Processes of naming, storytelling, architectural
construction, the layout and use of space, archives of cultural memory, ritual
practice—these are all ways of creating and maintaining locality, of creating
local identities, local subjects.

Appadurai distinguishes between locality and neighborhoods, the later
being the concrete social forms and practices in which locality is realized. The
Wedding Umzug has become part of the neighborhood, an annual practice, a
social form that both encourages and realizes broad community participation.
The particular form of the parade (and the larger festival in which it is centered)
creates a certain kind of locality. If we compare the Umzug with various processional acts in Wittenberg's history—the key ceremony of Kaiser Wilhelm II,
Nazi processions in the 1930s, communist parades in the DDR era—we can
see the dynamic to which Appadurai points.

These earlier parades and procession brought cultural elites to Wittenberg
in order that they could inscribe the spiritual and historical aura of the place
onto particular ideologies and effect nonlocal changes. A Nazi procession

through Wittenberg's streets marked the territory, and had local effects, to be sure. But the act radiated outward away from the small locale of Wittenberg to other power centers. The place itself was not important; what counted were the symbolic meanings that could be ritually created and then exported to a larger public—the nation—through mediated images. The Wedding Umzug, in contrast, is principally for the people who live and work in the neighborhood, and its force field works in reverse to the parades of civil, political culture. The Umzug creates a kind of magnetic field that pulls local people back, people who have a familial or cultural (through the Lutheran tradition) connection to the city but who, in the modern, global world, live and work elsewhere.

Locality has generally been theorized in relation to transnational cultures, diasporas, immigrant communities, and ethnicity. The dialectic, the tensions, the flows between the place one is from (by birth, by religion, by ethnic origins) and the place one works and lives are the foci of attention. Such considerations are not irrelevant to contemporary Wittenberg. Since 1989, there has been a minor diaspora of people, especially young people, to greener pastures or the bright lights of a bigger city. With the population of Wittenberg and the surrounding area continuing a slow decline because of people leaving for school and work, the annual festivals, especially Luther's Wedding, provides the occasion to return, to meet up with family and friends, to exchange stories, to remember and create a variety of traditions. Luther's Wedding, in addition to galvanizing local residents around a large, communal event, serves as a kind of homecoming occasion. In 2005, the wedding couple were former residents of Wittenberg. A woman studying at the university in Halle, specializing in the conservation and restoration of monuments, played Katharina; an engineer living in far-off Freistaat Bayern played Luther. The Wedding festival thus has a dimension of kinship reunion, gathering the folk, and creating a sense of shared locality by virtue of being from a place deemed special.

A second dimension of locality involves situating and linking Wittenberg to the larger sphere of heritage and cultural tourism in Germany and Europe. Groups from heritage and cultural cities are invited and participate in the Umzug and the larger festival. In 2006, for example, Heidelberg contributed a marching band, and official wedding guests were invited from Einbeck (who brought with them a flask of dark beer as a gift to the wedding couple), as well as partner cities in Denmark, Italy, Austria, and Belgium. In 2006, representatives of the Wittenberg Culture Society traveled to Italy, to represent the city and advertise the Wedding festival. Wittenberg was in the running for the 2010 title of European Capital of Culture, an annual title given out by the European Union to promote cultural and economic development across Europe. Wittenberg's nomination as a UNESCO World Heritage site and its considerable cultural capital places it on a map of Europe's important historical, heritage, and cultural spots. Wittenberg, in other words, is a Kulturstadt, a cultural city. Moreover, Wittenberg, as the home of the Reformation, makes it a site for Lutheran pilgrimage. Another dimension of locality involves the continual flow of Lutherans from around the globe, and the presence of the international institutions needed to support and manage these flows. Life in Wittenberg is subject to an endless round of visitors, visitors who come with their own vision of what Wittenberg is and means.

David Lowenthal popularized the notion that the "past is a foreign country," analyzing how we relate to the past in a manner analogous to our relation to far-off places and locales. Wittenberg's festivals create a sense of locality that is intimately connected with its Reformation past, a kind of foreign country, given the decline in religion over the past half century, not to mention the centuries that lay between then and now. Lowenthal's argument is that the loss and rebellion against inherited traditions has also generated a tremendous nostalgia for the past. In times of change, such as the post-Wende era, when the future is less than clear, we often turn to the well-worn tracks of the past. "Its vestiges in landscape and memory reflect innumerable details of what we and our ancestors have done and felt. The richly elaborated past seems more familiar than the geographically remote, in some respects even more than our own nearby present; the here and now lacks the felt density and completeness of what time has filtered and ordered."[12] The Reformation, like oil in the ground, is a local resource in the stones and the imagined past of Wittenberg that can be mined, refined, and circulated; like any resource, Wittenberg's cultural capital shapes local life, shapes neighborhoods.

One of the few official criteria for selecting the couple to play Martin and Katie at Luther's Wedding is knowledge of the city's Reformation history. It means something to be from Wittenberg because Luther and Cranach and Bugenhagen and von Bora were from Wittenberg. Life today in Wittenberg—in the visual culture of the city, in the hotels that cater to tourists, in the buildings being constructed and renovated, in the very name of the place, Lutherstadt Wittenberg—revolves around its past; locality is deeply related to an imagined place and time. One's identity and locality are shaped by memories and performances of the past. Playing Luther in the 2007 Wedding was a descendant of Martin Luther's brother. Selling herbs and liqueurs on the Marktplatz is a descendent of Luther and Katie. It is not that the Reformation era is purely fictive; there are artifacts, documents, buildings, a church community, and blood lines tracking back to the past. But "the original dramatic stage of the Reformation," as marketing material describes the city, is the dominant story line contributing to a sense of locality.

The year 2007, for example, saw the beginning of a new marketing program—the "Luther decade," an effort to encourage tourism and build momentum towards 2017, the five hundredth anniversary of the Reformation. The director of the marketing agency behind the project noted: "Every man and woman in Wittenberg should be ambassadors and promoters of the city." Like it or not, one's life and livelihood in Wittenberg is linked to Luther. Hence, a local bar throws a blues night on Reformation Day, and one of the customers, in response to my query, "Blues and the Reformation?" replies: "Not everyone is 'in' to Luther. There are normal people that live here too." In the DDR times, the state penetrated every nook and cranny of daily life; now, for better or worse, it is Luther and the Reformation. Unlike the DDR era, however, a blues night as an implicit way to resist the Lutherization of the town is not only permissible; it is a going concern. The "modes of localization most congenial to the nation-state have a disciplinary quality about them. . . . The nation-state localizes by fiat, by decree, and sometimes by the use of overt force."[13] Contemporary Wittenberg localizes around Luther largely out of necessity, though since the success of Luther's Wedding, a new kind of invented tradition has produced its own momentum.

The Public Sphere

Humanist philosophers and some sociologists have been interested in the question of sociability precisely because one feature of modernity has been the shrinking—some would argue the collapse—of a vigorous, embodied public sphere. Alexis de Tocqueville, writing about mid-nineteenth-century America, coined the term "individualism" to describe the emerging "American character" in a social context of a growing market economy, an emphasis on personal autonomy and equality, and democratic government. De Tocqueville described the phenomenon of individualism:

> Each person, withdrawn into himself, behaves as though he is a
> stranger to the destiny of all the others. His children and his good
> friends constitute for him the whole of the human species. As for his
> transactions with his fellow citizens, he may mix among them, but
> he sees them not; he touches them, but he does not feel them; he
> exists only in himself and for himself alone. And if on these terms
> there remains in his mind a sense of family, there no longer remains
> a sense of society.[14]

A similar dynamic was at work in Europe, hence Simmel's concern, working in a German context, with sociability. In the nineteenth century and on into the twentieth, private, domestic life, a tending to intimate relations within one's family and circle of friends, and work on one's self-project came to dominate and eclipse a less intimate, but far more sociable public domain. One of the features of modernity has been the decline in an embodied, performed public sphere.

The term *public sphere* is usually associated with the thought of Jürgen Habermas. Habermas describes the post-Enlightenment emergence of a public sphere, consisting primarily of the forums that carry public debate and shape public opinion within civil society: print journals, newspapers, electronic media, nongovernmental organizations. The style of this sphere is inherently discursive, with private individuals submitting their reasoned views and criticisms, principally texts of their ideas and their words, to the arena of criticism and debate. The title of Habermas's pathbreaking work is *The Structural Transformation of the Public Sphere—An Inquiry into a Category of Bourgeois Society* (1962). He rightly recognized and unpacked the history of this transformation. It is a history related to de Tocqueville's observation of a shrinking "sense of society" and the rise of individualism, to Richard Sennett's analysis of *The Fall of Public Man* in European bourgeois society, and to Peter Burke's analysis of the enervation of Carnival and popular culture in the wake of the Protestant Reformation. The public sphere, for the past two centuries, has been one where atomistic individuals address one another via the disembodied, desensualized, and ideologically controlled vehicles of modern media.

Although in principle this bourgeois public sphere is inclusive, in practice it has been the domain of intellectual, political, and economic elites. Discussions of "religion and the public sphere" usually revolve around theological, political, ethical debates, and are carried on in journals, editorials, and at conferences. The debates are focused on politically contentious issues: gay marriage, stem-cell research, the representation of religion in the media, religion and politics, religion and violence. My point is that within academic and political life, the term *public sphere* does not generally refer to public performance, ritual, the arts, travel and tourism, film festivals, parades, concerts, and the like. These activities are perhaps studied as "popular culture" or in departments of "cultural studies," but they are not typically imagined as an integral part of the public sphere; rather, they represent the special interests and proclivities of individuals and subcultures.

What the public sphere of texts, manifestos, charters, and newspapers fails to consider (and, moreover, fundamentally lacks) is sociability, performativity, face-to-face interaction, embodiment, the senses, decorum, conviviality. The general trajectory of the modern West has seen the erosion of public life and the rise of a narrow, intensely intimate, and personal domain of the family and private life. "Intimate vision is induced in proportion as the public domain is abandoned."[15] The decay of public space and life in the modern era was magnified in East Germany. In the DDR era, public life was radically eroded as techniques of ideological control and surveillance threw the individual back onto him or herself, and perhaps a small circle of family and friends—though it was not unusual that even members of families would spy and report on one another's thoughts and activities. The Stasi operated one of the most invasive systems of surveillance ever created; it is estimated that roughly one of every fifty citizens in the DDR had at one time or another served as a Stasi informant, monitoring and reporting political dissent. "When everyone has everyone under surveillance, sociability decreases, silence being the only form of protection."[16] In public, one had to play a role (loyal servant of the state) that in no way could be thought of as being performed. Masks, personas, the interpersonal rites of deference and demeanor were stripped away, leaving one with a bare self, and "human beings need to have some distance from intimate observation by others in order to feel sociable."[17]

A festival is about as sociable occasion as one can imagine, precisely because one can disappear in the crowd. One engages with, interacts with, one's fellow citizens, but the festival ground is not a place where "everybody knows your name." A festival, on the whole, gathers a people together not on the level of personal intimacy, but rather community and sociability. Play and jest are the paradigmatic gestures, and "jest is a piece of nonsense in the service of solidarity rather than isolation, but one which promotes fellow-feeling exactly by being an end in itself."[18] Festival culture in Wittenberg reintroduces and sanctions role playing. It allows for diverse performances, creating an occasion during which citizens can present themselves and their doings to one another on a public stage, but in a framed, stylized, even conventionalized fashion (not self-revelation but self-presentation). One does not feel exposed because no one is watching, everyone is performing (more or less), and knows they are; the performer-audience boundary collapses, at least to a degree.

One of the defining characteristics of the genre of "spectacle" is the presence of a sharp distinction between audience and performers. "Spectacles institutionalize the bicameral roles of actors and audience, performers and spectators. Both role sets are normative, organically linked, and necessary to the performance." Second, a spectacle is something primarily watched or observed. The actors perform the event, the spectators watch—at a distance. In festivity, in contrast, everyone is called to celebrate, together. Watching is part of festival action, but only a part. Finally, to call an event a spectacle is to introduce a certain suspicion or criticism—"he is making a spectacle of himself." A festival is different. Rather than generating a sense of diffuse awe and wonder, emotions that captivate while distancing the spectator from the action (think of gladiatorial games), festivals are joyous occasions, or are meant to be so. The "genres of spectacle and festival are often differently valenced. While we happily antici-pate festivals, we are suspicious of spectacles, associating them with potential tastelessness and moral cacophony."[19] The French sociologist Guy Debord argues that modernity is a "society of the spectacle," which is to say, "an epoch without festivals."[20] The distinction here is between the production of spectacle by elites for nationalist, consumptive-commercial purposes versus a more organic, cyclical domain of festivity that emerges from a people's productive labor.

Festivals are often thought of as events or cultural performances, but they are also social institutions and tools. Annual festivals become embedded in the social-cultural life of the city and region in which they take place, repeated, worked on, anticipated year after year. "Tools," writes Ivan Illich, "are intrinsic to social relationships. An individual relates himself in action to his society through the use of tools that he actively masters. . . . To the degree that he mas-ters his tools, he can invest the world with his meaning; to the degree that he is mastered by his tools, the shape of the tool determines his own self-image." Illich's definition of a convivial tool or institution is precise: "Convivial tools are those one which give each person who uses them the greatest opportunity to enrich the environment with the fruits of his or her vision." Wittenberg's festi-vals fit such a criteria; they are tools that promote broad participation and encourage self-expression; in so doing they "enrich the environment." Convivi-ality, writes Illich, is the opposite of "industrial productivity." The notion refers to the presence of "autonomous and creative intercourse among persons, and the intercourse of person with their environment. . . . Conviviality [is] individ-ual freedom realized in personal interdependence and, as such [is] an intrinsic ethical value."[21]

The "invention of tradition" school, exemplified in the work of Eric Hobsbawm and David Kertzer, has greatly influenced the study of public ritual. Both scholars focus on political ceremony, and conceive ritual as a tool for cre-ating ideology and maintaining hegemonic power. To be sure, ritual may serve such ends, but not necessarily so. There are different kinds of ritual tools. In Wittenberg, ritual experimentation has led Luther festivity away from the indic-ative, didactic, monologic, spectacle-like ceremony of earlier generations toward the festive mood, characterized by broad participation, diversity, spontaneity, and improvisation. That Luther's Wedding, a city-festival, has become a new tradition demonstrates how quickly traditions can emerge, and how a self-conscious, reflexive awareness of inventing a ritual tradition in order to achieve particular ends is in no way a liability. (Hobsbawm argues that the invented nature of tradition must be hidden, in absolutes or timelessness, in order for that tradition to have authority.) Ritual may acquire strength by virtue of being a hallowed, time-honored, ancestral, normative practice. But it may also be embraced because it is effective at achieving certain goals, or simply because it is enjoyable. Wittenberg's Luther's festivals have been and continue to be important tools in the creation of sociability and conviviality in a city and region that was desperately in need of a revived public sphere.

Excarnation

In his recent study of the coincidence of modernity and secularity, Charles Taylor draws special attention to the category of the "festive," and its relevance to what he terms a "modern social imaginary." A social imaginary is the way "we collectively imagine . . . our social life." The modern social imaginary is the product of the multitude of interlocking changes that constitute the modern world: the consequences of the Reformation for ritual and religion; the revolutions and emancipation programs of the Enlightenment; the rise of the nation-state as a new political entity; the withdrawal of religion from the public spaces and public life; the rapid changes, innovations, and problems associated with industrialization; an aggressive mercantile, industrial, and now global capitalism; the language of universal rights.

An important feature of this modern social imaginary is the decline of embodied, public life, what Richard Sennett refers to as "the fall of public man." Sennett tracks the erosion of an embodied, performed public sphere and the rise of a hyperbolic domain of private life in Paris and London during the nineteenth century. His concern has largely been with city planning and design, the ways in which built spaces encourage or deny the impulse to sociability. But Sennett also pays attention to bodily gesture, speech, and dress, and develops a model of public life based on the relationship between a performer and his or her audience. In fact, he demonstrates how the stylizations of theatre and the social interactions of the street paralleled one another in eighteenth-century France and England, especially in the larger cities, where an individual needed to relate and interact with strangers. Matters of deference and demeanor, stylized gestures, dress, and rhetoric created a kind of order, a way of interacting in the public realm, modeled on the stage. People could interact and "read" one another, playfully engage with one another, put on roles and masks, without having to expose or reveal the self. In the nineteenth century and into the twentieth, outward performance and ritual were eclipsed by the inwardness of feeling; persona became personality; self-presentation fused with self-revelation, and "public man" retreated into the confines of the home and the circle of the family.

The history of the suppression of Carnival and popular culture, which I discuss in the next chapter, is another dimension of the erosion of public life. It is a dimension that Sennett gives little attention to, but of late this chapter of the story is garnering greater attention. Charles Taylor, who is hardly fearful of trying out grand narratives, enfolds the eclipse of Carnival into his study of modernity as a "secular age." Taylor refers to the trajectory of the modern world as a process of "excarnation," the "transfer of our religious life out of bodily forms of ritual, worship, practice, so that it comes more and more to reside 'in the head.'"[22] These forms of public religious life Taylor associates with Victor Turner's discussion of communitas, the "intuition that we all share that, beyond the way we relate to each other through diversified coded roles, we also are a community of many-sided human beings, fundamentally equal, who are associated together." This breaking out of "coded roles" occurs most visibly in large-scale, public rites of reversal, inversion, transgression, and festivity, which "release fellowship" and "sets free our spontaneity and creativity. It also allows free reign to the imagination."[23]

If the narrative proposed by Taylor, Sennet, and others has merit, one way of understanding Wittenberg's contemporary festival culture is in terms of an impulse to revitalize, reincarnate a public sphere, through public, carnivalesque festivity, a notion to which we now turn.

6

The Carnivalesque, Processing Change

Carnival is the people's second life, organized on the basis of
laughter. It is festive life.

—Mikhail Bakhtin, *Rabelais and His World*

Wittenberg's festivals exemplify a broader cultural phenomenon,
the widespread enthusiasm for heritage-themed fairs and festivals.
Contemporary Renaissance and medieval fairs in Europe and North
America include arts and crafts, booths selling food and drink,
historical reenactment, and different kinds of performance art—
musicians, theatre troupes, jugglers, magicians, soothsayers, palm
readers, and fools. People wander through the stalls and streets,
watch the performances, taste regional and specialty foods, shop,
try their hand at a traditional craft, drink, eat, and socialize. Period
costuming is the norm for vendors and performers, and visitors often
dress up too; among those walking the streets are fictive merchants,
town criers, prostitutes, mimes, singers, nobility, clergy, knights,
squires, and other medieval or Renaissance-era figures. Renaissance
fairs tend to be a British and North American phenomenon; in
Germany, medieval fairs are the rule.

The word *medievalist*, not so long ago, referred principally to
academics who studied the Middle Ages. Today, medievalism is an
element of popular spirituality. Medievalists are those who attempt to
access and transport elements of premodern life and culture (often in
an imaginative and eclectic, if unhistorical manner) into the present,

for the purposes of personal and cultural renewal. Books, Web sites, societies, hobbyist groups, and medieval fairs are the institutional and public forums for contemporary medievalism. Many of the larger fairs and festivals in Europe contribute to and reflect New Age and neopagan spiritualities, but they also generally incorporate local traditions and history; in part, this is done to give a festival a theme that is distinct from other similar festivals. In Wittenberg, the theme is obvious—Luther and the Reformation—but both Reformation Day and Luther's Wedding include a prominent medieval theme.

A second influence on the festival is the carnivalesque. By *carnivalesque* I mean public events that: (1) feature masking and costuming, indulgence in food and drink, music and dance, bawdy humor and laughter; (2) take place in the streets and open-air plazas, featuring an eclectic mix of performances, entertainments, and "traditional" arts and crafts; (3) are marked by a spirit of revelry, excess, satire, play, heterogeneity, and sociability; and (4) are consciously informed by cultural memories, practices, narratives, and objects linked to the era of European Carnival in the early modern period. As Clifford Geertz has discussed, the term "ethos" refers to the "moral (and aesthetic) aspects of a given culture. . . . A people's ethos is the tone, character, and quality of their life, its moral and aesthetic style and mood; it is the underlying attitude toward themselves and their world that life reflects."[1] Something of this ethos, perhaps the heart of it, is on display in large-scale cultural performances, such as a public festival. The notions of style and mood are important; they emphasize the expressive dimension of festive celebration. In Wittenberg's festivals, the tone, character, and moral and aesthetic style is carnivalesque.

Just as carnivalesque festivity has a prominent place among contemporary public events, the term has also become part of the theoretical lingo of the social sciences and humanities, chiefly through the work of the Russian literary theorist Mikhail Bakhtin (1895–1975); my use of the term, then, is not simply descriptive but also carries theoretical implications and claims. Through Carnival, writes Bakhtin, people created a "second life," entering, for a time, a "utopian realm of community, freedom, equality, and abundance."[2] In Bakhtin's view, convivial relations and the performance of Carnival were one and the same. Historical understandings of medieval and early modern-era Carnival recognize the context of a hierarchical class system and feudal political structure. Carnival, it has been argued, was a means to suspend or alleviate tensions within these stratified relations, at least for a time—a kind of safety valve that released social pressures associated with class.

Bakhtin was living and writing in the age of the Stalinist terror, and in his writings on the relationship between Carnival and feudal society, we can detect a critique of Soviet autocracy and monoculture. The hierarchical, authoritarian,

even despotic cultural, political, and economic system of the former DDR suggests the relevance of applying Bakhtin's narrative of medieval Carnival to
festive celebration in post-Wende Wittenberg. Easter, when Carnival was (and
is) enacted, was an annual marking and celebration of death and resurrection,
so the resources existed within Carnival for processing larger social dramas.
"Moments of death and revival, of change and renewal," writes Bakhtin, "always
led to a festive perception of the world."[3] The revival, change, and renewal of
life in the former East Germany demands the creation of convivial relations,
and the carnivalesque is a tool to such an end.

The Eclipse of Carnival

Carnival, in a narrow sense, is a practice intertwined with the Roman Catholic
liturgical cycle, and continues to thrive in Latin America, Brazil, and pockets of
traditionally Catholic areas in Europe. In contemporary Wittenberg, carnivalesque festivity is something new, emerging only since the fall of the Berlin
Wall in 1989. The history of Carnival and the carnivalesque in Protestant
Germany is an important context for interpreting and understanding the action
that characterizes Luther's Wedding and Reformation Day.

Carnival and carnivalesque performances were central to European social-
cultural life in the late medieval and early modern eras, the result of the church
assimilating and adapting the seasonal feasts of pagan culture into its rites and
liturgical calendar. Carnival was the institution around which life revolved; people lived "in remembrance of one festival and in expectation of the next."[4]
Carnival was performed prior to Lent, the period of fasting preceding the high
liturgical Easter celebration. In another of Pieter Brueghel's well-known paintings, he captures the atmosphere of early-modern Carnival (fig. 6.1). Brueghel
depicts the figure of Carnival as a bawdy, beer-drinking, flesh-eating, rotund
man, sitting astride a beer barrel, holding (or wielding like a lance) a pig on a
spit, and surrounded by festive revelers. Carnival is pitted against Lent, a frail,
withered old woman, carrying a bundle of switches used to scourge penitents,
and displaying two fish on a baker's paddle, with the aged pious training behind.
In addition to revelry, performance, and indulgence, there was an agonistic
element to Carnival, encouraged by the presence of clowns and fools.

Three chief themes characterized the era of early-modern Carnival: "food,
sex, and violence."[5] For these reasons, clergy, nobility, and politicians tended to
view Carnival with suspicion and derision. Carnival was the domain of the
lower or middle classes, a "world turned upside down," a time to symbolically
invert and skew gender roles (travesty was common) and class structures,

FIGURE 6.1. *Battle between Carnival and Lent*, by Peter Brueghel the Elder, 1559. Kunsthistoriches Museum, Vienna.

impugn the haughtiness of religious and political elites, and get a bit ritually crazy, perhaps so as not to go really crazy. Carnival emphasized masking, costuming, processions, the overconsumption of food and drink, farcical plays and skits in the streets, music, carousing, and dance in the streets and market squares. The bearers of society's moral compass generally viewed indulgence in food, drink, and sex as a threat to the fiber of the folk. Those holding the reigns of temporal power knew that during Carnival, the horses might run wild—the ritualized violence, burnings, symbolic killings and inversions that accompanied Carnival could always threaten to turn into the real thing; occasionally, they did.

Carnival was integral to social-cultural life in Reformation-era Wittenberg. In fact, the Reformation was driven in part by carnivalesque satire and symbolic violence, as Robert Scriber has demonstrated. In December 1520, Luther publicly burned the papal bull condemning his writings, along with the books of church canon law. Later that same afternoon, a hundred students from the university erected a mock float, using a giant papal bull as a mast.

> The float was filled with students, one clad a charioteer, another as a
> trumpeter, some as scholars, others as musicians who provided
> music for the procession. The trumpeter held the papal bull affixed to

his sword, and another mock bull was stuck up on a stick. . . .
Accompanying students gathered firewood as they went, tossing it
into the wagon along with the books of Luther's opponents. . . . The
float returned to the embers of the morning fire, the students kindled
it and threw onto it the bulls and books. . . . Someone was dressed as
the pope, and threw his tiara into the flames.[6]

During the *Fastnacht* celebrations in February of 1521, university students carried an effigy of the pope through the city's streets, and pelted it
with dung on Wittenberg's Marktplatz.[7] Luther reported in a letter that
along with "cardinals, bishops, and servants," the mock pope was "hunted
through the streets with great merriment." Students also staged a "Latin
carnival play ridiculing the pope and indulgences."[8] Scribner has catalogued
more than twenty such carnival events enacted during Luther's lifetime,
consisting primarily of processions and plays that emphasized symbolic
inversion, and usually held on the dates of traditional church festivals. As
Scribner comments, Reformation-era acts of carnival, through "mockery,
mimicry and parody of official life, culture and ceremonies" aimed to "over-
turn the official world by exposing it to ridicule."[9] Carnivalesque rites and
performance may be understood as a safety valve that releases the tensions
of social hierarchies and inequalities, but they can also be a crowbar that
shakes up the status quo.

Luther himself was relatively tolerant of popular culture, and had no major
objections to Carnival: "let the boys have their games." After all, Carnival acts
served the Reformers well in their struggles against church authority. In time,
however, a new status quo solidified. Lutherans "were stricter than Luther," and
in post-Reformation Europe, as historian Peter Burke has shown, reformers of
all stripes (Lutheran, Calvinist, and Catholic) took heavy aim at the popular
practices and rites of the "simple folk." I quote Burke at length:

The reformers [mostly Protestant, but some Catholics] objected in
particular to certain forms of popular religion, such as miracle and
mystery plays, popular sermons, and, above all, religious festivals
such as saint's days and pilgrimages. They also objected to a good
many items of secular popular culture. . . . Actors, ballads, bear-
baiting, bull-fights, cards, chap-books, charivaris, charlatans, dancing,
dicing, divining, fairs, folktales, fortune-telling, magic, masks,
minstrels, puppets, taverns and witchcraft. A remarkable number of
these objectionable items could be found in combination at Carnival,
so it is no surprise to find the reformers concentrating their attack at
this point. . . . This cultural reformation was not confined to the

popular, for the godly disapproved of all forms of play [including, for example, theatre]. Yet one is left with impression that it was popular recreations which bore the brunt of the attack. . . . What, according to the reformers, was wrong with popular culture? . . . In the first place, [as Erasmus explained] Carnival is "unchristian" because it contains "'traces of ancient paganism." In the second place [again, according to Erasmus] it is unchristian because on this occasion "the people over-indulges in license."[10]

The history traced by Burke is one that sees Carnival and other forms of popular culture and religion sharply curtailed across much of Europe, especially Protestant Europe, by 1800.

The above passage demands a second reading, and some reflection. The expurgation of these practices and pastimes meant radical changes to the cultural domain we are focusing on in this chapter. Civitas, the domain of the people, the life of ordinary folk, was radically transformed in the wake of these reforms. Imagine drawing up a comparable contemporary list of the kinds of activities engaged in (aside from work) by the average person living today in Europe or North America; then imagine eliminating these from social-cultural life, and you'll have some sense of the enormity of the changes that took place within what we now call popular culture.

In nineteenth-century Germany, Carnival traditions persisted in pockets of the primarily Catholic southwest, but they disappeared in the Protestant northeast. France invaded southern Germany in 1794, and the Prussians invaded from the northeast in 1815. Like the church before them, these state powers worked to suppress Carnival. During the nineteenth century, Carnival became institutionalized and secularized in the southwest through the founding of Carnival associations (*Vereine*). In the Nazi era, Carnival all but disappeared, or was strictly employed for ideological purposes; travesty, satire, parody, masking, transgression—these were anathema to the Nazis. Similarly, in the communist-controlled East Germany, Carnival was suppressed.

Mikhail Bakhtin argues that in the early modern era, as the actual practice of Carnival across Europe (especially Protestant Europe) declined, its spirit found a new home in literature; the spirit of Carnival helped create a new genre of literature—the novel. Parody, the grotesque, the sensual body, travesty, dismemberment, inversion, scatology, orifices, holy fools and picaresque wanderings, banquets, ritualized violence, and portrayals of corrupt clerics and officials—the bread and butter of traditional Carnival—worked its way into European culture through the novel, a rule-less, cannibalizing, self-recreating, formless literary mongrel. But in the second half of the twentieth century, the carnivalesque has leaped out of the text and returned to European social-cultural life on a large scale—and it has recently returned to Wittenberg, the heartland of German Protestantism. Costuming, satire, mockery, fools, masks, inversion, theatrical skits in the streets, farces, folktales, dances, drum and pipe music, long hair, boots, buckles, beer, and bratwurst—all this is standard fare at both Luther's Wedding and Reformation Day, but it is new fare, or rather, old fare made new again.

As mentioned earlier, socially and theologically conservative Lutherans are at not entirely at peace with the resurgence of the "medieval Marktplatz," seeing in the carnivalesque a kind of backsliding into values, morals, and a worldview deemed problematic. If popes and the curia were the target of Reformation-era carnival, today Luther is king. In Roman Saturnalia, the festival king was ritually "killed." The satire and parody centered around Luther and clergy that takes place in the Marktplatz is an echo of this long tradition of inversion, mockery, and ritualized transgression.

The Medieval Market Spectacle

The geographic center of old town, the Marktplatz is also the hub of Wittenberg's festivals, home to the medieval market spectacle. The square is framed by the castle church to the north, the town church to the south, the old Rathhaus (City Hall), and other significant historic buildings, such as the Cranachhaus museum. The twin spires of the town church, located just off the Marktplatz, tower over the square. A curb, three or four inches high, raises the square above the streets that bound and define it. Elevation is one way of creating stage-space, of demarcating a performance site from ordinary space.

Applying the typology developed by Lindsay Jones introduced earlier, market squares in European towns and cities are examples of ritual-architectural priorities III A and II C. Such spaces are "architecture as ritual context," specifically "theatre," as they provide a "stage setting or backdrop for ritual performance." Market places are also forms of "architecture as commemoration." Many include objects—monuments, plaques, fountains—dedicated to mythical or historical figures, and are framed by heritage and civic buildings and the façades of churches and museums. Market squares are outdoor stages; meeting grounds for conversation, food, and drink; literally a marketplace for buying and selling; and a potential rallying point for political action and protest.

Tellingly, when Jürgen Habermas defined the bourgeois public sphere of the modern era, he trimmed off the life of the German Marktplatz, the Italian Piazza, the French Place du Marché. In spite of using the language of private individuals "coming together" to discuss and debate matters of mutual concern, the kind of togetherness that takes place within the sphere Habermas describes is of an odd sort. This public sphere is a mediated (usually textual), disembodied space; a realm of discourse, talk, and public opinion that lacks sociability. People do not talk to one another, but at or past the positions or views of faceless others. The sphere of public opinion making involves little actual togetherness. Television media tries to give an impression of sociability, through the use of the "town hall" forum. In this artificially created scene of coming together, a few hundred people are selected (rarely at random) as representatives of the public, meeting in an auditorium-like space. They are stuck in chairs, yoked to the rhythms of advertising breaks, cut off from the sociable influences of food and drink, music and art, tastes and smells, linked (usually via satellite) to a talking head projected on a screen (the body ends at the shoulders), and encouraged to assume and defend to the death one-sided positions by an institution that thrives on the contested hot button issue. The architectural features and the embodied (i.e., disembodied) style of such spaces and gatherings (familiar to academe, business, and government) makes authentically sociable, convivial relations a near impossibility. Moreover, in the era of media spectacle and concentrated, corporate ownership of the tools and institutions of media, propaganda has largely replaced open discussion and the sharing of and access to information. (The Internet and other technological revolutions perhaps offer the hope of a renewed, Habermasian public sphere.) Neither does the public sphere (as it is described by Habermas) touch the realm of commodity production, social labor, or the market. The public sphere as Habermas understands it is distinct from economic concerns.

Clearly, Habermas describes a central phenomenon of social-cultural life in the modern West. The problem is that his description of a certain kind of public sphere has come to have normative implications. When academics, for example, utter the phrase "religion and public life," they tend to have a very narrow conception of where these domains intersect—and it is not on festival grounds, pilgrimage routes, or market squares. A theory and model of the public sphere that neglects the occasions on which thousands and even tens of thousands periodically come together for festive celebration, travel together to religious or otherwise special destinations, or simply wander the streets and squares of larger cities in the evenings is woefully inadequate to understanding public life in today's global world. A Marktplatz and the festival life it hosts are an integral part of the public sphere.

Wittenberg's Marktplatz is an open-air stage; its location and slight elevation, the presence of the Luther and Melanchthon statues, the surrounding, framing architecture, the banners and actual elevated stages set up for the festivals mark actions that take place on it as both central and special. The Marktplatz feeds into two main streets that intersect at either end of the old town; for the festivals, they are lined with outdoor, medieval, and historical-themed stands and shops. These main streets in turn feed into smaller squares and courtyards, hosting exhibits, stages for music and performance, and more sellers. This market territory and dimension of the festivals is the location of the carnivalesque, the actions and performances that constitute what is referred to as the medieval market spectacle.

Two chief features of the Wittenberg festivals create a carnivalesque, medieval feel. First is the presence of performers and sellers from around Germany. The Spielleute—literally, "play-people," descendants of the wandering musicians, minstrels, jugglers, clowns, and improvisational dramatists of the Middle Ages, provide entertainment. The streets and squares are their territory. Most of these Spielleute contract their services through Heureka, a large firm based in Leipzig that specializes in medieval-themed fairs. The city hires Heureka to arrange stage settings and subcontract performers. Along with the Spielleute, the sellers from around Germany who pour into Wittenberg at festival time to set up their stands, hawk their wares, and ply their trades contribute to the carnivalesque feel. In addition to beer and food stalls, there are many shops selling various crafts and wares, jewelry and art, much of it "traditional" or "medieval." Selling, consumption, and exchange are integral to the life of the festivals. A beer stand in the Marktplatz for Luther's Wedding costs roughly 6,000 euros for the weekend, and a garlic-bread stand 1,200. The Marktplatz is an "arena for market relations," but is also a venue for debate, display, and expression. Many of the sellers set a medieval theme for their booths and products: a smithy, a fortune teller, puppeteers, glassblowing, woodworkers. For some of these performers and sellers, medievalism is both a philosophy and a way of life, part of the widespread contemporary interest within white, Euro-centric society for New Age spiritualities and practices. The Wittenberg festivals are in large measure constituted by the open-air market of diverse goods and performances brought into being by the performers and sellers.[⊙]

Second, one thing that makes the Wittenberg Luther festivals work, makes them successful, I suggest, is the ambivalent status of Luther; ambivalence was a central feature of traditional Carnival, combining praise and abuse, seriousness and levity, piety and malice, the sacred and the profane. Part of what gave (and continues to give) Carnival its edge and excitement is that it ran counter to (or alongside of) normative rules and codes, the civility and good manners of elites, the austere piety of the religious. Traditional Carnival took place within a

⊙ DVD: The Animators

context of official religious and civic festivity, but was in large measure a lay phenomenon, a festival of and for the people as a whole. The dichotomy or tension between low and high culture was typically symbolized in figurative differences between the lower and upper bodies; the former a world of indulgence and sensual pleasure, the later of manners, morals, and godliness. Luther remains enough of an ecclesiastical and civil figure—a symbol of "official" religion and elite culture—that the carnivalesque impulse toward mockery and inversion has something to push against. The satire and inversion characteristic of Carnival is relatively mild in Wittenberg's festivals (paint bombs aside), but it is present, and an example of it is the scene I earlier described and dubbed "A Beer for Martin," and to which we turn once again.

A Beer for Martin (II)

A frame analysis of "A Beer for Martin" is charted in table 6.1. The scene is an example of the "medieval," carnivalesque ethos of Wittenberg's Luther festivals. The performance of a bawdy, beer-guzzling Martin Luther that afternoon in Wittenberg's Marktplatz lasted all of ten minutes, but the scene is a small window that opens on to the dynamics of contemporary Luther festivity. "A Beer for Martin" taught me that bracketing out the medieval Marktplatz and focusing on ecclesiastical and civil religion—historically, the bread and butter of Luther festivity—would result in a very limited perspective. In witnessing the scene, my conceptualization of the festival crossed over from the liturgical and ceremonial into aesthetic performances and the carnivalesque.

"A Beer for Martin" was itself an exercise in framing. Unlike Luther's Wedding, the Reformation Day festival does not have a formal opening or ending. Coming at the beginning of the festival, it set a tone for those present, a tone of playful—for a few, offensive—merry-making. Significantly, the scene was not on the scheduled event-program.

The historical market spectacle was on the 2004 program, but scheduled to begin on Sunday, which happened to coincide with October 31, the traditional date of Luther's posting of the ninety-five theses. Performers and vendors set up the market on Friday evening and Saturday morning. By Saturday at noon, enough people were beginning to congregate in the old town that most of the stalls selling food, drinks, and souvenirs were up and running. An unofficial printed poster and word of mouth announced a 4 p.m. festival opening in the Marktplatz, and roughly two hundred people were present to witness the performance. The impromptu opening of the festival was primarily

TABLE 6.1. Framing "A Beer for Martin"

Time
    unofficial beginning of the festival
    symbolic time: late medieval; pre-Reformation Wittenberg
    enfolding of times (historical Martin in the contemporary Marktplatz)
    message: as he is today (a beer drinker, one of the folk), so he was then

Space
    outdoors; in the streets; public space
    Marktplatz (marketplace): place for games, food & drink, conversation, buying, sell-
        ing, aesthetic performances (dance, street theatre, heritage performance, music)
    symbolic: "old Wittenberg"; the festival's center or heart

Senses
    spectacle—visually compelling & sensuous (smells, tastes, movement, sounds
        concentrated and intensified)
    taste & smell employed metaphorically; "lower" senses = low culture
    kinesthetic/metaphoric: off-balance, spinning, tipsy

Performance Type
    street theatre; aesthetic performance
    carnivalesque; ludic
    Spielleute (players), not Schauspieler (actors)
    performer–spectator boundary collapsed; viewers also participants/performers
    performance space—city plaza as stage
    aesthetic: low; gutter humor; sexual innuendo; anti-authoritarian

Objects; Images
    beer; loved by Martin; challenges Martin as elevated celebratory object
    trumpet: traditional symbol of royalty; here, inverted, used to probe, listen & smell,
        rather than announce/pronounce

Persons
    The Fool: a foil to Martin
    Martin Luther: present among festival-goers; one of the people; brought down from
        imposing pedestal of the Luther monument

Domains
    public; popular culture; entertainment
    economic: Marktplatz—the marketplace; cultural performance as commoditized
        product

satire of "medieval," Luther-era clergy and monastics; by implication, the performers satirized the liturgical dimensions of contemporary Luther festivity.
Coming on the eve of Reformation Day, the opening in the Marktplatz pushed
the traditionally liturgical basis of the festival in the direction of the carnivalesque. The performance marked the festival as an occasion for play, entertainment, and socializing, rather than commemoration, worship, and speeches.

"A Beer for Martin," as a piece of street theatre, was primarily visual: People watched it. Gustatory, olfactory, auditory, and kinesthetic qualities were also present, both literally and metaphorically. "A Beer for Martin" was expressive, it was entertaining, aimed at getting people into the mood for celebrating; but it also embodied meanings. Historically, the herald trumpet was used to signal orders during military combat, and to announce the arrival of royalty. Its contemporary use by clowning festival performers suggests social inversion. Turning it end for end and using it not in conjunction with the mouth (the origin of speech, words, texts, and *logos*, the tools of Lutheran tradition) but as an instrument to expand the sensitivity of the ear and nose to detect the production and presence of smells amplified this inversion.

Beer is an object with a ubiquitous presence at festival time, so conspicuous that its significance might be easily overlooked. Ritual action is everyday action elevated, stylized, condensed, formalized. During festival time in Wittenberg, beer drinking (an ordinary, perhaps even everyday occurrence) becomes ritualized action and beer a ritual object. Beer is given as a gift; it shows up in rites and performances; it is balanced on the head, like a crown; the drinking of a beer marks the opening and closing of events; the strewn (at night) and stacked (in the morning) empties in Wittenberg's streets are testaments to a voracious appetite for and ability to consume vast quantities of the golden, amber, or dark liquid; the act of drinking beer with friends while sitting at the foot of Schadow's *Luther* monument on Reformation Day is a form of teenage protest.

Beer has the effect of altering normal sensory states. The spinning of Martin, coupled with the chugged beer, played havoc with the man's kinesthetic sense. Martin was off balance, and almost fell over—a model of and for the carnival-like, topsy-turvy atmosphere of contemporary Luther festivity. The kinesthetic sense of the scene was one of derangement, the sensory focus was on the "lower" senses associated with the genitals, mouth, gut, and bowels. Martin, the culture hero who posted the ninety-five theses, became for a moment something of a beer-loving, paunchy, farting, stumblebum. Reformation Day is marked on the liturgical and civic calendars in Sachsen-Anhalt. It is an elevated, special, extraordinary occasion: Its liturgical focus is on the text and the preaching of the Word. The meaning embodied in the postures and gestures that Saturday afternoon seemed to be: Let's not forget that Reformation Day, however elevated it may be, is also an event of and for the folk; a time to praise, but also to poke fun—maybe there is even something about Luther or the festival that stinks.

In writing about smells (however metaphorical and symbolic they may have been) I am not trying to be flippant, crude, or provocative; we ought not to trivialize or lightly pass over this probing for smells in the Marktplatz. The scene demands attention for two reasons: first, for some, the play of the Spielleute was mildly offensive, and second, such actions were not a part of traditional Luther festivity in the nineteenth and early twentieth centuries. In earlier eras of Luther festivity, the man was not the butt of jokes, at least not publicly. At a conference dealing with "religion and the senses," I presented a paper that included a reading of the scene "A Beer for Martin." A German philosopher, presenting after me, commented, "my paper doesn't deal with anything quite so entertaining as farts and beer; my paper is about Being rather than beer." The comment is telling, indicative of cultural attitudes toward smell, "low" culture, and body humor. Alain Corbin complains that Western history, as written, is "odorless," an observation that points to the suppression of senses other than visual that accompanied modernity. Various cultural theorists have argued that a central feature of modernity is the loss of the full range of the human sensorium, a loss that carries with it a cost: the repression of diverse perceptual dispositions, which in turn facilitates authoritarian control of the political subject and a narrowing of potential worldviews. The language betrays the point: who today has a "worldtaste"? Twentieth-century fascism and totalitarianism were, if nothing else, obsessed with the clean, the polished, the shiny, and relied heavily on the professionally stage-managed visual spectacle.

"A Beer for Martin" drove home to me Paul Stoller's plea that ethnographers attend to the "sensuous body—its smells, tastes, textures and sensations." Stoller arrived this methodological conclusion on the basis of fieldwork in Niger, during which he realized that perception "devolves not simply from vision (and the linked metaphors of reading and writing) but also from smell, touch, taste, and hearing." These "lower senses," as Stoller calls them, "are central to the metaphoric organization of experience."[11] Stoller and others have suggested that non-Western cultures tend to employ and value these "lower senses" more than those of the West. But such a conclusion is probably the product of decades of relative disinterest in using an ethnographic approach to study religion and culture in the West (the study of Christianity and Western philosophy emphasizing texts, theology, and Being), coupled with academe's historical fascination with the great books of the Western tradition and with high culture. The players in the Marktplatz brought my gaze and attention down from the reaching towers of the Stadtkirche that loom over the town square to the bodies in the streets.

What was the purpose or function of "A Beer for Martin," and how did it do (or fail to do) its work? What is its place and role in the larger festival? To ask functional questions of "A Beer for Martin" may be to commit a serious category error. After all, the scene involves Spielleute (players) at work, and their work is play, which is usually defined as a noninstrumental, non-goal-directed activity (that is, the opposite of work). Rites and performances characterized by play may not mean or do anything; play is an end in itself, rather than a means to something else.

When scholars have turned their attention to rites and performances marked by the qualities of play, there has often been a reluctance to think about the functions of play. Both Johan Huizinga and Roger Caillois, two influential theorists of play, use words such as "free," "unbounded," "unproductive," "useless," "frivolity," and "ecstasy" in describing play.[12] In this same tradition, Herbert Marcuse claims that the "play impulse does not aim at playing 'with' something; rather it is the play of life itself, beyond want and external compulsion—the manifestation of an existence without fear and anxiety, and thus the manifestation of freedom itself. . . . Play is unproductive and useless because it cancels the repressive and exploitive traits of labor and leisure; it [play] 'just plays' with reality."[13] We play because we play. As Huizinga writes, "the fun of playing resists all analysis, all logical interpretation. As a concept, it cannot be reduced to any other category."[14]

Why is the literature on play characterized by a reluctance to assign play functional value? The answer probably has something to do with the trajectory of modernity. In the language of Max Weber, modernity is characterized by an iron cage of instrumental reason, bureaucratization, and utilitarian values. The "non-goal-directed" theory of play advanced by Huizinga and others is probably influenced by the desire to cordon off a personal and cultural space free from the instrumentality and material interest of the modern world—a world that would turn play into "recreation," valued as a form of mental hygiene or a product to be consumed. For a society driven by the cycle of production and consumption—a mode of life that many critics view in terms of alienation—free play returns us to ourselves, to activities that are not means to getting ahead or enhancing status but expressions of life itself.

Festivity has often been theorized in terms of precisely such notions of free play. Josef Pieper describes festivity in terms of expressive joy and jubilation, a time of "being in tune with the world." Studies of festivity tend to be either highly theoretical on the one hand, or descriptive case studies on the other, but most of the most influential works on festivity are of the former variety, which means they are not grounded in the nuts and bolts of an actual festival but are rather discourses about festivity.

Though I am sympathetic with those who seek a more nonreductive understanding of play and human performitivity—and "A Beer for Martin" did indeed manifest a kind of expressive freedom—Huizinga and others are "surely wrong when [they see] play as divested of all material interest."[15] The Spielleute who performed "A Beer for Martin" were earning a living, and the city of

Wittenberg hired the Leipzig-based firm Heureka because the company puts on a good show, a show that delivers people to the city.[16] Without taking a too large, reductive, or explanatory leap, the primary aim of the performance was entertainment, and it achieved its aim. What was it that made the performance entertaining?

Characterized by spontaneity, improvisation, and a weakening of the performer-audience boundary, "A Beer for Martin," was not "pure" play, but something in between play and theatre; Spielleute (players) are not *Schauspieler* (actors). There was no script for this performance, but rather a scenario around which the players and spectators improvised. The scenario was something like this: An important, esteemed, well-known man (on the precise day set aside to publicly honor him) drinks too much, gets horny (the herald trumpet was briefly transformed into a phallus, and pointed at a "nun") and dizzy, farts, and makes a fool of himself in public—an age-old tale. Performed on Reformation Day, the effect was that of lowering Martin Luther from his pedestal in the Martkplatz. Bakhtin notes that "debasement" and "degradation" are forms of "grotesque realism," a chief aim of which is to "bring down to earth, [to] turn their subject into flesh."[17] For a few minutes, the man in the crowd was not just Martin, but Martin Luther, who in turn is fashioned as a man of the people, a bit bawdy, gustatory, a roguish connoisseur of fine beer, a man who appreciates a good festival. The scene allowed the public to poke fun at the high and mighty, while simultaneously using the figure of Luther to emphasize certain features of "German" character.

Martin played his role well. Upon finishing his beer, with an exaggerated sweep of his arm across his mouth, Martin mopped up of the golden liquid running down his chin, and proudly thrust out his chest. Drinking the mug down in one fell swoop was a performance of German beer-drinking prowess. Drinking a beer is a common enough activity in Germany. In the Marktplatz on Reformation Day, called upon by Spielleute, surrounded by fellow festival-goers, the smell of roast pig, and the sounds of trumpets in the air, banners waving in the wind—in such a situation drinking a beer becomes a scene, that is, theatrical and emplotted in a narrative structure. I use the term *scene* in both a colloquial and technical sense. In everyday speech, a scene is a happening, an event that captures our attention. Performance theorist Richard Schechner identifies a continuum of perspectives from which we can consider ritual and performance: brain event, microbit, bit, sign, scene, drama, and macrodrama, each drawing on and presupposing the former. Schechner refers to this continuum as the "magnitudes of performance."[18] Though Schechner is interested in ethological perspectives (the first four magnitudes), he tends to focus on the later end of the spectrum, those magnitudes of performance that can be characterized as the showing of doing, more or less self-conscious display. The scene is the point on the continuum where drama, theatricality, and narrative enter into play. The difference between just drinking a beer and the beer that Martin drank is in the narrative theatricality of the action; the framing, the fit between the play and the expectations of the audience, made for a successful, entertaining performance.

Another factor that made the performance fun and entertaining is that it drew the spectators into the play. The crowd formed a performance space in the Marktplatz by gathering in a semicircle, and people were thus on the border between being on and off stage, between being an audience member and being part of the production. Martin, one of the crowd, served as the crowd's representative, and others contributed with shouting, clapping, comments, and catcalls. One of the characteristics of festivity is that festival-goers are part of the production; this active participation is quite unlike, say, proscenium theatre, where an audience-performer boundary is demarcated and maintained throughout the performance. In festivity, spectators or consumers are also performers and producers. If you can consume a large mug of beer in a single, long gulp, if you dress up and perform your character, if you spend beyond your means, you amplify the ethos of festive celebration. A good festival is partly dependent on the willingness of the audience to engage in festive behavior.

The degree of separation between performers and audience is one feature often used to distinguish ritual from theatre. Where a high degree of separation exists, we have formal theatre; at the other end of the continuum, where spectator becomes participant, is ritual. Play is also characterized by the absence of a performer-audience boundary: If you are watching, you are not playing. Festivals that move in the direction of audience participation head in the direction of ritual and play, and those attending the event also play a part in its production; where the audience is passive, we have a cultural performance, looked upon and consumed by spectators.

Entertainment and Efficacy

Richard Schechner distinguishes performance in terms of an efficacy-entertainment dyad. To call a performance efficacious is to emphasize that its "purpose is to effect transformation" at a social, personal, or even physical level; a rite of passage, an ecstatic trance, and a healing rite are examples of such purposeful performance. Schechner's basic focus is not on the opposition between ritual and, say, theatre, but on the degree to which any type of performance slides one way or another on the efficacy-entertainment dyad. Since the pioneering work of Victor Turner, ritual is understood as a potential motor for transformative social processes, but games, theatre, and music tend to be viewed primarily as forms of entertainment (though avant-garde and experimental theatre attempt to push back in the other direction). Where does "A Beer for Martin" fall on Schechner's continuum? Is it doing any kind of ritual work? If, as I have claimed, festival culture in Wittenberg is implicated in processes of social change, must not this change be processed in the particular scenes, rites, and performance that comprise the larger abstraction called a festival?

Consider that the former East Germany was a repressive state. People lived in a world where the Stasi (secret police) would entice or coerce family members to spy on one another. Speaking out against authority or the state was an act that could have serious repercussions. Extending this historical context further back, we encounter the Holocaust, the Second World War, the era of Nazism, the depression of the 1930s, the legacy and waging of the Great War. The past century in eastern Germany has been a period of protracted of suffering, and not very playful. It has also been a time of quiet or forced acquiescence to the authority of the state, an authority incarnated in the public and near god-like stature and power of individual men, among them the heroic Luther.

Broadly speaking, "one's religion is . . . one's way of valuing most intensively and comprehensively."[19] Such a conception draws attention to the importance of values, as opposed to beliefs, in religious life. If you value democracy; or equal pay for equal work regardless of ethnicity or gender; or clean air; or, like Socrates, wisdom—and if you value these intensively and comprehensively, that is, the act of valuing is fundamental to one's larger life-world—then you have found your religion. In the context of the authoritarian state in Germany, the ability to defy and laugh at authority is intensively and comprehensively valued by many, though also still being internalized in the post-Wende era. "A Beer for Martin" embodied this value; it was playful, but also serious, also doing work.

Laughing at authority figures or playing around with prominent cultural-religious symbols may seem trivial, but the ability and willingness to engage in the public performance of political satire and critique is a measure of the health of democratic process. Historically in European culture, carnival provided the occasion for the public display of popular sentiments, ideas, and opinions, and this tradition continues in the Fasnacht and Fasching traditions in southern Germany and Switzerland. It is important to realize that the carnivalesque character of "A Beer for Martin" is a relatively new experience in Wittenberg. In the post-Reformation era, festive celebration based on the tradition of Carnival, an element of which included satire of authority and the inversion of social classes and roles, was suppressed and eventually banned in Lutheran territories. The suspicion of Carnival held by both the Lutheran Church and state continued unabated through the Nazi period and then on into the communist-controlled DDR. "A Beer for Martin" exemplifies the return to popular, street culture of a kind of playful, irreverent performance rooted in genres of mockery, parody, satire, and clowning. Spielleute once again, after several hundred years, walk the streets at festival time. Sylvia, a consultant and member of the performance group Scharlatan, explained to me the connection between historical and contemporary Spielleute in terms of the tradition of poking fun at officialdom. "What we do is basically try to transport what the medieval Spielleute did—to transport this into modern times. Because what we do is make fun of the system sometimes . . . and of political things, and combine this with music and fun. And this is what they did in earlier times." Luther, the raison d'être of the festivals, is also the target of the Spielluete's slings, arrows, and barbs. Bakhtin emphasizes that in the early modern era, "Carnival festivities and the comic spectacles and ritual connected with them" were intertwined with, though "sharply distinct from the serious official, ecclesiastical, feudal, and political cult forms and ceremonials." A "festive laughter" was the organizing principle of Carnival. Laughter, though often derisive, is not merely so. Laughter is "deeply immersed in the triumphant theme of bodily regeneration and renewal."[20]

A sure indicator that the Spielleute and other performers in the Marktplatz are doing something, and not only or merely playing around, is that not everyone is thrilled with what they do. Events in Wittenberg's Marktplatz, streets, and *Hofs* (courtyards) constitute the public face of both annual festivals, where cultural performances such as "A Beer for Martin" often bump into the attitudes and values embodied by liturgical and ceremonial rites, which generally take place indoors. In conversations with local church members or Lutheran visitors to Wittenberg, I heard concerns expressed over the carnivalesque nature of both Reformation Day and Luther's Wedding. One consultant, a trained, unemployed pastor, associated the ethos of the "medieval Marktplatz" with a wider medieval movement afoot in German culture. She was referring to neopagan forms of spirituality that are present not only in Germany but also around the globe. An American visitor noted, with contempt, that in Wittenberg bars Halloween parties were taking place alongside Reformation Day celebrations. Another consultant, in response to a question about the role of the church in planning Luther's Wedding, made a distinction between a Volksfest and religion: "Luthers Hochzeit," she said, "ist ein Volksfest. Es hat nichts mit religion zu tun." Lurking in the background to such critical comments is a very old cultural tension in Protestant Europe, the relationship between the feast days of ecclesiastical religion and the ethos of Carnival, as well as assumptions regarding the nature of true religion.

Mimesis, Magic, and the Carnivalesque

The scholarly theorizing of festive celebration has generally taken one of two tracks, each employing a fundamental root metaphor. One approach, following the tradition of structuralism, emphasizes the manner in which public festivity models (and in so doing, establishes, reinforces and legitimates) social structures, status-quo values, and hierarchies. A model is a representation in miniature of some larger structure or pattern. A model airplane is a model of the real, functioning thing that flies. But a model may also be developed as a blueprint for the real thing; a new airplane design is first modeled, and then built from the model. Similarly, a celebration has this dual nature; it is a model both *of* and *for* society.

A second slant to theorizing festivity utilizes the metaphor of the mirror. A chief tenant of structuralism is that ritual symbols and processes reflect or express social structure, that public ritual, performances, and symbols are more or less social and political control mechanisms. Victor Turner, who took this tradition of structuralism with him into the field, added to the mirror metaphor the notion of public and plural reflexivity. If a celebration is a mirror held up to a social world or group, it is not just passively reflecting social arrangements but also producing an image that can be seen, experienced, and in turn reflected upon. If we tell someone, "take a good look in a mirror," we are imploring that person to think about who they are, their behavior and actions, their lifestyle, their past actions, and their hopes and plans for the future. Similarly, in Turner's view, celebrations need not be understood as an epiphenomenon of social structure—a view that privileges an abstract "society" over its more concrete manifestations; they may also be vehicles of reflexive insight, resistance, and social change. Turner called such qualities "liminal." Clifford Geertz was also reared on the tradition of structural-functional analysis. Like Turner, as a result of his field work, Geertz was led to abandon structuralism as a comprehensive approach to the study of symbolic forms. Ritual and performance, according to Geertz, are "carriers of meaning, [or] bestowers of significance," as well as a form of metasocial commentary.

Geertz and Turner have both been taken to task for a model of religion and culture that emphasizes meaning, purpose, worldview, significance. But neither Geertz nor Turner, as their critics suggest, overlooks questions of power, contestation, and struggle. Stories, festivals, rites, performances, drama, art—it is these "contrivances" that "enable [religious] imaginings and actualize them, that render them public, discussable, and, most consequentially, susceptible of being critiqued and fought over, on occasion revised."[21]

From this Turnerian perspective, a celebration is not so much a model or mirror as a crucible, arena, or stage in or on which meaning is produced and social dramas are enacted. Applied to celebration, the language of performance is not merely metaphorical, since most celebrations include theatrical elements—costuming and staging, for example, or the fictive presence of historical figures and the reenactment of foundational stories. Celebrations are "ritually polychromatic. They are 'happenings' and thus emphasize the event end of the event-structure continuum."[22] Celebrations are put on, they take place, they occur. Like a stage drama, they are planned, rehearsed, come into being, and then pass away—only to reappear, when the right and proper time rolls around.

Model and mirror theories are relevant to Wittenberg's Luther's festivals, but I want to consider the reemergence of the carnivalesque in terms of performance, specifically in terms of magic. Ronald Grimes writes, "Magic . . . does not refer to only other people's rites but to ours as well." Magic shows up in most typologies of ritual; but, taking a cue from Grimes, we can also think of magic as a ritual attitude or sensibility. Grimes identifies six ritual modes, among them, magic. (The others are ritualization, decorum, ceremony, liturgy, and celebration.)[23] The set of sensibilities is a heuristic tool allowing us to explore the dimensions of a rite beyond those features typically associated with its label: A liturgy may be ceremonial, or a celebration magical.

The aspect of magic that interests me is its mimetic basis. The theory of magic developed by the armchair anthropologist James Frazer (d. 1941) is burdened with the language of primitivism and cultural evolution, but he introduced an idea that others have picked up on and developed. Frazer develops two classes of what he calls sympathetic magic: "If we analyze the principles of thought on which magic is based, they will probably be found to resolve themselves into two; first, that like produces like, or that an effect resembles its cause; and second, that things that have once been in contact with each other continue to act on each other at a distance after the physical contact has been severed."[24] The first, Frazer calls the Law of Similarity, the second, the Law of Contact or Contagion. The two actually go together, since the presenting and recognizing of similarities requires sensual contact. Frazer was trying to understand not magic but the workings of the "primitive" mind; magic is based on "principles of thought."

Then, we read in Frazer this sentence: "From the first of these principles, namely the Law of Similarity, the magician infers that he can produce any effect he desires merely by imitating it."[25] How Frazer knows what the magician infers, I don't know. But this is an interesting notion, provided we turn it inside out: Rather than follow Frazer's theory of magic (which is a psychological theory of

FIGURE 6.2. Puppets for sale in Wittenberg's Marktplatz. Photograph by Ronald Grimes.

ritual), we might consider the magic of imitation (which is more of a performative approach); rather than begin with the association of ideas as the fundamental human faculty, we might consider the mimetic faculty. In the dictionary, the word *faculty* refers to "members of a learned profession," to "the powers and capacities of the human mind," but also to "the ability to perform or act."

Perhaps the magician does not infer anything but uses the power of mimesis to generate a desired effect (fig. 6.2).

Walter Benjamin and Theodore Adorno turned this implicit insight of Frazer's into the notion that mimetic behavior involves becoming something other that what one is. The original Greek meaning of *mimesis*, they tell us, consists in "making *oneself* similar to another."[26] The stick bug looks like a stick, the killdeer feigns being wounded, the shaman becomes the first shaman, and—a personal example—my kids dress up and play Harry Potter. My children are also quite fascinated and then irritated when I mime them, a fact of some significance, I think. Why? As Michael Taussig has emphasized, for Benjamin, in copying or imitating, "a palpable, sensuous connection between the very body of the perceiver and the perceived," is made possible.[27] The heart of mimetic behavior is becoming something other than what one is. For this reason, mimesis, going back at least to Plato, has provoked both fascination and enmity, since it disrupts a stable ontology and straightforward epistemology. Critics who drink their Descartes neat will argue that one cannot really become something other than what one is. But anyone who has watched a mime working the street—or worse, has had the misfortune of being the mime's subject—knows the potential or power of mimicry. Mimesis is infectious.

It is also fundamental. "Nature creates similarities," wrote Benjamin in 1933. "One need only think of mimicry. The highest capacity for producing similarities, however, is man's. His gift of seeing resemblances is nothing other than a rudiment of the powerful compulsion in former times to become and behave like something else. Perhaps there is none of the higher functions in which his mimetic faculty does not play a decisive role."[28] This is high praise for primitive, childlike behavior. Note that Benjamin links the abstract and heady "seeing resemblances" (what we might call "thinking") to what he terms a "compulsion" to become something else by behaving like something else. That is, thinking, not just playing Harry Potter, is grounded in ritualization; thinking is mimicry.[29]

Ethnographic research is often, perhaps inevitably, informed by a mimetic longing to represent and show to others events witnessed, people encountered, and stories heard in the field. Film can achieve this showing in a powerful way. Film is a sensual medium. The written text, no matter how thick or transparent, is, in the end, a translation of what one perceives; film is an analogue of what one perceives. A difference between text and film is that between conceptual and perceptual knowing. Bertrand Russell describes this difference in terms of "knowledge by description" versus "knowledge by acquaintance."[30] In general, academic study has deemed this latter kind of knowledge to be superfluous, off-limits, inaccessible, or, at best, merely illustrative. But performance scholars and ritologists ought to concern themselves—not exclusively, but certainly—with the prospects for a sensuous knowledge, with what Adorno and Horkheimer, working the repressed body-side of the dialectic of Enlightenment, called "yielding."[31]

Charles Darwin was intrigued by mimesis. Anchored in the Bay of Good Success in 1832, observing the people of Tierra del Fuego, Darwin noted: "They are excellent mimics, as often as we coughed or yawned or made any odd motion, they immediately imitated us. Some of the officers began to squint and make monkey like faces; but one of the young Fuegians (whose face was painted black with white band over his eyes) succeeded in making far more hideous gestures. They could repeat with perfect correctness each word in any sentence we addressed them, and they remembered such words for some time. . . . All savages appear to possess, to an uncommon degree, this power of mimicry . . . the Australians, likewise, have long been notorious for being able to imitate and describe the gait of any man, so that he may be recognized."[32]

Notorious? There can be something notorious about miming: Parody and satire, mockery, clowning, and magic draw their strength from this notoriousness. If you desire to cause an effect, try miming someone. Darwin's thoughts here on mimicry are framed, we should note, in a historical narrative—"they" can do it, "we" can't, at least not nearly as well. Today, grand narratives are daring acts of academic suicide. But Durkheim and Eliade and others were not so timid, so let us be bold: In the wake of Protestantism, Positivism, and Pragmatism, the West has experienced a loss of the sacred and decline in its ritual interests and abilities; if so, this might have something to do with a decline in mimetic behavior.

A second example of the power of mimetic behavior is found in Claude Levi-Strauss's widely read essay, "The Sorcerer and His Magic." Levi-Strauss does not deny the physiological efficacy of certain magical practices, their ability to act on what he calls the sympathetic nervous system, but the full "efficacy of magic," he writes, "implies a belief in magic"—that is, magic and shamanism are psychological phenomena.[33]

A few pages later, we stumble across an odd paragraph—odd because it seems important, seems to reframe the general thread of both his approach and argument, and odd because Levi-Strauss drops the matter as quickly as he takes it up:

> In treating his patient the shaman also offers his audience a performance. What is this performance? Risking a rash generalization on the basis of a few observations, we shall say that it always involves the shaman's enactment of the "call," or the initial crisis which brought

him the revelation of his condition. But we must not be deceived by the word performance. The shaman does not limit himself to reproducing or miming certain events. He actually relives them in all their vividness, originality, and violence.[34]

"We must not be deceived by the word performance"—a warning to the reader not to gloss performance as "mere" performance, as secondary to mental processes. There is a power in the performance, and to ignore it, Levi-Strauss implicitly warns, is to ignore something crucial to how shamanism works. This paragraph, oddly enough, undercuts the representational approach to ritual that is characteristic of structuralism.

Also: The shaman "actually relives" his call—a pairing of two words that sets my mind, at any rate, reeling. Again, setting aside the problem of just how Levi-Strauss knows what the shaman experiences, we might ask, what does it mean to "actually relive" something, as opposed to simply reliving it? Why the "actually," if not to press home the ontological reality of the performance? On the verge of a full-blown dramatistic approach to his topic, Levi-Strauss pulls back to compare the shaman's work with that of the psychoanalyst—but more than that, by sleight of hand he hierarchically orders them.

Levi-Strauss does not just write on mimicry, imitation, representation, and performance; his essay is an example of the very thing. Levi-Strauss uses shamanism as an illustration of the efficacy and correctness of psychoanalysis: "Psychoanalysis can draw confirmation of its validity, as well as hope of strengthening its theoretical foundations and understanding better the reasons for its effectiveness, by comparing its methods and goals with those of its precursors, the shamans and sorcerers."[35] In other words, mimesis happens not just in ritual practice but also in the study and theorizing of ritual. Levi-Strauss does what Benjamin says we do: he "sees" a resemblance. In Levi-Strauss's hands, psychoanalysis acquires universal power by being a copy, an imitation, a resemblance (though an upgraded, modernized one) of Ur-practices of healing. It strikes me that in reading some of the classic accounts of magic, the explanations and theories offered achieve their power by the very thing they attempt to explain, that is, through the magical means of similarity. The principle of association (A is similar to B) was the lynchpin in explanatory theories of magic. Tyler, Frazer, and others perceived at work a faulty logic in that what the primitive associates in his mind is thought to hold for external, material reality. Scholarly procedures, however, are similarly homeopathic; what is associated in the mind is taken for historical or psychological or social reality.

Mimesis is epistemological; it is a way of knowing. Anytime we give an example, refer to a concrete case, illustrate an idea with a diagram or chart, project an image during a lecture, we are being mimetic and messing with a kind of magic, since the representation becomes, perhaps even acquires the power of, the represented. Hence the problematic of voice and representation in ethnographic work, work done with living bodies. We are now aware that "once the mimetic faculty has sprung into being, a terrifically terrifying power is established; there is born the power to represent the world, yet the same power is a power to falsify, mask, and pose. The two powers are inseparable."[36] Magic is contact, producing an effect, making a connection to something or someone through mimetic behavior. Magic is a power that a copy extracts from an original, or the power a copy has to influence or infect the original; thus, it involves a relationship between self and other, which is why Michael Taussig, following the thought of Benjamin and Theodore Adorno, connects mimesis with alterity.

Just how just mimesis establishes a connection to others is, of course, a complex question. No doubt psychological, social, cultural, and biological factors are all involved. What I do know is that in Wittenberg people, as part of the effort to deal with the problems and prospects of reunification, have of late been dressing up as their ancestors, enacting foundational myths of the city and region, and recreating, a couple of times a year, a medieval world on the verge of tipping into the modern—and they do so out of some sort of sense that this will make a difference. We might call this magical; it certainly is not, to borrow the language of Clifford Geertz, "commonsensical"—it is not ordinary, everyday behavior; which is to say that the quotidian, commonsensical, everyday world leaves something to be desired, and magic is, above all, driven by desire. But desire for what? In this case, perhaps mimesis itself.

Discussions of mimicry, mimesis, and magic are, as I have hinted, often framed in a historical narrative. Walter Benjamin, like Darwin, tells a "once-upon-a-time-we-were-mimetically-adept" story, as evidenced by dance, the mirroring of microcosm and macrocosm, and practices of divination based on correspondences between things like entrails and constellations, all of which he takes as characteristic of "primitive" societies. The trajectory of the West, claims Benjamin, was characterized by a repression of mimetic relations to the world, to self, and to others. Modernity, argued the Frankfurt School critics, involved the repression of mimetic behavior, and then the return of it in highly controlled and organized spectacle forms: a mimesis of mimesis, an imitation of imitative behavior, the extreme form of which is fascism. For Adorno, writes Michael Taussig, fascism was but an "accentuated form of modern civilization which is itself to be read as the history of the repression of mimesis."[37]

What is modernity? The question has been given many answers, but here is one: Modernity is the iconoclasts and bans on graven images, the persecution of gypsies, the Pietists' closing down of theaters and opera, the Puritan's denial of the body, the smug fear of religious fervor and emotionalism, and, in the words of historian Peter Burke, the "triumph of Lent over Carnival"— mimesis under siege.

Benjamin also notes that "language may be seen as the highest level of mimetic behavior." This is not necessarily a complement, because under the reign of modern linguistics in which the relation between the signifier and the signified is completely arbitrary, language becomes "the most complete archive of non-sensuous similarity: a medium into which early powers of mimetic production and comprehension have passed without residue, to the point where they have liquidated magic."[38] Benjamin is somewhat ambivalent whether this change should be viewed as "decay" or "transformation."

At any rate, magic was making a comeback. "Every day," writes Benjamin in prophetic tones, "the urge grows stronger to get hold of an object at very close range by means of its likeness, its reproduction."[39] Mimetic capacities and expressions were resurfacing in modernity he thought, willy-nilly, through technology, specifically the camera and film. The word C-A-T is nothing like a cat (that's "liquidated magic"), but the image of it on film is. Language, Benjamin suggests, has both a mimetic and semiotic basis; but the semiotic rules the roost in modernity. The sensuousness of film, he hoped, could make contact with the senses; the still and moving image would be routes to a sensual, magical kind of knowing—what Roland Barthes called not semiology but seismology—shock waves. "[P]eople whom nothing moves or touches any longer," writes Benjamin, "are taught to cry again by films."[40] Film can metaphorically and quite literally, through the phenomenon of involuntary mimicry, move people. I have shown the Luther's Wedding montage (on the DVD) on several occasions, and inevitably a few people watching begin to move. Film has the power to generate in viewers involuntary mimicry. So too does performance. As Adam Smith observed, watching a high-wire act, spectators "naturally writhe and twist and balance their own bodies as they see him do."[41] And if film can achieve this, what of ritual?

Festivals as Sympathetic Magic

To get hold of something "at very close range by means of its likeness, its reproduction": This is sympathetic magic. And what are the witches, nuns, minstrels, and fools in Wittenberg's street trying to get hold of if not the carnivalesque ethos of the early-modern era they are copying, imitating, playing with, and representing? Frank Manning, writing in the early 1980s, claimed that "throughout both the industrialized and developing nations, new celebrations are being created and older ones revived on a scale that is surely unmatched in human history."[42] Manning may have been overstating the case, but there is evidence that festive celebration in Europe and North America has experienced a renaissance.[43] What is going on here? Why are cities and regions turning back to earlier forms of popular culture? Why is Carnival experiencing a revival? Why the intense interest in heritage and history that accompanies festive celebration?

There are two typical answers given to this question. First, festival renewal is a response to modernity: to feelings of placelessness and the loss of tradition; to secularization and inability of the church to serve as a center for collective identity; to the shrinking of social life to the family and workplace; to the loss of seasonal rites with the shift from agriculture to industry, and the attempt of urban populations to get back, however metaphorically, to roots and the land. This is called the "performance of heritage." Second, festivals are understood an example of the commoditization of culture—Lutherland as a kind of Disneyland, or Reformation-era theme park; instead of Mickey, Luther walks the streets.

But if we consider Peter Burke's list of what Reformers and others went after, a common denominator is mimetic behavior: dressing up, masking, puppets, charlatans, mystery plays, magic, role playing. People are doing these things, once again—the return of the repressed. In a way, the actors and festival-goers in Wittenberg's streets at festival time are telling a story. In assessing the spiritual and cultural predicaments and possibilities of the present, there is an implicit understanding that the past is relevant piece of the puzzle. In knowing where we stand, we have to know where we have come from. The notion of disenchantment developed by Max Weber to describe the spiritual condition of modernity is related to the suppression of Carnival, myth, and magic in Western culture. Wittenberg's festivals are attempts at recovering and reinventing lost mimetic traditions.

Richard Schechner writes about "twice-behaved behavior" or "restored behavior." "Restored behavior is symbolic and reflexive" and comes down to a single principle: "the self can act in/as another. . . . Restored behavior offers to both individuals and groups the chance to rebecome what they once were—or even, and most often, to rebecome what they never were but wish to become."[44] Reformation-themed festivity in Wittenberg reenacts what the Reformation would ultimately do away with, what the people, who for centuries now have located their origins in Luther and the Reformation, never were but wish to become: the "battle" between Carnival and Lent that was medieval Carnival. Like Levi-Strauss's magician, Wittenbergers "actually relive" a pivotal historical-mythical moment in and through mimetic performance. This is not photographic replication, but more like streaming metaphors and metonyms, live streams;

not magic by likeness but magic by contact and contagion. Spielleute mock priests and nuns, they turn the everyday man in the street into Martin Luther, and vice versa, bringing Luther down off his heroic pedestal in the Marktplatz, and pillorying him with satire. Meanwhile, the pious complain about drums and pipes, a "medieval movement" in the Marktplatz, the contamination of Reformation Day with Halloween celebrations; and try to uplift Luther's Wedding in a renewal of vows ceremony while the sounds from outside flow inside to disrupt the service. Is Luther now the occasion for a kind of modern, secularized magic, a drumming and dancing into being the spirit of a lost world?

Could the renaissance of the carnivalesque be an attempt to "get hold of something by means of its likeness"? In "transporting" this and other aspects of carnivalesque performance, in mimicking "lost" forms of popular culture, do the Spielleute also transport (and make manifest) another worldview and ethic into the contemporary celebration of Luther? Is there, as Tom Driver suggests, "magic" in ritual performance?[45]

Peter Burke sees in the battles between Carnival and Lent that were per-formed in the streets during the Carnival season "two rival ethics or ways of life in open conflict." On the side of Lent rested the values of "decency, diligence, gravity, modesty, orderliness, prudence, reason, self-control, sobriety, and thrift, or to use a phrase made famous by Max Weber, 'this-worldly asceticism.'. . . . [This] ethic of the reformers was in conflict with a traditional ethic which is harder to define because it was less articulate, but which involved more stress on the values of generosity and spontaneity and a greater tolerance of disor-der."[46] Ironically, Wittenberg's fame as a site of Lutheran heritage and tradition is occasioning festive celebration informed by the traditions of popular culture that still existed at the time of Reformation.

Charles Taylor, in reviewing various theories of Carnival, finds in them a common theme: the idea of "complementarity, the mutual necessity of oppo-sites . . . of states which are antithetical, can't be lived at the same time"—except during the periodically created and bounded times of liminal, festive celebration. Carnival-like events and moments, and their persistent presence in human cultures, indicate a fundamental individual and social need for what Turner calls "anti-structure." The notion that a social code or order ought to leave "no space for the principle that contradicts it, that there be no limit to its enforcement . . . is the spirit of totalitarianism,"[47] and East Germany has known, in its recent past, enough of that spirit. "In human history," Turner writes,

> I see a continuous tension between structure and communitas, at all
> levels of scale and complexity. Structure . . . holds people apart,
> defines their differences, and constrains their actions . . . [this] is one

pole in a charged filed, for which the opposite pole is communitas, or anti-structure . . . the desire for a total, unmediated relationship between person and person, a relationship which nevertheless does not submerge one in the other but safeguards their uniqueness in the very act of recognizing their commonness. Communitas does not merge identities; it liberates them from conformity to general norms, though this is necessarily a transient condition if society is to continue to operate in an orderly fashion.[48]

Festival culture evokes or is underpinned by this quality of commonality or communitas that is difficult to identify or describe precisely. It is partly created by collective action, by the sociable qualities of mutual, public display. In Turner's descriptions of communitas is a latent element of bearing witness to one's own tastes, interests, and activities, in the context of a wider collective display. Our everyday, normative doings and identities are somewhat suspended, and our creative acts and personas, our imaginative life and our buffoonery, quirks and special talents, are given presence before and with others, and thereby validated.

Beyond an occasion for mutual public display and sociability, festivity aspires to a feeling of common emotion or experience. In Wittenberg, this happened one night in the Marktplatz, as the band began performing its closing number, Dylan's "Blowin' in the Wind." The three or four hundred people still present in the square for a moment gave up their individual and small-group discussions and pursuits, and joined in collective song, bodies swaying to the rhythm. Such moments of common action and feeling "both wrench us out of the everyday, and seem to put us in touch with something exceptional, beyond ourselves." Charles Taylor, whom I am quoting here, calls this the category of the "festive," and it is inherently related to the development of a more immediate, active, face-to-face public sphere. It is also, suggests Taylor, "among the new forms of religion in our world."[49]

7

Pilgrimage, Sacred Space

In their path-breaking work on Christian pilgrimage, Victor and Edith Turner observe, "a tourist is half a pilgrim, if a pilgrim is half a tourist."[1] Pilgrims, no matter how devout and religiously motivated, also act like tourists, seeing the world, satisfying curiosity, buying souvenirs, stepping outside normal day-to-day routines. And the tourists, for their part, may well be religious subjects, traveling and visiting places because of a site's historic or contemporary religious significance, or for religious reasons. The categories of "pilgrim" and "tourist" often overlap.

Tourism is one of the world's leading industries. For the year 2008, as I write, projected revenue of world travel and tourism is expected to top 8 trillion U.S. dollars, and rise 15 percent in the next decade. By the year 2018, more than 10 percent of the planet's GDP will be generated from tourism, and one out of every ten jobs will be in the tourism sector.[2] Given the historic pervasiveness of religion, it would be odd indeed if religion did not have a presence in the world of travel and tourism, a prominent part of global culture. Tourism is usually defined in terms of leisure, pleasure, play, and entertainment. Over the last two decades, however, the tourism industry and academe alike have discovered the phenomenon of "spiritual" or "religious" tourism, a subgenre of the larger tourism pie. In Sachsen-Anhalt, for example, the state in which Wittenberg is located, the Ministry for Industry and Labor published, in 2006, a study titled *Spiritueller Tourismus in Sachsen-Anhalt*. The study analyzes the potential of "spiritual tourism" as a "special tourism form," and makes recommendations to develop the region's potential, namely, the area's rich religious history associated with the Reformation and the Pietist movement, incarnated in the numerous religious sites and routes that dot and crisscross the landscape. The use of the word "spiritual" in the study's title is significant. It marks out a form of travel not necessarily grounded in confessional belief, church membership, or fidelity to a particular religious tradition. "Spirituality," we read, "connotes authenticity, deepening, slowing, insight, and restoration. . . . In our study, 'Spiritual Tourism' is described as 'sacred and embodied' travel, a form appealing to those searching for the experience of transcendence, for life's meaning and value."[3]

In figure 7.1, I map the variety of visitors to Wittenberg in terms of four interlocking poles: people, place, performance, and outcome. Action in the outer ring is informed by entertainment, recreation, diversion. The next two rings, in contrast, comprise the mix of spiritual, heritage, and cultural tourism found in contemporary Lutherland. The inner ring more narrowly defines the Lutheran and Protestant pilgrim. Spiritual tourism in Lutherland is worthy of study, but my interests and data collected in the field limit me to a discussion of the inner ring of figure 7.1, Lutheran pilgrimage and Wittenberg as sacred space.

Wittenberg receives roughly 350,000 visitors each year; more than 2,500 groups tour the old town. Between 15 and 20 percent of these visitors are from the United States. Since the majority of the visitors from the United States who travel to Wittenberg do so because of a connection to the Lutheran tradition, a conservative estimate would place the number of American pilgrims visiting the city each year in the neighborhood of 40,000. My discussion below is necessarily selective, drawn from my interaction with a few North American visitors to the city. Nevertheless, I believe the themes and issues raised have a general currency. Protestant pilgrimage is out there; Protestants are visiting religious sites for religious reasons, but the phenomenon has received little scholarly attention. Travel, tourism, and pilgrimage to Wittenberg and Lutherland will only increase in the coming years, as the 2017 jubilee approaches. If my initial efforts here can encourage others to pick up the Lutheran pilgrim trail, then my aims will have been achieved.

Protestant Pilgrimage?

The desire to journey to distant places, across religious, ethnic, and territorial divides, seems to be a pervasive human need; pilgrimage to sacred sites is a

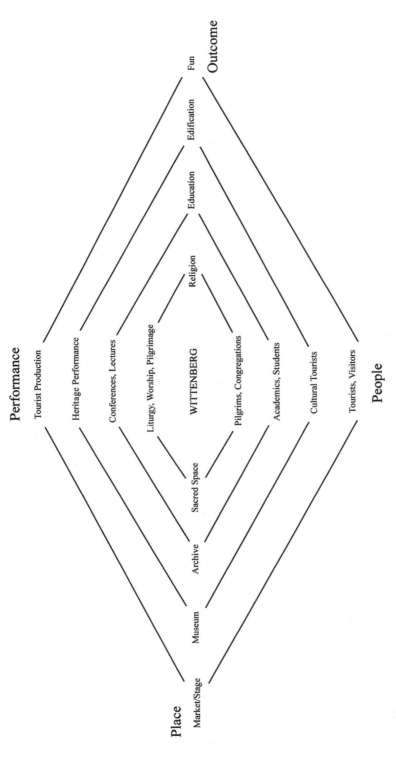

FIGURE 7.I. Travel to Wittenberg.

persistent manifestation of religious life. Such sites include the birthplaces and tombs of religious founders and saints, special places in the landscape (rivers, caves, mountains), the geographical settings of mythical and historical events, and places where the sacred is said to have manifested in the temporal, mundane, material world. Pilgrims, according to one concise definition, are "religiously motivated travelers who undertake infrequent round-trip journeys to sites they consider sacred."[4] Wittenberg is such a place for Lutherans around the globe—the place of origins, the resting place of the founders, the Lutheran "Mecca," an analogy I frequently encountered. But does pilgrimage really exist in the Protestant world? Isn't pilgrimage one of the "abuses" that the Reformation did away with?

The first elector of Saxony, Rudolf I (d. 1356) incorporated a relic chapel into Wittenberg's fortress complex, and determined to make Wittenberg a sacred place. Rudolf acquired a thorn from Christ's crown, the first of many relics that would help transform Wittenberg into a devotional center. In 1486, when elector Frederick III (the Wise) took the reigns of power, he transferred the electoral capital to Wittenberg and began a massive building campaign. Frederick had the old fortress torn down and replaced with a Renaissance complex befitting an elector of the Holy Roman Empire. Frederick developed Rudolf's relic chapel, spending a good deal of money stocking it with an impressive collection. In 1509, the chapel housed more than 5,000 relics. By 1520, when Frederick decided to give up collecting, he had gathered more than 19,000 items. Liturgical objects, books, and vestments used in Wittenberg's castle church were of the highest standards, and lavishly decorated. In 1505, Frederick brought Lucas Cranach to the city, turning it into a center for fine art. Cranach's workshop built the main altar for the castle church, plus nineteen side altars, adorned with the finest in European art, including four paintings by Albrecht Dürer. Frederick founded a cult of St. Mary and another for St. Anna, Mary's mother. In 1519, the year that marked the end of this form of Catholic piety in Wittenberg, 1,138 masses were sung, and 7,856 masses were read in the castle church (more than twenty masses per day!).[5] All this aesthetic and devotional activity marked Wittenberg as a place worthy of visit, and it became a stopping point on the long pilgrim trail from Eastern Europe to Santiago de Compostella in Spain. And then, precisely at the moment when Wittenberg came into its own as a magnet for pilgrims, reformers like Luther came down hard on the practice.

In his "Appeal to the Ruling Class," Luther argued, "pilgrimage to Rome should be disallowed. No person actuated merely by curiosity or his own religious feelings should be permitted to make a pilgrimage. . . . I do not say this because pilgrimages are wrong, but because they are ill-advised just now;

for what one sees in Rome is not exemplary, but scandalous." Rome, in Luther's view, was corrupt, a cesspool of vice, and nothing of merit could come from visiting such a place. Moreover, Luther thought pilgrimage to be unbiblical— not one of God's commandments—and only served to bring financial hardship on families. A man undertakes a pilgrimage to Rome; "it costs him 50 or 100 guilders more or less, while his wife and child, or his neighbors, suffer from distress at home. And yet the silly fellow thinks that his disobedience to, and contempt for God's [actual] commandments will all be atoned for by the pilgrimage, which he undertook on his own responsibility, although it was pure, self-willed, or Satanic seduction." The potential pilgrim's "pastor" or his "liege lord" must ascertain motivations for pilgrimage. If it "turns out that his purpose is to do a good work, then let the pastor or the liege boldly trample the vow and the work underfoot as a satanic delusion." The authorities should "tell the man to apply the money and effort required for the pilgrimage to fulfilling God's commandments, and to doing works a thousand times better than a pilgrimage, namely, meet the needs of his family and his poor neighbors." However, somewhat surprisingly, we read that if the motivation is "to satisfy his curiosity and go sightseeing in country and city, let him have his way." So long as merit aimed at salvation was not the motivation, pilgrimage, in Luther's view, was relatively benign. Finally, Luther criticizes the way in which the popes stirred a desire to pilgrimage to Rome through their "deceitful, trumped-up, foolish 'Golden Years' [jubilees]," an earlier form of tourism marketing.[6]

In the wake of the reforms initiated by Luther and by Calvin, Protestant culture associated pilgrimage with a theology of works, and staunchly rejected the practice. The chief concern was a perceived spiritual hubris, the idea that the individual could lift themselves out of a state of sin through penitential acts. Pilgrimage, to the extent that it was practiced in Protestant culture, shifted away from matters of healing and penance toward the satisfaction of curiosity, the desire to see the world, the pleasures and satisfactions of sightseeing.

The faith/works distinction remains central to Lutheran theology. Pastors proclaim it on Reformation Day, and in speaking with American Lutherans in Wittenberg, occasionally a "grace not works" position would be invoked in discussions over pilgrimage. Invariably, those reluctant to think of their visit as pilgrimage were LCMS members. When I mentioned to one couple my being in Wittenberg to study Protestant pilgrimage and sacred space, I received a rather impassioned response centered on "Luther's discovery of salvation by grace through Christ." The notion that works had anything to do with religion was offensive to the couple, and they associated pilgrimage with a faulty theology. Luther's "grace not works theology is a fundamental truth" and the basis for the "superiority of Protestantism over other religions." "Are there Protestant pilgrims?" I asked. "No. Works have nothing to do with Protestant faith of salvation by grace. Pilgrimage is a mistake." "Then what are you doing in Wittenberg?" I dared query. Momentarily stumped for an answer, the husband, in his early fifties, replied, "Well, I'm not exactly sure. We came for our daughter's wedding, and decided to take in Luther's sites, too. To see the history of the place, to see where the Reformation began. But it is not pilgrimage. I don't gain any merit by coming." In the Protestant worldview, to support pilgrimage is to support a Catholic sacramental theology; venerating persons or objects at a site deemed sacred challenges the radical message of salvation by grace revealed in and through the Gospel.

But as Thomas Tweed has shown in the case of American Methodists, there does exist a pattern of travel, and a sacralizing of locations and sites. The same is true of Lutherans. In spite of Luther's theology of grace, Calvin's rejection of sacramental theology, and the historic opposition within Protestant traditions to pilgrimage, the notion that Protestants do not have pilgrimage sites and routes has been overstated. "Protestants . . . are less anomalous in the history of religion than most scholars have assumed."[7] In the second half of the nineteenth century, encouraged by the new modes of transportation (steamship and rail) and the desires of modern tourism, Lutherans began seeking out religious roots and heritage in the places of Luther and the sites associated with the Reformation. The work done by Johann Gottfried Schadow and others through the nineteenth and early twentieth centuries created the contemporary Luther landscape of monuments, heritage homes, museums, and routes winding through the cities in which Luther lived and worked. Pilgrimage to this newly created Lutherland was not for the purpose of penance. Rather, it was to experience firsthand the places that define the story of the Reformation, and to deepen understanding of Luther's personal spiritual pilgrimage by physically traversing those sites linked to his life. This remains the crux of Lutheran pilgrimage today.

An important part of a city or region's pilgrimage landscape is the on-the-ground institutions that exist to support it. Since 1997, the Wittenberg English Ministry (WEM) has been operating during the tourist season, serving the needs of pilgrims and religiously motivated tourists. In 1999, the Evangelical Lutheran Church of America (ELCA) opened a permanent center in Wittenberg, working with local and international partners to bring Lutherans from around the globe to their spiritual homeland. The WEM, the ELCA Center, and the German church readily use the language of pilgrimage, as do most Lutheran visitors to the city; Protestants are no longer as suspicious of pilgrimage as they once were. In fact, the Evangelical Church in Germany is actively involved in planning Luther tourism, including the so-called Luther Decade, a series of events building toward the five hundredth jubilee of the Reformation in 2017. There are vague echoes in the notion of a Luther Decade to the papacy's "Golden Years," but time, it seems, has tempered the antagonisms of the past.

The Wittenberg English Ministry

In the fall of 1996, Reverend Keith Loesch, a pastor with a Lutheran Church Missouri Synod (LCMS) congregation in Virginia, took a sabbatical year to "recharge the batteries." He decided to spend two months in Wittenberg, a "personal pilgrimage," he explained to "connect my faith in Christ to my life-long connection to Dr. Martin Luther, and to soak up the atmosphere, to be here in this town." He began to interact with tourists visiting the historic sites, and in the process the idea for a ministry took root. The "German guides leading the tours," Loesch explains, "were atheists, the legacy of communism, and I began accompanying some of the groups in order to add a spiritual, faith dimension to what was otherwise a cultural and historical itinerary." On one particular day, a visiting group asked if they might sing Luther's hymn "A Mighty Fortress" in the Schlosskirche. Reverend Loesch mediated between the group and the church officials, whom he had come to know, and permission was given. Reverend Loesch sang with the group, and "halfway through the organist started playing and continued playing. It was a charged, electric moment, and I had a powerful experience of mission. I saw the possibility of an English ministry on the ground in order to develop spiritual connections to Luther." The city invited Loesch to set up a "worship and outreach ministry in English at the historic castle and town churches associated with Dr. Martin Luther. It was envisioned that this ministry would serve the hundreds of thousands of tourists who visit Wittenberg annually and develop into an ongoing international mission society."

Loesch identified a divide between German visitors to Wittenberg, who come chiefly for reasons of culture, history, and heritage, and groups from outside Germany, who come as church members, typically with fellow congregants. The "town saw in me the potential to increase tourist numbers, but also the value of having a ministry for faith-based visitors and to aid in rebuilding the church, which had been destroyed by communism." It is a little-known fact that according to federal census data, more Americans trace their ancestry to Germany than to any other country. Tapping the contemporary quest for "roots" by establishing "routes" to ethnic and cultural homelands has been one way of cultivating tourism in historic regions such as Lutherland, so the city's desire to promote pilgrimage by inviting the WEM is understandable.

The presence of the ministry, however, complicates the religious dynamics in Wittenberg.

Loesch describes himself a "servant" or "bridge" between "two communities," that is, between the local church and American Lutherans. The focus of the ministry is to offer "worship in Luther's church" to visitors, but a second aim is to combat secularism and reinscribe Luther's town with an aura of faith. "Luther's Hochzeit," Loesch mildly complains, "is contrived as a giant party, with beer drinking and bratwurst. The renewal of vows ceremony was introduced in order to uplift the festival." The ministry thus serves a dual purpose, supporting pilgrims but also doing mission work in the former East Germany, reseeding the region with Lutheran faith.

The WEM serves the needs of pilgrims and Protestant visitors principally through arranging and conducting worship in English for those visitors who happen to be in the city between April and the end of October. Pastors rotate through Wittenberg during the tourist season on two-week stints. Worship services conducted by the WEM are held in either the Stadtkirche or Schlosskirche on Saturday evenings, and on Wednesday afternoons and Friday mornings a devotional service is conducted in the small Corpus Christi chapel, located next to the Stadtkirche. The number of visitors on any given day is variable, but tends to be small, with even the occasional no-show; in such situations, the small number of congregants becomes the overwhelming fact of the worship service. Six or eight individuals gathering for worship in a church that seats several hundred makes plain the struggle of the church to find a place of relevance in contemporary Wittenberg. One Wednesday afternoon WEM service I attended had only three visitors. The presiding pastor, a Canadian, put on a brave face, but in speaking with him afterward, I could tell he was somewhat disappointed with his experience in Wittenberg:

"Have you been disappointed at all?" I asked. "There was a near no-show today."

"No, not really. If I was coming here and only had a couple of hours, would I want to sit in a church and listen to some guy? Saturdays have been good though. Last Saturday there were fifteen people, a couple from Brazil. It isn't so much quantity but quality, the different people you meet and get to touch. . . . The first couple of days [here] are great, but then, okay, now what? In the evenings and on weekends, the place really shuts down. There isn't much to do. Two weeks, for me, is a bit too long. Three quarters of the [WEM] pastors [who come to Wittenberg] are retired, so they see it differently, I think."

"Do you think of Wittenberg as sacred space?"

"This is something I think a lot of people have to be very careful of. I've seen too many people come to Wittenberg and they hold Luther higher than

Christ. They worship Luther higher than Christ. For me, I like to come and see where the Reformation started, and what Martin Luther did. But I don't view it as a sacred site. It is a historical site, not sacred. Obviously the church, in that sense is [sacred]. I wouldn't take my shoes off in Luther's house."

"Is visiting Luther sites is important for faith?"

"My wife, when we did the service on Saturday night, she said that hearing the music, being there in the church [Schlosskirche]—it made her feel closer to God. I think when people come here it becomes more real, not just history, but real."

"What do you make of the Luther phenomenon, Luther as a tourist draw?"

"I get a little disappointed . . . you come here and everything is Luther. Luther socks. I think this takes away from the historical aspect. It is nice to go home with a Luther mug or something, but it has gone to the extreme."

Several people associated with the WEM expressed to me disappointment with the commoditization of Luther. They feel it distracts from the religious significance and importance of Luther and the Reformation. As one of the WEM's associates explained: "Those people who participate in Luther's Wedding may not understand the treasure or the significance [of the city's Reformation heritage]. Or the tour guides. Many of them are very good; they know what to say. But that doesn't mean they have a real [religious] sense of what is going on."

The WEM hosts pilgrims and conducts worship, but it is also in Wittenberg to renew the local church. The theme of renewal is an integral part of the WEM's narrative of itself, and this mission of renewal is communicated to residents and visitors. As a WEM bulletin puts it, "God is using the Wittenberg English Ministry to be a fresh voice of the Gospel of Christ into the hearts of Germans who have lived with decades of Communism, Socialism, and Secularism." There is some hubris in such claims. The local, native Lutheran church has existed in Wittenberg for nearly five hundred years, and knows a thing or two about the decades of communist rule and secularization. American Lutherans often frame the low church membership and participation in Lutherland's churches in terms of the region's communist past. The "communist, godless East Germany," as one American visitor plainly summed-up the situation, is in "need of an infusion of Lutheran faith." To be sure, communism played a role in the declining fortunes of the church in the decades following the Second World War. On the other hand, secularization is a fact across Western Europe, and to invoke communism as an explanation for the state of the church and faith in eastern Germany is somewhat facile. The readiness with which American Lutherans visiting Wittenberg use communism and socialism as an explanation for "secularism" is filtered through the experience of the cold war, and American attitudes toward the "Evil Empire." President Ronald Reagan famously labeled the former Soviet Union as an Evil Empire, in a speech given, not coincidentally, to the National Association of Evangelicals in 1983. The majority of Lutheran visitors to Wittenberg grew up with the cold war and its rhetoric. One of the features of Lutherland that makes the region interesting to American visitors is the association of the region with the Iron Curtain.

That the WEM claims to speak with a "fresh voice" suggests that the local church is stale, a position that leads to mild antagonisms. The Lutheran community is diverse but, like many denominations, it divides into different wings: conservative, mainline, liberal. The use of such categories points to the limits of describing differences among the world's Christians in terms of denominational affiliations or religious families. Catholics, one rightly supposes, are different from Lutherans; but liberal Catholics have much in common with liberal Lutherans. Liberals, for example, are pro-choice on the abortion issue, conservatives pro-life. The "fresh voice" rhetoric used by the WEM is in part a jab at the liberal German EKD. The WEM is, relative to both the local German church and the American ELCA Center, theologically and socially conservative, and there is little cooperation and interaction between the WEM and these other church bodies.

A senior member of the Evangelische Akademie, when I asked if they did much work with the WEM, described to me the academy's awkward relationship to the WEM this way:

> No. We have, of course, our official ecumenical partners, like ELCA and UCC. . . . We had some questions from Missouri Synod to use the academy and we replied, "Of course, it is open to you also. But, you have to know, we have ordained women, we have a very open heart for gay and lesbian people in the church" . . . and we have never seen them again in the academy. . . . The academy is a lay center. It is on the borderline between church and society. It is a very liberal place. And if they [the WEM] agree with these conditions, everybody is welcome here. So, they made their own decision, and I can respect that. But it is their decision [to not work together], not ours.

Similarly, one of the leading figures of the local church felt that the "rotating pastor scheme—to preach in Luther's church—has an element of vanity. The wait list is long with the WEM, five or six years. To preach here is to be important." Another local church member lamented the presence of the theologically and socially conservative WEM, suggesting, "We don't need outsiders here creating divisions within the church. We've had too much division in the past."

People associated with the LCMS and WEM, for their part, have few kinds words for the Evangelische Akademie or the ELCA Center. Friedrich Schorlemmer, one of the academy's directors, I was told by a WEM associate, "is a mouthpiece for radical views; [the academy is] a biased group, which is clear from Schorlemmer's public rebuke of the conservative [German free] churches." The same man spoke of troubles with a female German pastor, as well as the former, female director of the ELCA Center. "Women should not be ordained; gays and lesbians should not be married. Conservative Lutherans come to Wittenberg very interested in such questions." Ironically, even though Wittenberg is the "authentic" site of the Reformation, the conservative North American Lutherans associated or affiliated with the WEM and LCMS tend to perceive their version of Lutheranism as the true carrier of authentic Reformation principles, values, and beliefs.

Shrine as Religious Void

Overall, the tensions I am describing here are relatively mild, and have little impact on the majority of Wittenbergers. They do, however, raise questions about the nature of sacred space and pilgrimage. Although most of the Lutheran visitors I spoke with in Wittenberg were quite willing to think of their visit as a pilgrimage, many demurred from naming Wittenberg as "sacred space." Nevertheless, the old city does have the qualities of a shrine, a "sacred site that houses holy artifacts, promotes ritual practice, and attracts religiously motivated travelers, who often mark the time and extend the space of the journey by returning home with mementos."[8] The centerpieces of pilgrimage to Lutherland are visits to the Schlosskirche, the Stadkirche, the Lutherhaus museum, as well as a stroll through the old town's streets, which are marked with plaques and monuments dedicated to famous Reformers, and lined with cafes and shops offering food and drink, and selling, among other things, Luther and Reformation souvenirs.

Earlier, in chapter 3, in my discussion of the WEM's renewal of vows service, I suggested that religious visitors to Wittenberg have their particular beliefs, narratives, and theological and moral views reinforced by the power of the place and the practices they enact. John Eade and Michael Sallnow have argued that pilgrimage sites and shrines often act as a kind of empty signifier that "officials, pilgrims, and locals invest [with] . . . meanings and ideas which are determinately shaped by their political and religious, national and regional, ethnic and class backgrounds." This investment gives a shrine its "religious capital. . . . The power of a shrine . . . derives in large part from its character as almost a religious void, a ritual space capable of accommodating diverse meanings and practices." Shrine sites, Eade and Sallnow continue, are akin to a vessel into which "pilgrims devoutly pour their hopes, prayers, and aspirations. And in a perfect illustration of the classic Marxist model of fetishization and alienation, the shrine then appears to its devotees as if it were itself dispersing the divine power and healing balm which they seek."[9]

The WEM's work in Wittenberg is, naturally enough, refracted through the conservative, traditional theology and worldview brought to the Wittenberg from America. The WEM is not an official organ of the LCMS, but its tenor is largely in keeping with its conservative theology and moral views. Worship bulletins have titles such as "God's Agents of Repentance" and "The Cross—Our Way to Deliverance." In a brochure advertising the ministry we read: "It is a great joy to hear the Gospel of Christ as it is proclaimed in this place. It is most meaningful to visualize Dr. Luther preaching from the Bible and pointing to Jesus on the Cross as the world's only savior from sin and eternal death. We trust that you will long remember this experience as you consider Luther's important role as the Great Reformer of the Church." The passage makes implicit reference to the Cranach altarpiece in the Stadtkirche, one of the highlights of a visit to Wittenberg, and the setting for the renewal of vows service.

The Stadtkirche St. Marien is a smaller, less grandiose, more intimate space than the castle church. Located in the center of the old town, just off the Marktplatz, the Stadtkirche is popularly known as Luther's church,' since it is here that Luther preached some 2,200 sermons. In 1522, Luther's colleague Andreas Bodenstein von Karlstadt (to Luther's chagrin) led what is now considered the first act of Protestant iconoclasm, a riot in the Stadtkirche that stripped the church of its medieval works of art. Twenty-five years later, an altarpiece by Lucas Cranach the Elder was installed in the church. Today, the altarpiece is one of the city's prized works of art, and one of the items on tourist and pilgrim agendas.

The structure of the altarpiece closely resembles its medieval antecedents; a predella and triptych over a table.[10] The content, however, is distinctly Lutheran. On the façade facing the nave, from left to right are images of the Baptism, the Lord's Supper, and the Confession. The predella depicts Luther, right hand outstretched pointing to Christ on the cross, preaching to a congregation in an otherwise unadorned, stark church (fig. 7.2). Replacing the artwork torn down by the iconoclasts, the altarpiece both draws from and instructs new emphases and forms in theology, belief, and liturgical practice. Of the seven Catholic sacraments, Lutherans retained two: Baptism and Communion.[11] In the center panel, a depiction of the Last Supper, Luther takes a place at the table as one of the twelve apostles. The predella encodes the emphases on the preaching and hearing of the word, of the saving work of Christ, and links the figures

FIGURE 7.2. Gazing at the Cranach altarpiece in Wittenberg's Stadtkirche. Photo by Ronald Grimes.

of Christ and Luther. Like the image above the Thesenportal that locates Luther and Melanchthon at Golgotha, the Cranach altarpiece places the Reformation in continuity with the Gospel narratives. Preaching a theology of the cross to pilgrims—"Jesus on the Cross as the world's only savior from sin and eternal death"—in front of the Cranach altarpiece inscribes that message with authority, the altarpiece reflecting back what is spoken to it. As one WEM pastor put it, "When you are in Wittenberg, it brings all sorts of memories back. The days when we learned something about Luther from our catechism. . . ." Walking with a German tour group one day, I heard quite a different interpretation of the altarpiece given by the guide. "They would have," the guide said, "baptized the child," the beginning of a completely historical account of a supposedly long-disappeared religion and faith. For one group, the altarpiece encodes the heart of the faith and presence, for another, the eclipse of religion and perhaps nostalgia. The sites, practices, artwork, and symbols of pilgrimage locales are polysemous; their meanings and uses are multiple and at times conflictual.

Ideological tension between secularism and faith occasionally rears its head, and has an impact on the tenor and content of Luther tourism. One consultant, Anika, an ordained pastor and graduate of Wittenberg's Predigerseminar, was faced with unemployment after not being able to find a church posting. The church is in poor financial shape, and declining church membership and participation meant that two-thirds of Anika's graduating class were unemployed. She attempted to hire on as a tour guide with the Wittenberg Tourist Center, thinking that her knowledge of Lutheran history and theology would aid her chances. On the contrary, "they didn't really want me because the office is run by old-guard socialists, and they don't want to include in Lutherstadt Wittenberg guided tours with faith. Only one of the guides there is a member of the church community." So Anika set up a small business, a travel-tour service, Glaube und Reise ("have faith and travel"). She printed brochures, put up a Web site, and offers specialized services to incoming pilgrims, but traffic has been slow. Ironically, the American Lutheran groups working in Wittenberg are there to aid in church renewal, yet their hosting and operating ministries and pilgrim tours may take potential clients away from the efforts of Anika and others to build a viable business and apply her training.

David Chidester and Edward Linenthal have argued for a situational approach to studying sacred sites. The influential essentialist models of the sacred developed by Mircea Eliade and Rudolph Otto "might be regarded as attempts to replicate an insider's evocation of certain experiential qualities . . . but a situational analysis, which can be traced back to Emile Durkheim, has located the sacred at the nexus of human practices and social projects." For Eliade and Otto, the sacred irrupts into human communities at precise places, "causing [those places] to become powerful centers of meaningful worlds." For example, in Exodus, God speaks to Moses at the burning bush, proclaiming, "Do not come near; put off your shoes from your feet, for the place you stand is holy ground" (Exod. 3:5). An essentialist view would understand this as a hierophany, the in-breaking of the divine or transcendent into the world. A situational analysis, in contrast, points to the creation and maintenance of sacred space through ritual action. Taking off one's shoes marks a place as special, extraordinary, qualitatively different from the profane world of dirt and labor. However sacred a tradition may declare a particular place, its qualities and meanings are maintained through narratives and built architecture, and through use, including ritual. These three actions—telling stories, marking a place with buildings and material culture, and ritual—are the chief elements constituting a pilgrimage landscape. That the sacred is the product of symbolic labor means that sacred sites are often "contested sites where negotiated contests over the legitimate ownership of sacred symbols" take place. A sacred site is the product of "the human labor of consecration . . . involving the hard work of attention, memory, design, construction, and control of a place." Sacred space, Chidester and Linenthal emphasize, is "not merely discovered, or founded, or constructed; it is claimed, owned, and operated by people advancing specific interests."[12]

The renewal of vows service and the broader aim of the WEM to speak the faith of Luther with a "fresh voice" represents the efforts of one group to shape the symbolic dimensions of Luther and the town that bears his name. The interests of outsiders in pilgrimage sites are not necessarily at odds with the local population, and the WEM does have a small number of committed residents who support its work and mission. But one of the dynamics pilgrimage sites and shrines seem to breed is tension between church and government, or between different faiths, or even among wings of the same religious tradition.

In 2004, for example, the EKD invited the Catholic archbishop of Magdeburg to deliver the Reformation Day sermon in Wittenberg's Stadtkirche. This was the first time in nearly five hundred years that a Catholic preached in the church. The EKD made the offer in the spirit of reconciliation and ecumenism. Historically, Reformation Day festivals were occasions for anti-Catholic polemic and propaganda; having the archbishop preach in Luther's church was an attempt to heal old wounds. In his only direct reference to Luther, the archbishop referred to the "Augustinian monk" Martin Luther, a choice of words that struck some present as mean-spirited. A member of the Evangelische Akademie was less than enthusiastic about the occasion. "If it is a genuine gesture, then fine. But if it is an event, an event for the cameras and press, without any real ecumenical intent, then it is just show. And I think that is what was happening." One of the WEM pastors, in response to my description of the 2004 service, was even more perturbed: "What would Martin Luther think of consorting with the Catholic Church?"

If there have been some mild tensions between American Lutherans and the local church since the arrival of the former following the Wende, recent events provide even an even greater illustration of the relevance of "contesting the sacred" to on-the-ground dynamics in Wittenberg. Early in 2007, in cooperation and with the financial backing of the LCMS, another Lutheran body, the Selbständige Evangelische-Lutherische Kirche (SELK, the Self-standing Evangelical Lutheran Church), purchased an old Gymnasium near the Stadtkirche. The building, as I write, is being converted into a SELK church and welcome center for Lutheran pilgrims; the grand opening is scheduled for October 2008, timed with Reformation Day.

The stated goal of SELK is to establish a "truly Lutheran congregation in Wittenberg." The origin of the German free churches—churches with no state support—dates to the formation of the Union Church in the Prussian era. Because the Reformed (Calvinist) and Lutheran tradition varied on several points of doctrine, when the two churches were unified some congregations dissented, forming freestanding Lutheran churches. The contemporary Evangelical Lutherische Freikirche (ELFK) and the Selbständige Evangelisch-Lutherische Kirche (SELK) represent the legacy of this dissent. SELK has about 40,000 members and ELFK fewer than 2,000. The two groups are politically, theologically, and socially conservative, and have links with both the American LCMS and the even more conservative Wisconsin Evangelical Lutheran Synod. SELK describes itself as a "confessional Lutheran Church," which means that the historical Confessions of the Lutheran Church, as contained in the 1580 Book of Concord, are taken as foundational, authoritative, and the true explanation of God's Word. SELK and the LCMS have many of the characteristics of fundamentalist Christianity: They hold to biblical inerrancy and are socially conservative, rejecting, for example, the ordination of women.

Because the German church is a Union Church, accommodating both Reformed and Lutheran doctrine and liturgical practice, SELK refuses to enter into fellowship with churches of the EKD. Pulpit and altar fellowship are rejected on the basis of doctrinal differences. The same divide prevents fellowship between the ELCA and the LCMS. The ELCA, in contrast, has had fellowship with Reformed Churches for more than a decade, and the EKD is similarly ecumenical. The German state churches with Lutheran roots have retained a strong affinity to Lutheran tradition, theology, and practice. Bernhard Naumann, the Kirchenmeister of Wittenberg's Stadkirche, described to me the Union Church not as a fusion or blending of traditions, but as akin to two friends who join arms to walk together for a time, traveling in a similar direction while retaining their own identities. In every way but name—and this is likely to change in the near future—the Union Church in Wittenberg understands itself as Lutheran—but it is not, at least from the perspective of SELK, a Lutheran church. A lot can be invested in a name.

Heading the SELK project in Wittenberg is Pastor Wilhelm Torgerson: "You may be wondering why a Lutheran missionary is even necessary in

Wittenberg. The quintessential Lutheran town. That's where it all started, at that door, the door of the castle church in Wittenberg. . . . [Yet] when confessional Lutheran groups, particularly from America but also from other places, from Eastern Europe, [when they] came to Wittenberg they actually had no place where they could truly feel at home and say this is, these are, people with our own kind of religious conviction." Pastor Torgenson admits that founding a SELK congregation and chapel in Wittenberg is "highly in dispute, particularly by the Protestant leadership in the town. We, the SELK, the old Lutheran church in Wittenberg, would like to establish a mission center to reestablish a Lutheran congregation in Wittenberg. . . . Lutherans from around the world come to Wittenberg, and ask 'Where is the Lutheran church?' And I have to tell them, there isn't one." Such claims, coupled with the fact that the project was initiated without any discussion with the local church, have strained relations between SELK and the local Evangelical Church. The LCMS has published several polemical pieces in its magazine, *The Lutheran Witness*, promoting the new Wittenberg ministry and blog sites repeat the claims that there are "no Lutherans in Wittenberg." "A new ministry will bring the Gospel to 'Luther's City,'" we read, as though the Gospel is somehow missing. Or another example: "When Bruce Kintz visited Wittenberg last year, the president and CEO of Concordia Publishing House stopped in bookstores to see what was on the local shelves. But in this city so closely associated with Martin Luther and the Reformation, he could find very little about Luther or Lutheranism." Such comments are polemical, though there is a theological position informing them: Those who do not hold rigorously to the Book of Concord are in error. Wittenberg is becoming a site for contesting the sacred; as momentum builds towards 2017, it is likely that tensions will rise.

The local church in Wittenberg has been working tirelessly since the Wende to transform the city into a center for ecumenical dialogue. The arrival of SELK will strain these efforts, and will probably have the effect of further alienating an already distant public from the life of the church. If we ask what Luther would make of the growing controversy in the city that now bears his name, we could do worse than quote these lines from his "A Sincere Admonition from Martin Luther to All Christians," written in 1522 in an attempt to quell iconoclastic fervor in the Wittenberg:

> I ask that people do not make reference to my name. Let them call
> themselves Christians, not Lutherans. What is Luther? After all, this
> gospel teaching is not mine. Neither was I crucified for anyone. In 1
> Corinthians 3, St. Paul does not allow Christians to call themselves
> "Pauline" or "Petrine" but only "Christian." How then should I—the

poor, stinking bag of maggots that I am—come to have people call the children of Christ by my wretched name? Let it not be so, my dear friends. Rather, let us abolish all partisan names and call ourselves Christians, after him whose teaching we hold.[13]

The Gaze: Nineteenth-Century Luther

A pilgrimage is created partly by what one does, but also by what one sees. "When we 'go away,'" John Urry writes, "we look at the environment with interest and curiosity. . . . we gaze at what we encounter. And this gaze is . . . socially organized and systematised."[14] Tourist destinations are constituted by a system of signs that visitors visually absorb in a relatively passive manner. Urry argues that with the advent of tourist marketing—which relies heavily on the glossy image of a place disseminated through film, television, brochures, magazines, and Web sites—people arrive at a tourist locale with a predefined representation of the place. This imaginary construction of reality is in turn mirrored by the tourist destination, designed as it is by the tourism industry to provide an experience that authenticates those very images and representations created to draw visitors in the first place.[15]

As discussed earlier, during the the Prussian era the figure of Luther was instrumentalized for political purposes, and Wittenberg became ceremonial ground, its landscape transformed by the erection of monuments, the restoration of the Schlosskirche, the installation of the bronze Theses Door, and the opening of the Lutherhaus museum. One of the reasons given by UNESCO for the inclusion of the Luther memorials on their World Heritage List is that Wittenberg's commemorative sites "constitute outstanding examples of 19th century historicism." In particular, Wittenberg's castle church "became a national monument to the Reformation, with its late 19th century furnishings, and so it also bears witness to Wilhelmian ecclesiastical politics." While UNESCO may realize that images of great historical figures are culturally produced, visitors are less likely to be as historically aware. In gazing at the Thesenportal, visitors do not see the "ecclesiastical politics" of the Kaiserreich; they see the heroic Luther. Martin Treu, a director of the Lutherhaus Museum Foundation, put the matter this way:

> The question then is what kind of image do people have when they speak about Luther. . . . In my experience there is a huge gap between the public image and the historical Luther. The historical Luther is mostly formed still by the ideas of the nineteenth century. We have a display here [in the Lutherhaus museum] on the reception of Luther,

especially in pictures. If you look at the nineteenth-century images, they are like still shots of the 2003 movie [*Luther*, starring Joseph Fiennes]. I think most people still have quite [a few] legends in mind when visiting Luther.

This nineteenth-century Luther is incarnated in old Wittenberg's Luther sites, and a symbolic reading of these sites suggests the kind of meanings absorbed by the tourist gaze in Wittenberg. As Dr. Treu notes, "Taking visitors into this process of historical thinking, of weighing evidence, is a very interesting process, but interesting for only a minority. . . . Most people just want to be at the 'authentic' places. For this Wittenberg is an ideal place. Nothing much has changed, since the old city was protected by the fortifications, which only came down in 1873." Historical thinking, however, is necessary in studying the commoditization of culture and the received impressions of the tourist gaze.

Thesenportal: Positional Meanings

The third leg in Victor Turner's interpretation of symbolic objects is to examine a symbol in relation to other symbols; Turner refers to this as positional meaning. (The first two, discussed earlier, are the exegetical and operational dimensions.) The positional relationship of one symbol to another is a contributing factor a symbol's meaning. As the tradition of structuralism has demonstrated, symbols are often arrayed in antithetical or complementary pairs. Beyond the tight binary approach of structuralism, symbols exist in a field or cluster of other symbols, and the various features and meanings of one symbol may be transferred to or latent in another.

Structuralism is dominated by a concern for the organization, roles, and hierarchies of social groups, and culturally prominent symbols are understood to be overt or covert reflections of social relations. Typically, religion is studied with an eye to how it "holds society together, sustains values, maintains morale, keeps public conduct in order, mystifies power, rationalizes inequality, justifies unjust deserts, and so on." Like Clifford Geertz, who supplies this concise summary of functionalism in order to reject it, my approach to working with symbols, rites, and performance owes more to interpretive hermeneutics—a "bringing to light," not a "metaphrase or a decoding."[16] Nevertheless, an understanding of the situational or positional relationship between a culture's symbols grounds the study of rites and performances in important social-historical contexts.

We return then, for a last time, to Luther's Thesenportal. Literally, the Thesenportal is a structure, and its meaning is shaped by the other dominant built structures that, taken together, constitute Wittenberg as a UNESCO World

Heritage site. The two other symbols I will discuss in relation to the Theses Doors are the statue of Luther located in the Marktplatz and the Katharinenportal, located at the Lutherhaus museum.

In 1540, Luther had a sandstone Gothic-style portal installed in the Lutherhaus. He dedicated it to his wife, Katharina von Bora, and today it is know as Katharina's Portal. When the site was renovated in the nineteenth century, Katharina's Portal became the architectural focus of the large garden area in front of the entrance to the museum. Today, the garden and portal are a setting for the Luther's Wedding festival, newlyweds frequently use the portal as a backdrop for wedding photographs and receptions, and it is one of the sites taken in by visitors and pilgrims to the city.

Wittenberg's Schlosskirche and the Lutherhaus museum are located at either end of the old city. The Thesenportal is part of a complex of civil and ecclesiastical symbolism (the castle church), while the Katharinenportal is located in domestic space (the onetime home of Martin Luther and Katharina von Bora). The phallic tower of the castle church dominates the cobbled Schlossplatz, whereas an approach to the Lutherhaus is through an open, green, quiet garden area. Schadow's *Luther*, the heroic monument located in the center of the city, works to unify these domains. In the literal structure of the old city, we find a framing and conjoining of social-cultural domains and symbols: masculine and feminine, political/ecclesiastical and domestic, religious life and family life. In the middle is the Marktplatz—public, civic space. Monumental statuary is an allegorical statement of national narratives and values. The reach of the anchoring figure of a towering Luther in Wittenberg's Marktplazt extends to both the Thesenportal and the Katharinenportal. Here is one possible arraying of these symbols:

	THESENPORTAL	SCHADOW MONUMENT	KATHARINA PORTAL
Location	Castle Church	Marktplatz	Lutherhaus
Principal domain	church	civic	family/heritage
Gender	masculine	masculine	feminine

"Fatherland" (*Vaterland*) in German discourse has two distinct meanings. It can refer to the kingdom of heaven (the domain of the heavenly father) or to state authority. At times, these two meanings have been joined, the Prussian memorials to Luther being a case in point. Consider, for example, the words of the German historian Heinrich von Treitschke, in a publication produced for the 1883 Luther jubilee:

A stranger may inquire in bewilderment how it was possible for such striking contrasts to show themselves in the same human soul. Men wonder how it was possible to combine a capacity for towering anger with a pious and sincere belief, high wisdom with childlike simplicity, deep mysticism with heartfelt enjoyment of life, uncouthness and roughness with the tenderest goodness of heart. . . . We Germans are not puzzled by these apparent contradictions; all we say is, "Here speaks our own blood." From the deep eyes of this uncouth son of a German farmer there flashed the ancient and heroic courage of the Germanic races, a courage which does not flee from the world, but rather seeks to dominate it by the strength of its moral purpose.[17]

During the nineteenth century, the name and image of Luther became a kind of symbolic shorthand through which to bind notions of blood, land, sense of mission, progress, imperialism, enlightenment, and filial duty to God and state.

Another meaning of "Fatherland," however, is in relation to the domestic sphere. The Reformation was more than a theological or political revolution. The Reformers took on sexual revolution—practices considered problematic, such as celibacy and marital infidelity. Licentiousness was a social problem, and Protestants and Catholics alike deemed the institution of marriage as one in need of reform. Luther's wedding to Katharina von Bora, the wedding of a monk and a nun, scandalized many. For the Reformers, it signified and acknowledged the social and religious importance of marriage and family life. In the nineteenth century, this thread of the historical Luther was idealized through pastoral images of romantic love and domestic tranquillity. Luther as husband, father, and family man emerged as a popular subject in painting, Katharina von Bora herself garnered greater interest, and historians and laity turned their attention from Luther's published theological works and publicly performed sermons to his letters and table talks, that is, to the private, domestic sphere.

In Protestant German culture, the figures of Luther and his wife Katharina von Bora were instrumental in the construction and maintenance of gender identities and social roles. Though their status has declined with the declining fortunes of religion, within the Lutheran tradition the couple retains an important place. The "union of Martin and Katie was . . . blessed with the birth of the Protestant parsonage and the rebirth of a genuinely Christian ethos in home and community. Luther's marriage remains to this day the central evangelical symbol of the Reformation's liberation and transformation of the Christian daily life."[18] So concluded the Lutheran theologian-historian William H. Lazareth, writing in 1960. The figure of Luther, in other words, conjoined three cultural domains in Prussian-era Germany. Luther was father of the church, father of the nation, and father of the family.

If at the turn of the twentieth century, the Thesenportal, Schadow's *Luther*, and the Katharinenportal formed a web of signification linking the political, the religious, and the domestic, to what extent has this web remained intact in the contemporary situation? In the wake of world wars, the Holocaust, and scholarship that has drawn lines from Luther to Bismark to Hitler, is a structural rendering of the interrelationship between these three nineteenth-century symbols relevant today? Probably not, at least not at a national level. As Martin Treu noted in conversation, "The question of German identity is a very difficult one to answer. . . . Germans in Europe are quite unsure of who they are. I'm not really sure Luther is really a figure of identification for Germans, or even East Germans." Given that most Germans are not practicing, committed Lutherans, that they are disaffiliated and distanced from the church, and that the figure of Luther is a troubled one, it is worth asking whether and how Schadow's *Luther* remains an anchor of any sense of cohesive identity. And if it does not, then what is meaning and relevance of these UNESCO World Heritage sites? Are the phenomena of heritage tourism, Protestant pilgrimage, and public festivity in Lutherland anachronistic, given that they take place in a scenographic built landscape shaped by nineteenth-century nationalism and traditional gender roles? If the style, history, and ethos of monumental architecture in Wittenberg encodes and coveys primarily political, religious, and gendered narratives and values from over a century ago, do contemporary rites and public performances that use these as setting and stage reinforce or subvert their ideological limitations?

Several decades of critique in the context of dealing with the horrors of the two world wars, along with the secularization of society, have largely broken Luther's connection to the political state. Though one of Germany cultural luminaries, Luther and politics are no longer a happily married couple, as I discussed in chapter 4. But there is another thread in the braiding of Lutherland and Fatherland, one that has received little attention, namely, Luther as the father of children, the husband in a marriage, and the head of a household. Lutherland is still in many ways the land of the father, and festivals, pilgrimage, and tourism in Lutherland are implicated in the performance of gender, a theme I develop in a chapter of the DVD.$^{\odot}$

Communion

St. Paul's Lutheran is located in Oakland, an ELCA church. In October of 2005, pastor Ross Merkel led a group of twenty-five souls on a ten-day tour through

⊙ DVD: Lutherland-Fatherland

the cities of Luther. I met up with the group in Wittenberg, and traveled with them one afternoon to nearby Torgau, the resting place of Katharina von Bora, and home to the first Reformation church, built by the elector John Frederick "the Magnanimous." On the return trip, the discussion turned to "Lutheran identity" and the diversity and differences within the Lutheran community. One theme was communion:

"I attended an Episcopal church in Tokyo for a couple of years. There wasn't a Lutheran church there—there was a Missouri Synod church, but I'm not sure they're considered Lutherans" (laughter).

"I was raised Missouri Synod."

"I was raised Missouri Synod too. My grandparents were Wisconsin—we were Wisconsin and Missouri Synod. My family won't go to church with each other" (laughter).

"They won't commune with each other."

"They won't commune with each other" (laughter). "My aunt will not take communion in an ELCA church. She'll now come, with my mother. But she won't take communion. She wouldn't come for a long time. But now she'll go if there's something important going on, if someone's graduating or getting married or something."

"Confirmation?"

"Confirmation, she'll come. But she won't take communion" (laughter).

Communion can be a divisive issue within the Lutheran family. If altar and pulpit fellowship is a way of marking boundaries within conservative Lutheran circles, communion has for liberal Lutherans been a means of building ecumenical partnerships and recognizing the legitimacy of diverse religious, ethnic, and gendered identities.

In the late 1990s, the ELCA established fellowship with three Reformed churches in the United States, a move that in the same stroke both relaxed and intensified doctrinal differences within the Lutheran community. As a confessional church, that is, a church that finds its identity in the confessions, creeds, and statements of doctrine dating to the sixteenth century, the vote in favor of communion fellowship with some Reformed churches was a significant event. Perhaps it is a sign of a declining interest within "high church" Protestantism in matters of doctrinal propriety and belief, and a revitalization of liturgics and embodied forms of religion.

Communion was a central focus of the St. Paul's congregation. As they made their way through Lutherland, what transformed the trip from sightseeing into pilgrimage was the holding of communion services for the group in Wittenberg, Torgau, and Erfurt. St. Paul's is the only growing Lutheran congregation in the Bay area, in spite of—or perhaps because of—a running engagement with the ELCA hierarchy over issues of gay and lesbian ordination and same-sex marriage. Approximately one-quarter of the congregation is gay, lesbian, or transgender. The church's pastor, Ross Merkel, was defrocked and removed from the ELCA roster in 1995, after making public his long-term gay partnership. His parish refused to let him go.

Lutherland's religious sites can act like empty signifiers or religious voids, but they also provide a medium, arena, or stage for enacting rites. While the tourist industry has established "routes to Luther," and efficiently moves visitors through the region's heritage sites, pilgrims have the ability to cobble together activities and sites of special interest. Rather than being passive receptors of signs, tourists and pilgrims alike have a degree of agency; they do not simply or merely consume, they also produce. Tourism studies typically distinguish between consumption and production, the former focusing on the economic and cultural impacts of tourism on a locale, the later to matters of performativity, mobility, and the creative play of the traveler.

Drawing on Victor Turner's notion of liminality, some scholars have analogized tourism as a form of ritual practice. Turner was interested in the (potentially) universal traits of liminal practices such as pilgrimage, festivity, theatre, and rites of passage. Pilgrimage, argues Turner, has some of the qualities of liminality that characterize passage rites:

> release from mundane structure; homogenization of status; simplicity of dress and behavior; communitas; ordeal; reflection on the meaning of basic religious and cultural values; ritualized enactment of correspondences between religious paradigms and shared human experiences; emergence of the integral person from multiple personae; movement from a mundane center to a sacred periphery which suddenly, transiently, becomes central for the individual . . . movement itself, symbol of communitas, which changes in time, as against stasis, which represents structure.

These features of pilgrimage spill over into some forms of tourism in the modern era. As liminal phenomena, pilgrimage and tourism are occasions that generate "metasocial commentary," allowing for "implicit critique" of the "encompassing social order."[19] Movement and travel become metaphorical means to resist and transform social stasis and structure. Turner's ideas here are relevant to the trip of the St. Paul's congregation.

The St. Paul's communion services in Lutherland's historic churches distinguished their trip from others I observed, pushing the trip in the direction of production rather than consumption. There was something beyond leisure and learning at stake in their trip. The group came as Protest-ants—that is, visiting Lutherland in a spirit of protest against injustices to the gay, lesbian, and transgender community, sublimated as this protest was through museum and church visits, and worship services. The group was able to hold small, intimate communion services, away from the crush of tourists. Though their trip was relatively short, they stayed for an extended time in a few locations, rather than rush to a new site each day. Extending overnight stays slowed the pace, produced the time for special events, and allowed the group to build, through the ELCA Wittenberg Center, some links to the local community. Most pilgrims and tourists take souvenirs home with them—mementoes of places visited. The St. Paul's group left something behind, a trace of their presence in Wittenberg, in the form of a $4,600 donation to a local church-based organization that helps settle East European immigrants in Wittenberg and the surrounding region.

The St. Paul's communion services had the effect of uniting the group not just in Christ but in the tradition that is their faith. In Torgau, the group visited the grave of Katharina von Bora, and dedicated the communion service in Torgau's elegant Schlosskriche to the life and work of Katharina von Bora, in particular her commitment to the family. Communion while on pilgrimage introduced a tactility and silence into a liturgical form that can be dominated by the spoken word, and a gravitas to travel in a place that sometimes feels, as one of the St. Paul's group confessed, "like a Lutheran Disneyland."

At the two communion services I attended, special mention was made of the gay and lesbian community as full members of the church. Through these performative utterances and gestures, a place for the "other" at the communion table, in the geographical and historical places of the Reformation, was a way of affirming full participation for all in the life of the Lutheran Church. A place for the "other" at the communion table was amplified and validated by holding communion in the geographical and historical places that created a faith that historically has been patriarchal in orientation and resistant to accepting people whose sexual orientation deviates from recognized social norms.

Lutherland—Fatherland

The remembered Luther is a prototype of the contemporary traditional father, Katie the contemporary traditional mother, and together they are the prototype of the contemporary, traditional couple. Within Lutheranism, the marriage of Martin and Katie has played an important role in shaping traditional views on sexuality and gender. Through the nineteenth century and into the twentieth, a robust appreciation of domestic, heterosexual life came to characterize Lutheran tradition. In the words of church historian William Lazareth, "Luther's faith was simple enough to trust that after a conscientious day's labor, a Christian father could come home and eat his sausage, drink his beer, play his flute, sing with his children, make love to his wife—all to the greater glory of God."[20] Written in 1960, Lazareth's book offers a revealing glimpse into the way in which the changes wrought to marriage, sexuality, and gender during the Reformation would in time develop into a stable, even intractable complex of ideas, values, and practices connecting heterosexuality, marriage, religion, gender, patriarchy, and domestic life. The end of the 2003 film *Luther* leaves us not with a final image, but, fittingly for a Lutheran-made film, with text.[21] Sandwiched between hagiographical mention of Luther's pushing open the door to religious freedom and his revolutionary impact on education, politics, economics, music, and the German language, we read: "He and Katharina von Bora enjoyed a happy marriage and six children."

Riding the train one day between Weimar and Wittenberg, I stumbled across a passage from one of Luther's letters to his wife that brought the pilgrimage of the St. Paul's group into focus, for me, at any rate:

> Torgau, 27 Feb., 1532, To my beloved housewife Katharin Lutherin, for her own hands. God greet you in Christ! My sweetheart Kate. I hope that if Dr. Bruck gets permission to leave, as he consoles me that he will, I will be able to come with him tomorrow or the day after. Pray to God that he brings us home fresh and healthy. I sleep altogether well, about six or seven hours without waking, and after that two or three hours more. It is the beer's fault, in my opinion. But I am sober. . . . Kiss young Hans for me, and tell little Hans, Lenchen [Magdalena], and Aunt Lena to pray for our dear prince and for me. Even though it is the annual market here in the city, I cannot find anything to buy for the children. If I do not bring anything special, have something on hand for me to give to them.

Fieldworkers are supposed to avoid ethnocentrism, the seeing of the world and others through one's own eyes and images. Reading this passage was a form of culture shock. Usually, that term refers to confusion bred by a profound lack of familiarity. In my case, the confusion was bred by the recognition of a deep similarity and sympathy. It was a odd example of "going native," only I had seen the other, and he was me, or rather the other way around. Fieldwork has a dramatic, narrative pattern to it, and moments of shock, confusion, and distance, but also recognition, identification, and sympathy are part of that pattern. The anthropologist James Clifford describes such moments as "surrealist ethnography"—"that moment in which the possibility of comparison exists in unmediated tension with sheer incongruity."[22] This moment of recognition and identification intensified awareness of my own assumptions. Something I had understood intellectually—what Judith Butler calls the "performance of gender"—was made visceral. The model of father-husband-Doctor-theologian-pastor with the dutiful, committed, concerned, supportive housewife became the model for the newly emerging Lutheranism, and was later emulated in the university, a place first populated by secularized Protestant men. Some of us still emulate it; some of us owe Dr. Martinus a great deal.

Prior to the 10 a.m. Festgottesdienst in the Schlosskirche which I described in chapter 3, the ELCA hosted an English-language Reformation Day service at 8 a.m.[⊙] In spite of utilizing the same lessons and gospel reading as the Festgottesdienst, the ELCA service had a very different feel. The congregation was significantly smaller; most of those participating were from the St. Paul's group. Since most of the congregation knew one another, and were attending as Lutherans, the audience-congregation tension was not as apparent as in the Festgottesdienst. In the sermon delivered from the pulpit, the interim director of the ELCA Center, a bishop of the Evangelical Lutheran Church of America, spoke of an "inner Reformation." "As we continue in God's word, a Reformation can happen within us as well. We can become free enough to change things in our family, in our community, in our church." The words pointed to the power of the word to produce loving change, but the sermon was free of actual content. The service then moved from the elevated pulpit to the smaller lectern, where Ross Merkel offered prayers to those present, to a safe journey home, and to victims of natural disasters. Prayers were then opened up to the congregation, democratizing the service, and in so doing the call for change and reform was given concrete substance. One of the prayers uttered was: "May God continue to work with us to welcome in those who the church continues to exclude: the poor, the elderly, the disabled, the forgotten, gays and lesbians, too. Hear us O God." One of the central issues faced by Christian churches of all stripes is the place, role, and status of gays and lesbians in the church and society.

Among the congregants that morning was an LCMS member from Texas. When the prayer above was offered, he physically twisted the bulletin in his hands, angered, I presumed, at the prayer for the gay and lesbian community. Speaking the next day with him about the service, he commented: "I thought it was going to be an ELCA service. Even the ELCA doesn't tolerate homosexual

⊙ DVD: Worship–ELCA Service

pastors." When we turn from considering the place and the gaze to practices and performances, we discover that Wittenberg, rather than focusing and fixing meanings of Luther, constellates a variety of at times conflicting visions of what Luther and the Reformation mean.

The ELCA Center runs what is called a Lutheran identity program for incoming tour and pilgrim groups. As the former director of the center, Twila Shock, explains, the program "hopes to convey some core tenants, but what these become in interaction is open ended. Sometimes Lutheran identity doesn't necessarily mean people come away having a better understanding of justification by grace through faith. What it might mean is coming away with the understanding that, 'Oh my goodness, it means something very different to be a Lutheran in India than it does in Argentina.' There is an incarnational dynamic." Wittenberg draws Lutherans, but Lutherans are a diverse, global bunch, and recognition of this fact may be an outcome of a visit to the "authentic site of the Reformation." It may happen that, without intending it or wanting it, someone opposed to the ordination of women is in the pew when a woman ascends the pulpit. Travel to Wittenberg has the potential to present "metasocial commentaries" to individuals who might not otherwise be in positions to reflect on the processual implications of a faith grounded in protest and reformation.

The day after the Reformation Day service, on All Saints Day, the St. Paul's group held a communion service in the Stadtkirche. Pastor Ross Merkel ascended the pulpit and, over Luther's grave, delivered an impassioned sermon on the theme of "those left behind."⊙ The reference was to the thought of Tim LaHaye and Jerry Jenkins, who have written a series of apocalyptic novels that emphasize the how the wrath of God will rain down on those who do not toe their fundamentalist line. But the implicit reference was to the church's persistent policy of excluding gays and lesbians in general (if no longer by the letter, as is the case with the ELCA, still often in spirit), and from ordination and marriage in particular. Here was Ross Merkel preaching in Luther's church over Luther's grave—Luther, the prototypical father and straight man—about injustices and prejudices based on sexual discrimination, rejecting a worldview and value set that would make gays and lesbians among those "left behind." To top it off, sitting in the pews was one of the bishops who had voted in 1994 to strip Merkel of his ordination, after he made public his gay partnership.

Some Protestants say the Reformation is not yet, and never will be, complete; far fewer are willing to make attitudes and policies surrounding sexuality,

⊙ DVD: Lutherland-Fatherland

gender, and marriage part of this ongoing Reformation. The Reformation was driven in part by radical changes to conceptions of sexuality and gender. Lutherland need not be a place that reinforces traditional practices and beliefs with the weight of tradition. Rather, it is a site of transformation and change, and to remain true to its spirit of reform is to bring that spirit to bear on entrenched views about marriage, sexuality, and women's roles. The St. Paul's pilgrimage embodied this spirit, a spirit Paul Tillich called the Protestant Principle.

Appendix A: Processing Change

Since the Prussian era, much has changed in the celebration of the Reformation. In general, the trajectory has moved from officious ceremony to carnivalesque play. I have attempted to map these changes, with reference to Robert Wuthnow's conceptualization of public ritual, in terms of three social sectors: voluntary organizations, which include the church and Wittenberg's Vereine, such as the Cranach Foundation; the state, which we can further divide into civil and civic domains; and the market.

Once built around a mythic image of Luther as father of religious, domestic, and civil society, the tight braid between ecclesiastical and civil rites has been broken. Luther is an economic, religious, and cultural resource for a region continuing to deal with the problems and promises of reunification; but he is also now a troubled figure. For the church, Luther remains foundational; for civil society, he is of far less importance than he was a century ago, though he is still on the cultural map. For civic society, for the region, Luther is of central importance, a cultural and economic resource. In each of these social-cultural domains, memories of Luther are somewhat conflicted: Luther is both resource/ancestor and scar. Reformation festivals and heritage do include conferences and exhibits that attempt to deal with questions about the darker side of Wittenberg's best-known citizen. Those outside official institutions play their role too, their thoughts literally coloring the public spaces of Luther festivity, in the form of graffiti and paint bombs. The tension between Luther as scar and Luther as resource is palpable.

A second change in public ritual is found in the prominence of market performances. Today, Luther celebrations are driven by the market, and the outdoor, open-air performances of the medieval market spectacle do not always rest easy with the ritualized intentions of both church and civic society. The postmodernist scene of a crowd accidentally blocking the processional route, for example, upstaged the procession of the Academic Senate on Reformation Day, 2005. The crowd had gathered to watch Colombians and Peruvians dressed in Plains Indian garb, dancing a "native" dance, and playing Zamphir on the pan-flute; the gathered onlookers unwittingly forced the Senate to the edge of the street, where they squeezed by, with hardly a glance cast their way, and continued down the street. Reformation Day is not what it once was. The kaiser would never have been pushed off the street.

A third shift in Reformation festivity in Wittenberg is found in the confluence of the market and community organizations such as the Lucas Cranach Foundation and Art School, and this shift has created competition for ecclesiastical and civic religion. "Art," reads one of the postcards in the Cranach printing shop, "is what moves the soul of man." "No symbol other than religion," reads the graffiti painted on a poster advertising an art exhibit held in another of Luther's cities, Erfurt, that dealt with the symbolization of the German oak in nineteenth- and twentieth-century art. While the church is hanging on to Luther's theology of grace, trying to uplift the festivals through gospel music imported from America, struggling to reconcile commitment to an ancestor deeply implicated in difficult questions that hang over acts of memory in Germany, the Cranachhaus is a swirl of energy, activity, and enthusiasm. In twenty or thirty years, perhaps, if you travel to Wittenberg in June, you will be visiting the city of Lucas Cranach, and have the opportunity to attend Cranach's, rather than Luther's, Wedding.

Some churched individuals from Wittenberg and elsewhere—such as the American-based WEM and ELCA—are concerned over the secular nature of festivals associated with the name of Martin Luther and the event of the Reformation. Wild hair, leather, tattoos, heavy buckles, and pipe and drum music signify to some a regressive revisiting of pre-Christian pagan culture. But, like it or not, the carnivalesque, medieval Marktplatz is the driving force of contemporary Luther celebrations. The market is threatening to take control of Luther, or run past him all together, and the church wants its man back. Some conservative American Lutherans visiting the city on Reformation Day are taken aback by the Halloween parties thrown in a couple of downtown bars. The WEM introduces the renewal of vows service to "uplift" the festival. The procession of the confirmands on Reformation Day is partly an attempt to reinscribe the festival with its traditionally religious basis. In 2005, the planning committee of Luther's Wedding, under the influence of the Lutherzentrum, invited not the Dixieland and jazz bands of past years to headline the Saturday night concert in the Marktplatz, but a soul and gospel group: the Budapest Ragtime Orchestra was out, the American Jackson Family Singers in. The gospel theme was reinforced with gospel hymns, performed in English, at Sunday worship in the Schlosskirche—moves made to try and push the festival in the direction of what is taken to be Luther's chief discovery: salvation by grace through faith. In the end, however, it was a performance of Dylan's "Blowin' in the Wind" that created a feeling of communitas in the Marktplatz.

The church in Wittenberg and other cities of Luther faces a double bind of sorts. On one hand, Luther is the goose that laid the golden egg. Hotels offer Luther packages, restaurants offer Luther dinner theatre. For the church to harshly criticize the commercialization of its founding father is to distance itself even further from a populace hungry for economic revitalization and the simple pleasures of a night out, or festive celebration. On the other hand, Luther is part of Lutheran identity, and the commoditization of Luther can only be taken so far until it runs up against resistance. To make a mockery of Luther—one person, tongue in cheek, told me that in next year's yellow pages there will be a heading titled "Rent-a-Luther"—and to dumb Luther down to beer and bodily functions (I mean this quite literally: a line from an ad for a three-act Luther dinner theatre reads, presumably quoting Luther, "Why are you not passing wind and belching, is the food not satisfying?")—to use Luther simply as the occasion for fun and good times is to make a mockery of the church, and promote values that the church does not necessarily endorse.

An important question related to the changing dynamics of Luther-occasioned rites and performances is to what extent these actions are instruments of change, rather than merely passive reflectors of change. Do rites and performance merely formalize or reinforce social and other changes effected by other means and forces? Or do they have transformative power? In Victor Turner's terminology, is contemporary Luther festivity ceremony or ritual? There is no simple answer to such questions, other than, "it depends." In any large-scale festival there exists a mix of ritual and performance genres, and a diverse variety of individuals and groups; questions of ritual dynamics must be considered on a case-by-case basis.

Demonstrating casual links between the enactment of a particular rite and or performance, on the one hand, and cultural dynamics, on the other, is tricky business. An important question, however, is: Why does one want to demonstrate such links? The desire to identify the practical results of ritual and performance is partly driven by the need to appear useful, which means, given the dominance of positivistic, scientific paradigms, to develop interpretations of ritual that have explanatory and predictive power. Further, the desire to explain a rite's function is based on the premise that ritual, if it is to be of any value, must be able to do some sort of "work." The metaphor of ritual work comes from the sciences, on the one hand (and is related to notions of energy, power, force, a muscular, getting-thing-done kind of language), and the world of labor, on the other. The language of research and theory metaphorically positions the academic in the realm of science. This study has not been about creating predictive or explanatory models of ritual. Rather, my aim has been to insert the reader/viewer into the action comprising Luther-themed festivity and tourism, and to offer critical and interpretive readings of that action.

I have suggested that Wittenberg's Luther festivals, on the whole, variously affect or attempt to affect social-cultural-religious dynamics. The festivals, for example, are not reflections of conviviality—they are the very thing. The Cranach entry in the Wedding parade in 2005 was aimed at building momentum, money, and interest in the Cranach monument that would come to be in 2006. The procession of the confirmands attempts to inscribe Reformation Day celebrations with faith. A Blues Night on Reformation Day elides the importance of Luther to the city. The renewal of vows ceremony may not actually uplift the carnivalesque nature of the Luther's Wedding festival, but it attempts to; more to the point, it uplifts or redeems the festival for some, while others (most of those attending, in fact) see in the renewal of vows ceremony little of importance, if they see it at all. My own view is that the renewal ceremony helps constellate a "Carnival versus Lent" dynamic; those worshiping inside and those making the noise outside need one another. The festivals then are not merely passive reflectors of society, they are integral to the social-cultural life of the region. As with any complicated public rites and performances, it is impossible to provide any single functional or theoretical explanation of their workings.

Appendix B: The Camera, Theory, and Method

"Participant observation" is a catch-all phrase for a methodological approach. The researcher shows up, makes contacts, establishes rapport, observes, participates, asks questions, has conversations, takes photographs or video, collects primary source material (programs, posters, artifacts), tapes interviews, and jots or writes out notes in a field journal. The sprawling, fast-paced action of the Wittenberg festivals made detailed note taking an impractical strategy, so I relied on digital video to document the events. I shot the surfaces, speeches, colors, music, sounds, places, and bodies of the festivals, and this documentation became the data for my analysis. Rarely did I feel that participants experienced the presence of a camera as a violation, and so, following the good advice of a former professor, I "shot bravely." I also shot a lot, and working with the data required that it be organized in some fashion.

Description, analysis, theorizing—these are the three big steps of classical ethnography, and field-based study in general. These doings of the researcher define the kind of knowledge sought and produced: descriptive knowledge; structural-relational knowledge; explanatory-conceptual knowledge. Focused on a particular rite or cultural performance, these three steps entail: detailed documentation and description; understanding the functions, purposes, and meanings of a rite or performance; and interpreting or theorizing how the rite or performance works. In practice, however, these steps are rarely climbed one after the other. Theory and method always interpenetrate.

FIGURE B.I. The author, filming in Wittenberg. Photograph by Ronald Grimes.

Going out the gate, the imagination of what one is doing when entering the field shapes data. Documenting primarily with a video camera, for example, rather than by way of notes in a field journal, is connected to my immersion in scholarly works and discussions rife with terms like *scene, performance, enactment, behavior, reflexivity, play, front stage,* and *social drama.* Lutherland, I imagined before setting out, was a geographical place but also a cultural stage; the place was a scene, the camera was a way to shoot the action and actors.

What is at stake here is perhaps made clearer by comparison with Don Handelman's short study of the Palio festival in Siena.[1] In the first few pages, Handelman offers a description of the Palio, a centuries-old Italian festival built around a horse race. Terms such as *subsystem, structures, stratification, scale, connections, parts, axes, models, unit, levels,* and *position* are scattered throughout the description. This is the metaphorical language of structuralism. The point is that theory plants itself down into description. Stripping oneself of theoretical (metaphorical, imaginative, foundational) assumptions at the stage of method is an impossibility. The theoretical and methodological approach guiding both my fieldwork and analysis of the Wittenberg festivals is drawn from scholars who use a performative or dramatistic approach (rather than a structuralist one—the two are often theoretical competitors) to ritual and public events.

In my way of thinking, if fieldwork and method are a stage in scholarly production, this means not a level or point in one's research, but a role-playing within a certain framed space. While in Wittenberg, I spent most of my time in the old town, rarely venturing outside the geographical space marked out by the one-time existence of old city walls. The city of 50,000 bears the name Lutherstadt, but the concentration of Luther and Reformation material culture is localized in a geographical space than can be circled on foot in less than an hour. This space is the stage on which the performance of the Reformation takes place, and academic study is part of the performance. "Oh, here comes the fieldwork guy," one group of consultants would tease whenever I showed up and tagged along. The group members would at times reflexively talk of "playing tourist," and they reminded me that I too was playing a certain role. I was one of the actors circulating in the specially framed space of Lutherland. Part of Wittenberg's revitalization involves hosting academic culture and events, in the form of conferences, museum exhibits, lectures, and special programs at the once-prestigious Wittenberg University. Academics, like pilgrims and cultural tourists, travel to and perform in Wittenberg.

My carrying a camera, and a rather fancy one at that, influenced my participation. As I was often mistaken for a journalist, performers would ham it up before the camera; television camera operators and reporters would strike up conversations (often turning out to be excellent sources of information); and organizers, security staff, and ritual leaders would often grant me special access and position in order to film. The camera had the mysterious power to confer status on a rite or performance; the camera was itself a kind of actor. On several occasions (word gets around about what business one is up to) I was approached by people wanting me to record their impressions of the festival; putting thoughts on tape, I suppose, gives them an aura of facticity. When given permission to film a dinner theatre based on Luther's table talks, the actors felt my presence would be less intrusive if I dressed in historical costume. I became Justas Jonas (d. 1555), the reasoning being that I am, as Jonas was, a doctor of the university; moreover, the hotel I was staying in was once Jonas's home, located across the square from the Schlosskirche.

Festivals and pilgrimage sites are visually compelling, so the use of visual media for documentation and data collection makes sense. But a comprehensive process of data collection and observation of lived religion requires tending to the full range of the human sensorium. The sensual variety of the Wittenberg festivals includes: the tastes and smells of food and drink (and, on occasion, vomit); the blaring of trumpets and pounding of drums; the rhythms of jazz and the cantatas of Bach; the baking of bread, the odor of roast pig, and the cool, musty air of a twelfth-century church; the cadence of a marching drum-and-pipe band, and the crunching of broken beer bottles under one's feet. As paradoxical as it sounds, using video to document ritual and perform-ance need not privilege the visual. Rather, the combination of film and synchro-nous audio can encourage an appreciation of the multisensory nature of social life-worlds.⊙ Looking through a camera is not necessarily a voyeuristic gazing from a distance. In a shot of a bubbling pot of soup, one can see the food, hear the cooking, and almost feel the heat and smell the aroma; in a long, lingering shot of a communion table, the presence of bread and wine lead to matters of the tongue, taste, and the body. The visual evokes tactility and the kinesthetic sense. The visual "is equally a pathway to the nonvisible, and to the larger domain of feelings, intellect, and the remaining senses. . . . The individual is involved [in film] as a thinking and feeling person, but also as a body in relation to other bodies, to objects, to time, space, and place, and to the narratives of social interaction."[2]

In documenting the festival, I deliberately choose hotel rooms from which I had a bird's eye, photogenic view of events. I also walked the festival grounds. In an effort to cover as much festival territory as possible, I would at times liter-ally run, camera in hand, from one event to another. The view from on high and the running and scrambling for position in the thick of the crowd were two forms of observing; the former more observational and at-a-distance, the latter, more participatory—in tight, close, rubbing shoulders, one of the crowd or con-gregation. My observational style mirrored what I take to be a sound analytical approach: moving in close, giving attention to detail, backing out and up, to gain distance and perspective.

Once cumbersome monstrosities, video cameras are now easy to handle; just "point and click." Some academics, being self-reflexive animals, are quick to note that someone is always doing the pointing, and they probably have a good point. The images of film or photography are not raw data, since the cam-era operator is not transparently seeing what takes place, but actively looking. The manner in which the person behind the camera looks is a complex matter. How and where do you place yourself in relation to the action? How willing are you to get a particular shot? What kinds of things do you shoot? Do you wait for the cloud to pass, the rain to stop, or for the clock to strike twelve in order to have a "better" shot? Should a shot use wide angle, zoom, varying focal lengths, filters, tripods, camera harnesses? The ethnographer who uses digital video in the field may or may not give much thought to such questions; the answers given may be implicit or made on the fly, but they are constitutive of experi-ence, meaning, and knowledge. Film and photography are inherently reflexive:

⊙ DVD: Extras—Sensory Overload

"Corporeal images are not just the images of other bodies; they are also images of the body behind the camera and its relation to the world."[3] Watching the DVD material that accompanies this book, you see a record of bodies in motion; implicitly (occasionally, explicitly) you also see my body. Look closely and you will detect my movement, my foci of attention and lacunae, where and how I located myself (literally and metaphorically) in relation to my subjects.

Shooting and framing ritual and performance with a camera both enlarges and diminishes vision. Filming involves foregrounding a particular thing against a background, to call attention to it, to emphasize it, while simultaneously sacrificing background connections of no interest to (or unknown to) the person behind the camera. Even though a camera shot foregrounds, and thus selectively removes objects, buildings, and bodies, film and video nevertheless fill in more than does a text. The wealth of detail in a single photograph may require a dozen pages of written description. Moreover, textual description is once removed from the image; translation from image to text is a process of abstraction and translation. Film and photography, on the other hand, are analogues of the visual, not translations, and hence closer to sensate reality, to the tactility of surfaces. In reading a text, the imagination fills in a great deal; with film, a street becomes a particular street, bodies become particular bodies—this one face.

My combining text and DVD in studying the performance of the Reformation raises many questions. What, for example, "can pictorial images convey that words cannot? How do film images mean?"[4] The philosopher Bertrand Russell distinguishes between knowledge by acquaintance and knowledge by description. Film or video, I suggest, has the power to acquaint us with people, places, events, emotions, sounds. Film has presence; it is evocative. Film inserts both the fieldworker and viewer into a place and into people's lives in a manner that a text can rarely, certainly not easily, match. Film takes a step toward a more unified field of experience and knowledge, incorporating the visual, the verbal, the kinesthetic, and the acoustic in a single medium. As the viewer engages with the multisensory world of film, the object of study becomes more of a subject, figured, textured, and placed.

When Clifford Geertz calls for "thick description" as the methodological basis for field study, he is demanding that ethnographic accounts be richly detailed, rooted in the setting, scenes, and lives encountered in the field. One reason driving Geertz's desire for thick description is that good theory requires good data. This is not his only reason, however; theory building is important, but not all. Geertz writes that "the essential vocation of interpretive anthropology is not to answer our deepest questions, but to make available to us answers that others, guarding other sheep in other valleys, have given, and thus to include them in the consultable record of what man [sic] has said."[5] Good humanist that he is, Geertz holds that such representational work has moral value. Film has an important contribution to make here. The knowledge acquired from images is an affective, experiential, and mimetic knowing. Film makes available not just what people say, but how they look, how they move, the places they inhabit; the consultable record of film is inherently thick.

Ethnographies, whether textual or filmic, vary in their styles and aims. Some move toward assertions, conclusions, and theory building; in others, theory is a side issue, the chief aim being to present to the reader a sense of having been there, to communicate the encounter and the conversations. The best varieties of the former type advance our understanding of the workings of social-cultural life; increase our predictive powers; apply, test, and revise theories in relation to the concrete case. The worst simply reproduce existing theories, constricting, rather than expanding understanding, proving the theory correct like a dog chasing its tail. The best of the later type are informed by the genres of travel writing, autobiography, or documentary film; they present to the reader, through the eyes, voice, and experiences of the individual ethnographer (and, usually his or her subjects) a previously unknown or little-known world; ethnographic materials mediate life-worlds. The worst are simply vehicles for the authors to explore their own self, interests, and affectations; the setting is not valued for its own sake; there is little sense of an encounter with otherness, a lack of receptivity, and a failure to see the intricacies of surfaces and to sink into the ground on which one walks. This study, as is the case with many ethnographic-based books, combines elements of these two ideal types: It is not the best example of thick description, but neither is it a collage of personal reflection.

For the fieldworker, the aim, again to quote Geertz, is neither to "become natives" but "to converse with them, a matter a great deal more difficult, and not only with strangers, than is commonly recognized."[6] Geertz acknowledges that the encounter with other cultures, other ideas and values, may serve to expand, clarify, or critique our own. Part of doing fieldwork and cultural interpretation entails openness to the possibility that we may indeed be moved by (or repulsed by) a work of art, the enactment of a rite, our conversations with others. In representing the details and events of individual and group life, ethnography straddles the slippery border between fact and fiction. In writing up field notes or editing video, a move is made from telling and describing to showing and enacting. The ancient Greeks called this move *mimesis*, as opposed to *diegesis*. The former is not simply imitation, as it often understood in aesthetics, but refers to representational forms that include "make-believe, pretend, and ways of pretending."[7] Mimesis takes place in the subjunctive mood.

Contemporary scholarship refers to the performative qualities of ethnographic based texts as "writing culture." Ethnographers are not simply observers and presenters of information; they employ literary tropes, narrative forms, and styles that have a determinative impact on knowledge. Ethnographically informed writings are "fictions; fictions, in the sense that they are 'something made, something fashioned'—the original meaning of *fictio*—not that they are false, unfactual, or merely 'as if' thought experiments."[8]

There is desire in mimesis. As Walter Benjamin describes it, mimesis is the "urge . . . to get hold of an object at very close range by way of its likeness, its reproduction." For Benjamin, miming, copying, representing, imitating are rooted in the desire to know the other. In copying or imitating, "a palpable, sensuous connection between the very body of the perceiver and the perceived" is made possible.[9] Consider "A Beer for Martin." I chose to begin my representation of the Reformation Day festival with a rather off-center moment, a small slice of a festival whose dominant ethos (at least historically) is ecclesiastical and liturgical. In so doing, I am enacting in writing a narrative about the festival. The piece of street theatre caught my eye, ear, and belly; it got hold of me, and my writing it up is my attempt to get hold of it, even elevate to a position others may feel it does not deserve. A part of me identifies with the Spielleute, their stories and antics. Representing in writing their poking fun at Luther is a way to craft a connection between perceiver and perceived, between me and them. Witnessing the scene has led me to frame an approach to the festivals in terms of distinctions (even tensions) between high and low culture, between the rites and performances of the church and those that take place in the streets.

The traditions and cannons of scientistic objectivism balk at the pseudo-mysticism of this mimetic urge and its presumed power to generate "palpable, sensuous connections." (As Benjamin recognized, there is a secularized version of sympathetic magic implied here, a topic to which I shall return.) Moralists see in it a disturbing academic imperialism: In representing a performance, I fix it in words, capture it, in effect, and hence control it. Following the thought of Michael Taussig, who is turn indebted to Benjamin, I want to try to redeem the mimetic faculty from such criticisms, flesh out its implications for studying and theorizing ritual and performance, and develop a framework for thinking about a more developed role for visual technologies and media, one that moves our conception and use of them beyond the realist concerns of data collection.

In the past twenty years, much ink has been spilled in anthropology and allied disciplines and fields over the process and politics of representation and translation. For one, representation requires elimination; the researcher can never hope to fold everything observed, photographed, filmed, or taped in the field into their descriptions and analysis. A written chapter on a festival is clearly not the same thing as a festival; nor is a festival a text—the text is many steps removed from the real thing. Debates over representation and translation also include discussion of asymmetrical power relations between the field-worker and his or her subjects. The issue, as Geertz puts it, cutting to the heart of the matter, is whether "one sees poking into the lives of people who are not in a position to poke into yours as something of a colonial relic."[10] The location of my fieldwork, coupled with my focus on public events, pushed this issue somewhat into the background. Nevertheless, in both text and film, I am representing real events, describing and quoting real people, and offering interpretations, theories, and even criticism of their doings.

The recognition over the past twenty years that ethnographic writing and filming employs the mimetic faculty has been the bugbear of field-based scholarship. We are now aware that "once the mimetic faculty has sprung into being, a terrifically terrifying power is established; there is born the power to represent the world, yet the same power is a power to falsify, mask, and pose. The two powers are inseparable." Michael Taussig, whom I am quoting here, sees in the mimetic faculty the "prospects for a sensuous knowledge in our time, a knowledge that in adhering to the skin of things through realist copying disconcerts and entrances by spinning off into fantastic formation." These prospects are, however, entangled in the fact that mimesis is caught up in a naïve faith in human powers of representation, coupled with a history of conceptual and other forms of colonization. Mimesis (or representation) "is said to pertain to forced ideologies or representation crippled by illusions pumped into our nervous systems by social constructions of Naturalism and Essentialism. Indeed, mimesis has become that dreaded, absurd, or merely tiresome Other, that straw-man against whose feeble pretensions poststructuralists [a species of which is made up of postmodernists] prance and strut."[11]

Postmodernism, in acknowledging the pervasiveness of mimesis in human life, throws the proverbial baby out with the bathwater, refusing to play the mimetic game for fear of getting it wrong in trying to get it right. Representation becomes the great enemy, and postmodernists spare no effort at being nonrepresentational; they speak, but are at pains to not to "speak of" and certainly not "for" anyone. Postmodernist ethnographic writing is thus based on the model of the montage or collage; it plays with a surrealist juxtaposition of images, emphasized decenteredness, eschews the elucidation of symbolic meanings in favor of an endlessly receding deferral of meaning; it tends to blur boundaries and frames, seeks out edges and margins rather than centers, and labors over moral, political, and philosophical questions lying at the heart of field-based research.

The black hole analogy is truly apt in studying festivity. Black holes, so physicists tell us, may link alternate universes, function as a time portal, look like wiggling strings, and may not (as once thought) collapse to a singularity, but spew out a swirling, rotating ring or vortex of neutrons (neutral particles) that has been described with reference to the "Looking Glass of Alice."[12] The black hole is a postmodern object par excellence. If such a thing did not exist, a creative postmodernist would surely have invented it. A festival is akin to a black hole—a montage of images, a play and juxtaposition of ideas and performances, a spread-out, swirling din of sound, flashes of color, waves of smells. Festivity—global, cosmopolitan, sprawling, spinning, mediated, complicated— can play into postmodernist sensibilities and writing styles. The danger is that the collage or montage becomes the model and style for studying and writing about contemporary festivity, replacing thick description, explication, theorizing, and criticism. Festival-goers wander about the grounds, tasting this bit of food, trying that drink, purchasing an item here and there, attending this or that performance. Field researchers do this too, and they should; they should spin, and swirl, and taste, and mingle—and they should do so with the camera running. I did. But after the spinning, one stops, tries to get one's bearings, and makes maps; that a map is not the landscape is self-evident—but, if drawn with care, maps help us find our way about. Mapping the festivals in terms of cultural domains—ecclesia, civilitas, and civitas—is an intuitive way to impose some order on unwieldy events.

Appendix C: Timeline, Luther and Wittenberg

1483   Luther born in Eisleben
1490   Prince Frederick the Wise starts construction on the castle
          church, and begins acquiring a collection of holy relics for
          its chapel
1502   Wittenberg University founded by Frederick the Wise
1505   Luther enters the Order of Augustinian Hermits, in
          Erfurt
1505   Lucas Cranach (b. 1472) arrives in Wittenberg
1508   Luther is sent to Wittenberg by the Augustinians
1512   Luther receives his doctorate in theology from the University
          of Wittenberg, and is appointed lecturer in theology
1517   Luther pens the ninety-five theses
1546   Luther dies in Eisleben
1586   Giordano Bruno arrives in Wittenberg, and lectures for two
          years at the university
1600   Shakespeare pens *Hamlet*; in the play, Hamlet had attended
          the University of Wittenberg
1617   First Reformation jubilee, celebrated in Wittenberg
1808   Goethe's masterpiece *Faust* is published; Goethe sets Faust's
          home in Wittenberg
1817   The Predigerseminar, a training institute for clergy, is
          founded in Wittenberg
1817   Lutheran and Reformed churches in Prussia begin merging,
          forming the Union Church

1817   The universities of Wittenberg and Halle are merged, and the campus in Wittenberg closes

1821   Schadow's *Luther Denkmal* (monument) erected in Wittenberg's Marktplatz

1820s   Wittenberg emerges as a *genius loci* in the religious and national landscape of Germany

1856   The bronze Theses Door is installed in the Schlosskirche

1883   Lutherhalle (museum) is opened; jubilee year (400th anniversary of Luther's birth)

1918   The Luther Society is founded in Wittenberg

1933   Nazi party officials and church leaders participate in the celebration of the 450th anniversary of Luther's birth

1933   The German National Synod holds its first meeting in Wittenberg

1933   The University of Halle is renamed Martin Luther University Halle-Wittenberg

1935   Gerhart Hauptmann publishes his play *Hamlet in Wittenberg*

1945   Defeat of Nazi Germany

1948   The Evangelische Akademie is founded in Wittenberg

1983   Wittenberg hosts, and the government of the DDR actively designs, the 500th jubilee of Luther's birth

1989   The Wende; Friedrich Schorlemmer, pastor of Wittenberg's Stadtkirche, plays an instrumental role in the Peaceful Revolution

1990   The Lucas Cranach Institute is founded in Wittenberg

1991   The Luther Gedenkstätten (Luther Memorials Foundation) is founded, headquartered in Wittenberg

1994   The first Luther's Wedding festival is held in Wittenberg

1995   The Leucorea, affiliated with the University of Halle-Wittenberg, is founded in Wittenberg

1996   The Wittenberg English Ministry is founded

1999   ELCA Center Wittenberg opens its doors

2001   The Institute for Christian Art is founded in Wittenberg

2007   With the aid of the Lutheran Missouri Synod, SELK purchases and begins renovations on an old high school, with the aim of returning an "authentically" Lutheran church to Wittenberg

2008   The city of Wittenberg announces the Luther Decade, building momentum toward the 500th jubilee, in 2017, of Luther's "posting" of the ninety-five theses, the act that launched the Reformation

Notes

INTRODUCTION

1. John Calvin, the other Reformer to make the *Life* list, was fortieth.

2. The German *Wende* is often rendered into English as "peaceful revolution," though the term literally means "change." The term refers to moments of great import in history.

3. Wittenberg's Stadtkirche (town church) is sometimes referred to as Luther's church, since Luther preached most of his sermons from the pulpit of the Stadtkirche.

4. Wittenberg, as the seat of the German Reformation, has long been a destination of churchmen, artists, politicians. Its university was one of Europe's finest during the sixteenth and seventeenth centuries. The notables to have lived, studied, or passed through Wittenberg include Giordano Bruno, Lucas Cranach, Johann Faust, Peter the Great, and Johann Wolfgang Goethe.

5. In German, the term *Evangelisch* does not carrying the connotations and implications of the English "evangelical." The term refers to churches with a Lutheran heritage.

6. Bakhtin, *Dialogic Imagination*, 7.

7. The performance was directed by Fernando Scarpa, and the event gave birth to Bühne Wittenberg, a local theatre company.

8. The Nazi state officially granted the city of Wittenberg the title Lutherstadt in 1938.

9. Grimes, *Rite out of Place*, 35.

CHAPTER 1

1. "A portal is any gate or doorway insofar as it elicits ritual actions or becomes a locus for architectural symbolism. . . . Since a portal often

separates a sacred precinct from a profane one or a regulated from an unregulated zone, it is both a termination and beginning point. As a structure that is both inside and outside the same zone, it is a site of considerable ambivalence, attracting dangerous as well as beneficent forces" (Grimes, *Reading, Writing, and Ritualizing,* 67).

2. Basso, *Wisdom Sits in Places,* 7.

3. Scribner, *Popular Culture and Popular Movements in Reformation Germany,* 302.

4. Smith, "Numismatic Perspective," 197.

5. Jones, *Hermeneutics of Sacred Architecture,* vol. 1, xxviii; 41; emphasis in original.

6. Ibid., 191; emphasis in original.

7. SELK stands for Selbständige Evangelische Lutheranische Kirche, the "independent" or "free-standing" Lutheran church. The origins of SELK date to the early nineteenth century, when the Prussian state created a Union Church out of Lutheran and Reformed Landeskirchen.

8. Difficult economic times are likely to continue for some time in the former East Germany. As I put the finishing touches on this manuscript, global financial markets are tumbling.

9. I have placed the English translation of the published theses into the beggar's mouth (Dillenberger, *Martin Luther,* 494).

10. Burke, *Dramatism and Development,* 22.

11. Schieffelin, "Problematizing Performance," 194.

12. Burke, *A Grammar of Motives,* 14.

13. Greenwood, "Culture by the Pound," 178.

14. Eric Cohen provides a concise summary of theories and critiques of cultural commoditization that accompanies the production of tourist locales: "tourism is said to lead to 'commoditization' of areas of local community life. In particular, 'colorful' local costumes and customs, rituals and feasts, and folk and ethnic arts become tourist services or commodities, as they come to be performed or produced for touristic consumption. . . . Commoditization allegedly changes the meaning of cultural products and of human relations, making them eventually meaningless. . . . Further-more . . . since local culture can be commoditized by anyone, without the consent of the participants, it can be destroyed, and the local people exploited. . . . Commoditiza-tion is said to destroy the authenticity of local cultural products and human relations. It is replaced with a surrogate, covert, 'staged authenticity' in which contrived cultural events are staged for tourists. 'Staged authenticity' is said to thwart the tourists' genuine desire for authentic experiences. . . . Commoditization, engendered by tourism, allegedly destroys not only the meaning of cultural products for the locals, but paradoxically, also for tourists and that tourism is therefore a 'colossal deception.'" (Cohen, "Authenticity and Commodification in Tourism," 372–373.) Cohen recognizes the relevance of the commoditization critique, but his studies of tourism also push beyond this all too common approach.

15. Shepherd, "Commodification, Culture and Tourism," 185.

16. Goethe, *Italian Journey,* 390.

17. Ludic is an adjective meaning "playful." The term derives from the Latin verb *ludus*, "to play." The notion of thinking of social-cultural life and ritual in terms of play was developed by the Dutch historian and cultural theorist Johan Huizinga in his book *Homo Ludens* (1938), literally, "Man the Player."

CHAPTER 2

1. Among liberals in postwar Germany, a common interpretation of the division of the country into East and West by allied powers at the end of the Second World War has been that the act was punishment for the rise of Hitler, the waging of war, and the Holocaust.

2. The conditions that led to the collapse of communism and the roles played by various social institutions and individuals is a history far too complex (and contested) to summarize here. Equally complex are the social, political, economic, cultural, and religious changes that have taken place in the former East Germany since 1989. For those interested in dipping a toe in the vast literature of post-Wende Germany, with special reference to events in and around Wittenberg, see Schorlemmer, *Die Wende in Wittenberg*, and Rock, ed., *Voices in Times of Change*. Friedrich Schorlemmer was the pastor of Wittenberg's Stadtkirche in the years leading up to and following the collapse of communism.

3. Schechner, *Performance Theory*, 7. The notion of performance can be understood in many ways. In this study, I tend to follow Schechner's definition of performance as "an activity done by an individual or group in the presence of and for another individual or group" (*Performance Theory*, 22). Schechner bases this definition of performance on "certain acknowledged qualities of live theatre, the most stable being the audience-performer interaction." In applying the notion of performance to the study of public festivity, Schechner's emphasis on public "display" is relevant. At festival time, individuals and groups put their doings on display, performing on literal or metaphoric public stages. People watch. The element of display applies to liturgical rites, as well. Ordinarily, a church worship service is not a performance, since one of the features of worship is a collapsing of the performer-audience boundary: A congregation is not an audience, but participants in the rite. But a festival worship service, by definition, is not ordinary. The presence of media cameras, gawkers, tourists, and the merely curious turn a worship service in the direction of performance: The church presents itself to the public, many members of which are not church members.

4. Statistics from *Evangelische Kirche in Deutschland: Zahlen und Fakten zum kirchlichen Leben*, published online by the EKD. See www.ekd.de/statistik/zahlen_fakten.html.

5. Luther, in a letter to his friend and colleague Nikolaus von Amsdorf, written on All Saints Day in 1521, in *D. Martin Luthers Werke, Kritische Gesamtausgabe*, vol. 4 of *Briefwechsel*, (Weimar: Verlag Hermann Böhlaus Nachfolger, 1883–1929), 275.

6. Goffman, *Frame Analysis*, 10–11.

7. Grimes, *Ritual Criticism*, 92.

8. Wuthnow, *Producing the Sacred*, 1.

9. Geertz, *Interpretation of Cultures*, 113. The notion of cultural performance emerged in the 1950s in the work of Milton Singer. Doing fieldwork in India, Singer, in an effort to better understand Indian culture, turned to what he called "cultural performances." Singer's interest in specific, bounded performances (a musical performance, a wedding, a worship service, a speech in parliament) was a practical way to reduce complexity to a manageable size and the potentially abstract notion of culture to the specifics of particular events. It is impossible for an individual or even a large team of researchers to study a culture in its totality, so Singer assumed that a culture's performances offered a condensed, concrete, observable version of the larger, more abstract entity. I am making a similar assumption here: The Wittenberg festivals are a window onto the values and worldviews at play in a particular society, in a particular place, at a particular time. Since society today is rarely a homogenous body, public festivity offers insights into group dynamics. When the event site has a global presence, the attending group may consist of people from widely different locations and cultures. Richard Schechner identifies seven kinds of activities that, taken together, constitute public performances: ritual, theatre, sport, games, play, dance, and music. The Wittenberg festivals are composed of actions from each of these performance types.

10. Bellah, "Civil Religion in America."

11. Following the thought of Victor Turner, I will use the term "ceremony" to distinguish the rites and performances of civil religion.

12. Ferre, "The Definition of Religion," 11.

13. Grimes, *Deeply into the Bone*, 70.

14. Grimes, *Symbol and Conquest*, 43–44.

CHAPTER 3

1. The Reformers reduced the canonical seven sacraments of the Catholic Church (baptism, confession, Eucharist, confirmation, marriage, holy orders, and extreme unction) to two: communion and baptism. Oddly, in the sixteenth century, Reformers, who sought to rid themselves of much Catholic ritual, retained the word *mass* (G. *messe*), but the word detached itself from the celebration of the Eucharist. Communion was infrequently celebrated in Lutheran churches—perhaps once a month at most. A "mass" therefore was likely to be noneucharistic, consisting of biblical readings, hymns, and the sermon. In place of the term *mass*, the use of *Gottesdienst*, literally, service of God, became more common and eventually *mass* was reserved for services in which the Eucharist was celebrated. A Gottesdienst then is more the norm within Lutheran culture, but its form is premised on the more substantial communion service. See Karant-Nunn, *The Reformation of Ritual*, 124–125.

2. Grimes, *Beginnings in Ritual Studies*, 52.

3. Rappaport, *Ritual and Religion*, 265.

4. Statistics from *Evangelische Kirche in Deutschland: Zahlen und Fakten zum kirchlichen Leben*, published online by the EKD: http://www.ekd.de/statistik/zahlen_fakten.html.

5. Davie, "Is Europe an Exceptional Case?" 23–29.

6. For a discussion of emergence of "art" and "aesthetics" as conceptual categories and social institutions, see Hans-Georg Gadamer's *The Relevance of the Beautiful.*

7. Bateson, *Steps to an Ecology of Mind,* 129.

8. Luther's comment on the celebration preparations was recorded in the *Tischreden.* The original German reads: "Lebe ich noch ein jar, so muss mein armes Stublin hinweg, daraus ich doch das bapstumb gesturmet habe propter quam causam dignum esset perpetua memoria." Cited in Laube, "Der Kult um die Dinge," 11.

9. Thanks to Peter Erb for lifting out these meanings from Luther's comment on the process of his own memorialization.

10. Luther, "Vom Anbeten des Sakraments" (The Adoration of the Sacrament), in *D. Martin Luthers Werke, Kritische Gesamtausgabe,* vol. 11 of *Schriften* (Weimar: Verlag Hermann Böhlaus Nachfolger, 1883–1929), 422.

11. See Grimes, *Beginnings in Ritual Studies,* 40–57, for a discussion of the modes of ritual sensibility. My characterization of the Festgottesdienst as ceremonial is based in part on Grimes's discussion of the various ritual moods and modes.

12. The question of whether and precisely how the Reformation contributed to the liberation of women is complex. With respect to convent life, although it is true that some women were forced to enter and life could be oppressive, the convent was for some a way to escape oppressive roles associated with marriage, the raising of children, and domesticity.

13. It should be noted that the moderate position of affirming the blessing of same-sex couples and marriage is in no way an endorsement of what is usually referred to as a "lifestyle choice." Rather, blessings are framed within the context of pastoral work. The implicit message is that the church must embody Christ's love of all people, even if those people are somewhat flawed.

14. Butler, *Gender Trouble,* 25.

15. Jones, *Hermeneutics of Sacred Architecture,* vol. 2: 3.

16. Turner, *Celebration,* 18.

17. See Turner, *Celebration,* 12–20, for Turner's concise approach to the interpretation of symbolic objects.

18. By *multivalent,* Turner means that symbols are motivated by desire, a feature of symbolic behavior shared among animals. In addition, human beings encode symbols with ideational and ideological elements, a fact Turner emphasizes with the term *multivocal.* See Turner, *Celebration,* 12–20.

19. From the UNESCO Evalution Report, titled "The Luther Memorials in Eisleben and Wittenberg," recommending the inclusion of the memorials on the World Heritage list. The report is available on line: http://whc.unesco.org/archive/advisory_body_evaluation/783.pdf.

20. Turner, *Celebration,* 18.

21. See Tillich, *The Essential Tillich,* Part III, "The Protestant Principle," 69–100.

22. As Robert Scribner has discussed, popular literature and visual culture in Luther's era drew parallels between Luther and Christ. "To depict Luther as a living

saint of Christ-like stature seems paradoxical for a movement which rejected the cult of saints because it placed mere humans on the level of God. The contradiction with the Reformer's basic doctrines was so great that it was hardly likely to become an overt constituent element in Luther myth. However, it was always present as an undertone in the view of him as an exemplary Christian, a man of exceptional piety, and a chosen tool of God's purpose in showing the way to true salvation" (*Popular Culture*, 306).

23. Grimes, *Reading, Writing, and Ritualizing*, 39.

CHAPTER 4

1. My approach to civil religion and the political dimensions of public ritual has been influenced by a number of works. See Robert Bellah's seminal study of American civil religion, "Civil Religion in America" Clifford Geertz, "Centers, Kings, and Charisma: Reflections on the Symbolics of Power," in *Local Knowledge*, 121–146; Robert Wuthnow, "Public Ritual," in *Producing the Sacred*, 127–150; Eric Hobsbawm and Terence Ranger, eds., *The Invention of Tradition*; Sally Moore and Barbara Myerhoff, eds., *Secular Ritual*; and David Kertzer, *Ritual, Politics, and Power*.

2. See H. W. Smith, *German Nationalism and Religious Conflict: Culture, Ideology, Politics, 1870–1914*; Puschner et al., *Handbuch zur Völkischen Bewegung 1871–1918*; and Laube and Fix, eds., *Lutherinszenierung und Reformationserinninerung*.

3. Götz, *Johann Gottfried Schadow*, 133–138.

4. Boyer, *City of Collective Memory*, 33–34.

5. Schröder, "Die Baugestalt und das Raumprogramm des Berliner Doms," 144.

6. Ibid., 142.

7. Senf, *Die Reformationsfeier zu Wittenberg 1917*, 62.

8. Hobsbawm and Ranger, *The Invention of Tradition*, 2.

9. Adolf von Harnack, *Lehrbuch der Dogmengeschichte*, 3: 817; cited in Stayer, *Martin Luther, German Savior*, 12.

10. This excerpt of Auden's, poem, "September 1st, 1939" is from Auden's *Another Time* (New York: Random House, 1940).

11. Wallmann, Johannes, "The Reception of Luther's Writings."

12. Steigmann-Gall, *The Holy Reich: Nazi Conceptions of Christianity 1919–1945*, 134–140.

13. Tiefel, "The German Lutheran Church," 326–331. See also Richard Steigmann-Gall's *The Holy Reich* for examples of Nazi use of Luther's anti-Semitic writings.

14. See www.zdf.de/ZDFde/inhalt/31/0,1872,2085567,00.html.

15. Walser's speech was printed as "Die Banalität des Guten," *Frankfurter Allgemeine Zeitung*, October 12, 1998. For a discussion of the controversy, see David Kamenetzky, "The Debate on National Identity and the Martin Walser Speech: How Does Germany Reckon with Its Past?" For a broader perspective on dealing with the Nazi past in the former East and reunified Germany, see G. Christoph Classen, *Faschismus und Antifaschismus*, and Jeffrey Herf, *Divided Memory*.

16. Grimes, "The Lifeblood of Public Ritual," 273.

17. Jones, *Hermeneutics of Sacred Architecture*, vol. 2, 308–309.

18. Oberman, *Luther*, 296. As we have seen, Luther's tract *On the Jews and Their Lies* (1543), written toward the end of his life, is a scathing anti-Semitic attack that includes a call to burn Jewish synagogues.

19. Brinks, "Germany's New Right," 125.

20. Brinks, "Luther and the German State," 1.

CHAPTER 5

1. Schechner, *Performance Theory*, 114.

2. See Grimes, *Reading, Writing, and Ritualizing*, 63–67, for a discussion of processional action.

3. Costa, "Festivity," 542–543.

4. Todorov, *Imperfect Garden*, 80.

5. Simmel, "The Sociology of Sociability," 158–159.

6. Garner, *Apes and Monkeys*.

7. Schechner, *Performance Theory*, 172.

8. Huizinga, *Homo Ludens*, 2.

9. Bakhtin, *Rabelais and His World*, 11.

10. Pieper, *In Tune with the World*, 23.

11. Appadurai, *Modernity at Large*, 179.

12. Lowenthal, *The Past Is a Foreign Country*, 3.

13. Appadurai, *Modernity at Large*, 191.

14. Cited by Richard Sennett in his *The Fall of Public Man*, 2.

15. Sennett, *The Fall of Public Man*, 12.

16. See John O. Koehler's *Stasi: The Untold Story of the East German Secret Police*, 200. Florian Henckel von Donnersmarck's film *The Lives of Others* (2006) is a cinematic treatment of the impact of the Stasi on life in East Germany.

17. Sennett, *The Fall of Public Man*, 12–15.

18. Eagleton, *The Gatekeeper*, 113.

19. MacAloon, *Rite, Drama, Festival, Spectacle*, 243–246.

20. Debord, *The Society of the Spectacle*, 113.

21. Illich, *Tools for Conviviality*, 11–23.

22. Taylor, *A Secular Age*, 613. Also see Barbara Ehrenreich's *Dancing in the Streets: A History of Collective Joy*.

23. Taylor, *A Secular Age*, 50.

CHAPTER 6

1. Geertz, *Interpretation of Cultures*, 126–127.

2. Bakhtin, *Rabelais*, 9.

3. Ibid.

4. Quoted in Burke, *Popular Culture in Early Modern Europe*, 179.

5. Ibid., 186.

6. Scribner, *Popular Culture and Popular Movements in Reformation Germany*, 72–73.

7. The term *Fastnacht* translates as the "night before fasting," the night before Lent, which was a highpoint of Carnival. *Fastnacht* is the name given to contemporary Carnival celebrations in north Switzerland and southern Germany. *Fasching* is celebrated in Bavaria and Austria, taking place on Shrove Tuesday; the name derives from the term *vastschank*, which refers to the practice of emptying wine casks prior to Lent. Geographically, strong Carnival traditions tend to be associated with wine-producing areas.

8. Scribner, *Popular Culture and Popular Movements in Reformation Germany*, 73

9. Ibid., 93.

10. Burke, *Popular Culture in Early Modern Europe*, 208–209. The excerpt here is from Burke's chapter titled "The Triumph of Lent: The Reform of Popular Culture."

11. Stoller, *Sensuous Scholarship*, xvi.

12. Caillois was indebted to Huizinga. Caillois describes play as "free, separate, uncertain, unproductive, regulated, and fictive" (*Man, Play, and Games*, 43).

13. Marcuse, *Eros and Civilization*, 187, 195.

14. Huizinga, *Homo Ludens*, 3.

15. Turner, *Anthropology of Performance*, 125.

16. Beyond these rather obvious material interests, play, as some scholars have argued, may have adaptive functions—that is, play may enhance species survival. Richard Schechner, for example, links improvisational play to skill and success in hunting. Hunting is a situation whose outcome is not predetermined, and in which the creative, spontaneous application of learned behaviors enhances achieving the goal. To play at hunting makes an animal better at it. Whether contemporary festivity—ritual and performative events characterized by play—can be pushed or coaxed down the evolutionary tree, linked to the ritualization of animal behavior, and understood in terms of species adaptation and survival is a question worth pondering, but a line of inquiry too far afield from my interests here.

17. Bakhtin, *Rabelais*, 20.

18. Schechner, *Performance Theory*, 325.

19. Ferre, "The Definition of Religion," 11.

20. Bakhtin, *Rabelais*, 75.

21. Geertz, *Available Light*, 15.

22. Grimes, *Beginnings in Ritual Studies*, 55.

23. Ibid., 48.

24. Frazer, *The Golden Bough*, Part 1, *The Magic Art and the Evolution of Kings* (London: Macmillan, 1911), 52.

25. Ibid., 52.

26. Cahn, "Subversive Mimesis," 34.

27. Taussig, *Mimesis and Alterity*, 21.

28. Benjamin, "On the Mimetic Faculty," in *Reflections*, 333.

29. Jonathan Z. Smith, in his essay, "In Comparison a Magic Dwells," in *Imagining Religion* (Chicago: University of Chicago Press, 1982), 19–35, discusses the mimetic (that is, the associative and comparative) basis of thinking.

30. See chapter 5, "Knowledge by Acquaintance and Knowledge by Description," in Russell's *Problems of Philosophy*, Oxford: Oxford University Press, 1912.

31. Michael Taussig, drawing on Adorno and Horkheimer's discussion of mimesis, develops the concept of "active yielding," a "bodily mirroring of otherness and even ideas," that Taussig contrasts with the "Enlightenment science's aggressive compulsion to dominate nature." See Taussig, *Mimesis and Alterity*, 46.

32. Cited in Taussig, *Mimesis and Alterity*, 74–75. I'm indebted to Taussig's discussion of Darwin.

33. Levi-Strauss, *Structural Anthropology*, 168.

34. Ibid., 180–181.

35. Ibid., 204.

36. Taussig, *Mimesis and Alterity*, 44.

37. Ibid., 68.

38. Benjamin, *Reflections*, 333.

39. Ibid.

40. Benjamin, *Reflections*, 86.

41. Cited in MacDougall, *The Corporeal Image*, 23.

42. Manning, *The Celebration of Society*, 4.

43. See Boissevain, *Revitalizing European Rituals*, a collection of case studies on the resurgence of traditional celebrations across Europe.

44. Schechner, *Between Theatre and Anthropology*, 36–38.

45. Driver, *The Magic of Ritual*.

46. Burke, *Popular Culture in Early Modern Europe*, 213.

47. Taylor, *A Secular Age*, 50–51.

48. Turner, *Dramas, Fields, and Metaphors*, 274.

49. Taylor, *A Secular Age*, 482–483.

CHAPTER 7

1. Turner and Turner, *Image and Pilgrimage in Christian Culture*, 20. The Turners' study of Christian pilgrimage sites was the starting point for what is now a major, interdisciplinary academic subfield: the study of pilgrimage and religiously motivated travel.

2. Statistics from the World Travel and Tourism Council's Web site, www.wttc. travel/eng/Home/.

3. *Spiritueller Tourismus in Sachsen-Anhalt*, 7.

4. Tweed, "John Wesley Slept Here," 43.

5. See Junghans, "Luther's Wittenberg."

6. Dillenberger, ed., *Martin Luther*, 443–445.

7. Tweed, "John Wesley Slept Here," 42.

8. Ibid., 43.

9. Eade and Sallnow, *Contesting the Sacred*, 15–16.

10. A predella is a support for the larger panel; the predella, which contains a painting or image, sits on the altar, and the altarpiece panels on the predella. A trypitch is a three-panel altar piece.

11. At the time Cranach completed the altarpiece, the Reformers had yet to do away with confession.

12. Chidester and Linenthal, Introduction to *American Sacred Space*, 6–15.

13. Luther, "A Sincere Admonition by Martin Luther to All Christians to Guard against Insurrection and Rebellion" (1522). In *Luther's Works*, edited by Jaroslav Pelikan and H. T. Lehmann (St. Louis: Concordia / Philadelphia: Fortress, 1955), vol. 45: 51–74.

14. Urry, *The Tourist Gaze*, 1.

15. Urry's theory also emphasizes the agency of tourist. Urry acknowledges a process of negotiation between site and viewer.

16. Geertz, *Available Light*, 15–17.

17. Treitschke, "Luther und der deutsche Nation," 256.

18. Lazareth, *Luther on the Christian Home*, 1.

19. Turner and Turner, *Image and Pilgrimage*, 34–38. Strictly speaking, Turner distinguishes between the liminal and the liminoid, the former associated with the passage rites of traditional or tribal societies, the later with modern, Western societies. Turner's argument is that in the modern era, the sacred has fractured and scattered from well-defined institutional domains and socially obligatory passage rites into voluntary practices such as pilgrimage and tourism. For a fuller treatment of the distinction, see Turner's "Liminal to Liminoid, in Play, Flow, and Ritual: An Essay in Comparative Symbology," and chapter 1 of *Image and Pilgrimage in Christian Culture*.

20. Lazareth, *Luther on the Christian Home*, 145.

21. The financial company Lutheran Thrivent funded the making of the film.

22. Clifford, *The Predicament of Culture*, 146.

APPENDIX B

1. Handelman, *Models and Mirrors*, 116–119.

2. MacDougall, *Corporal Image*, 269.

3. Ibid., 3.

4. Ruby, *Picturing Culture*, 166.

5. Geertz, *Interpretation of Cultures*, 30.

6. Ibid., 13.

7. Kaufmann, *Tragedy and Philosophy*, 43.

8. Geertz, *Interpretation of Cultures*, 15.

9. Taussig, *Mimesis and Alterity*, 20–21.

10. Geertz, *Available Light*, 117.

11. Taussig, *Mimesis and Alterity*, 42–44.

12. In 1963 Roy Kerr proposed that black holes did not collapse to a point but were shaped more like a ring. This ring, known as the Kerr Ring, is analogized as Alice's looking glass, an entry point into alternate worlds and realities.

Bibliography

Appadurai, Arjun. *Modernity at Large: Culture Dimensions of Globalization.* Minneapolis: University of Minnesota Press, 1996.

Bakhtin, Mikhail. *The Dialogic Imagination: Four Essays.* Translated by Caryl Emerson and Michael Holquist. Austin: University of Texas Press, 1982.

———. *Rabelais and His World.* Translated by Helene Iswolsky. Cambridge: MIT Press, 1968.

Basso, Keith. *Wisdom Sits in Places: Landscape and Language among the Western Apache.* Albuquerque: University of New Mexico Press, 1996.

Bateson, Gregory. *Steps to an Ecology of Mind.* San Francisco: Chandler Publishing, 1972.

Bellah, Robert. "Civil Religion in America." *Daedalus, Journal of the American Academy of Arts and Sciences* 96 (1967): 1–21.

Benjamin, Walter. *Illuminations: Essays and Reflections,* edited by Hannah Arendt, translated by Harry Zohn. New York: Schocken Books, 1969.

———. *Reflections: Essays, Aphorisms, Autobiographical Writings,* edited by Peter Demetz. New York: Schocken Books, 1986.

Boissevain, Jeremy. *Revitalizing European Rituals.* New York: Routledge, 1992.

Bourdieu, Pierre. 1984. *Distinction: A Social Critique of the Judgment of Taste.* Translated by Richard Nice. Cambridge: Harvard University Press.

Boyer, Christine. 1996. *The City of Collective Memory.* Cambridge: MIT Press.

Brinks, Jan Herman. "Germany's New Right." In *Nationalist Myths and Modern Media,* edited by Jan Herman Brinks, Stella Rock, and Edward Timms, 125–138. London: I. B. Tauris, 2005.

———. "Luther and the German State." *Heythrop Journal* 39.1 (1998): 1–17.

Buc, Philip. *The Dangers of Ritual: Between Early Medieval Texts and Social Scientific Theory.* Princeton: Princeton University Press, 2001.

Burke, Peter. *Popular Culture in Early Modern Europe*. New York: Harper and Row, 1978.

Burke, Kenneth. *Dramatism and Development*. Worcester: Clark University Press, 1972.

———. *A Grammar of Motives*. New Edition. Berkeley: University of California Press, 1969.

Butler, Judith. *Gender Trouble: Feminism and the Subversion of Identity*. New York: Routledge, Kegan and Paul, 1990.

Cahn, Michael. "Subversive Mimesis: Theodore W. Adorno and the Modern Impasse of Critique." In *Mimesis in Contemporary Theory: An Interdisciplinary Approach*, edited by Mihai Spariosu, 27–64. Philadelphia: John Benjamin's Publishing, 1984.

Caillois, Roger. *Man, Play and Games*. Translated by Meyer Barash. Champaign: University of Illinois Press, 2001 [1958].

Chidester, David, and Edward Linenthal. "Introduction" to *American Sacred Space*, 1–42. Bloomington: University of Indiana Press, 1995.

Classen, G. Christoph. 2004. *Faschismus und Antifaschismus*. Vienna: Böhlau Verlag.

Clifford, James. *The Predicament of Culture: Twentieth-Century Ethnography, Literature, and Art*. Cambridge: Harvard University Press, 1998.

———. *Routes: Travel and Translation in the Late Twentieth Century*. Cambridge: Harvard University Press, 1997.

Cohen, Eric. "Authenticity and Commodification in Tourism." *Annals of Tourism Research* 15 (1988): 371–386.

———. "Tourism as Play." *Religion* 15 (1985): 291–304.

Corbin, Alain. *The Foul and the Fragrant: Odor and the French Social Imagination*, translated by Miriam L. Kocahn, Roy Porter and Christopher Prendergast. Leamington: Berg, 1986.

Costa, Xavier. "Festivity: Traditional and Modern Forms of Sociability. *Social Compass* 48.4 (2001): 541–548.

Davie, Grace. "Is Europe an Exceptional Case?" *Hedgehog Review* 8.1/2 (2006): 23–34.

Debord, Guy. *The Society of the Spectacle*. New York: Zone Books, 1995.

Dillenberger, John, ed. *Martin Luther, Selections from His Writings*. New York: Anchor Books, 1961.

Driver, Tom F. *The Magic of Ritual*. New York: Harper San Francisco, 1991.

Eade, John, and Michael Sallnow. *Contesting the Sacred: The Anthropology of Christian Pilgrimage*. Chicago: University of Illinois Press, 2000.

Eagleton, Terry. *The Gatekeeper: A Memoir*. New York: St. Martin's Press, 2001.

Ehrenreich, Barbara. *Dancing in the Streets: A History of Collective Joy*. New York: Metropolitan Books,

Ferre, Frederick. "The Definition of Religion." *Journal of the American Academy of Religion* 38.1 (1970): 3–16.

Gadamer, Hans-Georg. *The Relevance of the Beautiful and Other Essays*. Cambridge: Cambridge University Press, 1986.

Garner, Richard Lynch. *Apes and Monkeys: Their Life and Language*. Boston: Ginn, 1900.

Geertz, Clifford. *Available Light: Anthropological Reflections and Philosophical Topics.* Princeton: Princeton University Press, 2000.

———. *The Interpretation of Cultures.* New York: Basic Books, 1973.

———. *Local Knowledge.* New York: Basic Books, 1983.

Goethe, Johann Wolfgang. *Italian Journey.* New York: Suhrkamp, 1989.

Goffman, Erving. *Frame Analysis: An Essay on the Organization of Experience.* New York: Harper and Row, 1974.

Götz, Eckhardt. *Johann Gottfried Schadow, 1764–1850: Der Bildhauer.* Leipzig: Seemann Verlag, 1990.

Greenwood, Davydd. "Culture by the Pound: An Anthropological Perspective on Tourism as Cultural Commoditization." In *Hosts and Guest: The Anthropology of Tourism,* edited by Valene Smith, 171–186. Philadelphia: University of Pennsylvania Press, 1989.

Grimes, Ronald L. *Beginnings in Ritual Studies.* Rev. ed. Columbia, S.C.: University of South Carolina Press, 1995.

———. *Deeply into the Bone.* Berkeley: University of California Press, 2000.

———. "The Lifeblood of Public Ritual." In *Celebration: Studies in Festivity and Ritual,* edited by Victor Turner, 272–283. Washington, D.C.: Smithsonian Institution Press, 1982.

———. *Reading, Writing, and Ritualizing.* Washington, D.C.: Pastoral Press, 1993.

———. *Rite out of Place: Ritual, Media, and the Arts.* New York: Oxford University Press, 2006.

———. *Ritual Criticism: Case Studies in Its Practice, Essays on Its Theory.* Columbia: University of South Carolina Press, 1990.

———. *Symbol and Conquest: Public Ritual and Drama in Santa Fe.* Albuquerque: University of New Mexico Press, 1992.

Handelman, Don. *Models and Mirrors: Towards and Anthropology of Public Events.* Cambridge: Cambridge University Press, 1990.

Herf, Jeffery. *Divided Memory: The Nazi Past in the Two Germanys.* Cambridge: Harvard University Press, 1997.

Hobsbawm, Eric, and Terence Ranger, eds. *The Invention of Tradition.* Cambridge: Cambridge University Press, 1983.

Huizinga, Johan. *Homo Ludens: A Study of the Play Element in Culture.* London: Maurice Temple Smith, 1970 [1938].

Illich, Ivan. *Tools for Conviviality.* New York: Harper and Row, 1973.

Jones, Lindsay. *Hermeneutics of Sacred Architecture.* 2 vols. Chicago: University of Chicago Press, 2000.

Junghans, Helmar. "Luther Wittenberg." In *The Cambridge Companion to Luther,* edited by Donald K. McKim, 20–38. Cambridge: Cambridge University Press, 2003.

Kabus, Ronny. *The Jews of the Luthertown Wittenberg in the Third Reich.* Wittenberg: Luther-Zenturm, 2005.

Kamenetzky, David. "The Debate on National Identity and the Martin Walser Speech: How Does Germany Reckon with Its Past?" *SAIS Review* 19.2 (1999): 257–266.

Karant-Nunn, Susan. *The Reformation of Ritual: An Interpretation of Early Modern Germany.* London: Routledge, 1997.

Kaufmann, Walter. *Tragedy and Philosophy.* New York: Anchor Books, 1969.

Kavanagh, Aidan. *Elements of Rite: A Handbook of Liturgical Style.* New York: Pueblo Publishing, 1982.

Kertzer, David. *Ritual, Politics, and Power.* New Haven: Yale University Press, 1989.

Kirschenblatt-Gimblett, Barbara. *Destination Culture: Tourism, Museums, and Heritage.* Berkeley: University of California Press, 1998.

Koehler, John O. *Stasi: The Untold Story of the East German Secret Police.* New York: Basic Books.

Junghans, Helmar. "Luther's Wittenberg." In *The Cambridge Companion to Martin Luther,* edited by Donald McKim, 20–38. New York: Cambridge University Press, 2003.

Laube, Stefan. "Der Kult um die Dinge an einem evangelischen Erinnerungsort." In *Reformationserinnerung und Lutherinszenierung,* edited by Stefan Laube and Karl-Heinz Fix, 11–35. Leipzig: Evangelische Verlagsanstalt, 2002.

Laube, Stefan, and Karl-Heinz Fix, eds. *Lutherinszenierung und Reformationserinnerung.* Leipzig: Evangelische Verlaganstalt, 2002.

Lazareth, William. *Luther on the Christian Home: An Application of the Social Ethics of the Reformation.* Philadelphia: Muhlenberg, 1960.

Levi-Strauss, Claude. *Structural Anthropology.* Vol. 1. New York: Basic Books, 1963.

Lowenthal, David. *The Past Is a Foreign Country.* Cambridge: Cambridge University Press, 1999.

MacAloon, John, ed. *Rite, Drama, Festival, Spectacle: Rehearsals toward a Theory of Cultural Performance.* Philadelphia: Institute for the Study of Human Issues, 1984.

MacCannell, Dean. *Empty Meeting Grounds: The Tourist Papers.* New York: Routledge, 1992.

MacDougall, David. *The Corporeal Image: Film, Ethnography, and the Senses.* Princeton: Princeton University Press, 2006.

Manning, Frank E. *The Celebration of Society.* Bowling Green: Bowling Green University Press, 1983.

Marcuse, Herbert. *Eros and Civilization.* New York: Beacon, 1974 [1955].

Moore, Sally Falk, and Barbara Myerhoff, eds. *Secular Ritual.* Amsterdam: Van Gorcum, 1977.

Muir, Edward. *Rituals in Early Modern Europe.* Cambridge: Cambridge University Press, 1997.

Oberman, Heiko. *Luther: Man between God and Devil.* New York: Image Books, 1992.

Pieper, Joseph. *In Tune with the World: A Theory of Festivity,* translated by Richard and Clara Winston. New York, 1965.

Puschner, Uwe, et al. *Handbuch zur Völkischen Bewegung 1871–1918.* Munich: K. G. Saur, 1999.

Rappaport, Roy A. *Ritual and Religion in the Making of Humanity.* Cambridge: Cambridge University Press, 1999.

Rock, David, ed. *Voices in Times of Change: The Role of Writer, Opposition Movements and the Churches in the Transformation of East Germany.* New York: Berghahn Books, 1999.

Ruby, Jay. *Picturing Culture: Explorations of Film and Anthropology.* Chicago: University of Chicago Press, 2000.

Schechner, Richard. *Between Theatre and Anthropology.* Pennsylvania: University of Pennsylvania Press, 1985.

———. *Performance Theory.* New York: Routledge, 2003.

Schieffelin, Edward. "Problematizing Performance." In *Ritual, Performance, Media,* edited by Felicia Hughes-Freeland, 194–207. London: Routledge, 1997.

Schorlemmer, Friedrich. *Die Wende in Wittenberg.* Wittenberg: Drei Kastanien Verlag, 1997.

Schröder, Jochen. "Die Baugestalt und das Raumprogramm des Berliner Doms als Spiegel der Ansprüche und Funktionen des Bauherrn Kaiser Wilhelms II." PhD dissertation, University of Marburg, 2003.

Scribner, Robert. *Popular Culture in Early Modern Europe.* New York: Harper and Row, 1978.

———. *Popular Culture and Popular Movements in Reformation Germany.* London: Hambledon Press, 1987.

Senf, Max. *Die Reformationsfeier zu Wittenberg 1917.* Wittenberg, 1918.

Sennet, Richard. *The Fall of Public Man.* New York: W. W. Norton, 1992.

Shepherd, Robert. "Commodification, Culture and Tourism." *Tourist Studies* 2.2 (2002): 183–201.

Simmel, Georg. "The Sociology of Sociability." In *Theories of Society.* Vol. 1, edited by Talcott Parsons et al., 157–163. Glencoe, Ill.: Free Press, 1961.

Smith, Helmut Wasser. *German Nationalism and Religious Conflict: Culture, Ideology, Politics, 1870–1914.* Princeton: Princeton University Press, 1995.

Smith, Thurman L. "Luther and the Iserloh Thesis from a Numismatic Perspective." *Sixteenth Century Journal* 20.2 (1989): 183–201.

Spiritueller Tourismus in Sachsen-Anhalt. Ministerium für Wirtschaft und Arbeit. Magdeburg-Lutherstadt Wittenberg, 2006.

Stayer, James. *Martin Luther, German Savior.* Montreal: McGill-Queens University Press, 2000.

Steigmann-Gall, Richard. *The Holy Reich: Nazi Conceptions of Christianity 1919–1945.* Cambridge: Cambridge University Press, 2003.

Stoller, Paul. *Sensuous Scholarship.* Philadelphia: University of Pennsylvania Press, 1997.

Taussig, Michael. *Mimesis and Alterity: A Particular History of the Senses.* New York: Routledge, 1993.

Taylor, Charles, *A Secular Age.* Cambridge, Massachusetts: Harvard University Press, 2007.

Tiefel, Hans. "The German Lutheran Church and the Rise of National Socialism." *Church History* 41.3 (1972): 326–336.

Tilley, Christopher. *A Phenomenology of Landscape: Paths, Places, Monuments.* Oxford: Berg, 1997.

Tillich, Paul. *The Essential Tillich*, edited by F. Forrester Church. Chicago: University of Chicago Press, 1999.

Todorov, Tzvetan. *Imperfect Garden: The Legacy of Humanism*. Princeton: Princeton University Press, 2002.

Treitschke, Heinrich von. "Luther und die deutsche Nation." Translated as "Luther and the German State," in *Germany, France, Russia, and Islam*, 227–260. New York: G. P. Putnam's Sons, 1915.

Turner, Victor. *The Anthropology of Performance*. New York: Performing Art Journal Publications, 1987.

———. *Celebration: Studies in Festivity and Ritual*. Washington, D.C.: Smithsonian Institution Press, 1982.

———. *Dramas, Fields, and Metaphors*. Ithaca: Cornell University Press, 1974.

———. "Liminal to Liminoid, in Play, Flow, and Ritual: An Essay in Comparative Symbology." *Rice University Studies* 60 (1974): 53–92.

Turner, Victor, and Edith Turner. *Image and Pilgrimage in Christian Culture: Anthropological Perspectives*. New York: Columbia University Press, 1978.

Tweed, Thomas. "John Wesley Slept Here: American Shrines and American Methodists." *Numen* 47.1 (2000): 41–68.

Urry, John. *The Tourist Gaze: Leisure and Travel in Contemporary Societies*. London: Sage, 1990.

Wallmann, Johannes. "The Reception of Luther's Writings on the Jews from the Reformation to the End of the 19th Century." *Lutheran Quarterly* 1 (1987): 72–97.

Wuthnow, Robert. *Producing the Sacred: An Essay on Public Religion*. Champaign: University of Illinois Press, 1994.

Index

DATE DUE

GAYLORD   PRINTED IN U.S.A.